First published in Great Britain in 2016 by Soundcheck Books LLP, 88 Northchurch Road, London, N1 3NY.

Copyright © Martin Popoff 2016

ISBN: 978-0-9932120-2-4

A CIP record for this book is available from the British Library

Book design: Benn Linfield (www.bennlinfield.com)

Printed by: Bell & Bain Ltd, Glasgow

Time And A Word

And A

The Yes Story

by
Martin Popoff

soundcheck books
the stories behind the sounds

Dedicated to Chris Squire...
...the engine of Yes from the genesis.

Contents

Introduction

•••

I must say, it's been a pleasure writing a book on progressive rock pioneers Yes, having been a fan since the late 1970s. Indeed, Yes would've been one of the very first bands that wasn't a hard rockin' heavy metal (or punk!) band that I ever liked and respected and led into my fast-developing literary-inclined life, high school into university.

My gateway into Yes was that I was an aspiring drummer, and upon my white Pearl nine-piece set, I tapped away at the likes of *Going For The One*, *Drama*, and... well, definitely not *Close To The Edge*, *Tales From Topographic Oceans* or *Relayer*, because that would've been too difficult!

So here we are, looking at a book that was a joy to write because it allowed me to go back and play all this great music again, from so many different eras, with so many different lineups, and to put it into some kind of logical order. Or maybe that should be chronological order as I knew that if I was going to tackle a book on Yes, I had to use the timeline with quotes format.

What I like about the timeline format is that it applies particularly well when a band has as complex a history as does Yes. Because, as most pertinently shown with my *Deep Purple Royal Family* two-book set, the idea here was to include much of the solo album and side collaboration experiences so that one could see, using tight chronology, when these events happened in relation to Yes albums and tours. Just to clarify matters, I put limits on how extensively I would address solo careers. For example, Rick Wakeman has put out something like 100 albums! Additionally, I didn't include solo works by everybody who has ever been a part of Yes, but stuck mainly to the chief members of the band.

And then there are grey areas. People like original drummer Bill Bruford, who wasn't around for that long, but did a couple of solo records in the late 1970s that are essentially considered part of the progressive rock family, is of interest to most Yes fans. On the subject of solo work, I tried not to offer quotes for everything, even if it was a record by a major member of the band. Still, I get a kick out of the fact that this might be the only book where any of these ravaged tributaries of the Yes river are discussed to any degree at all. Suffice to say that, in general, we will more than dip our toe in the rolling solo waters, but we don't submerge fully lest the current... OK, enough.

Also, what I like to do with these timeline things, and I've done it here, is that I've included some major milestones from other big prog bands related to Yes, or even just considered part of the progressive rock story, and thus shed some mirrored light on Yes's career and *vice versa*. Also, in spirit of the *Royal Family*-type idea, I've pretty much given most of the Asia story, as well as covering GTR and then later, in lesser detail, things like Circa and Conspiracy.

A few other points of structure, just in case you noticed them and were scratching your head. If I only knew the year of an event, and not the month, that entry goes at the start of the entries for that year. Drilling down, October 1976 will be listed prior to the days in October where events of significance occurred. You will also see that I have introductions to each decade, and the thinking here is that I'm trying not to infuse too much opinion into the entries, leaving them pretty much informational, and then letting the subject say their piece, or in some cases, that entry provides a place to insert a general comment.

But I indeed wanted to say my piece, as that is one of the satisfying parts of doing these books, whether it be this way, or the typical narrative paragraph method, which I've utilized for over a dozen of these rock biographies as well. So, the introductory sections for each decade are the locales in which I get to reflect, shoot my mouth off, give you a glimpse of what I think of the band's material during this time, and indeed, give you an overview of the salient elements of what happened to the band over the 40-odd years period that you are about to wander amongst and relive.

I've also included a smattering of reviews I've written for various magazines as well, in anticipation of a book where I had planned to review all the Yes albums and most of the offshoot solo works. The aim here is, as above, to inject a little more analysis of the art on my part, in balance against the scholarly feel of our timeline with oral history approach. But although I've included quite a few of these, I didn't go too crazy, so as not to interrupt the running dialogue of the band too much. As well, I scattered 'em around, to provide a balance between band and satellite project. I figured it still felt right, given that I've included the odd review from outside journalists, as well as the fact that I've quipped a bit myself directly within entries. Where they show

Introduction

up, take 'em in the spirit of a sidebar, a pause to reflect a little more deeply on what matters the most in all this—the recorded works.

So that's about it. The utopian world Jon Anderson resolutely, if nowhere near methodically, created through his growing lyrical canon over the years... it can't be anything but good for the heart to be confronted with such optimism so enigmatically put year after year now for well on 50 of them.

As well, it's been rich and rewarding doing this book because it reminded me of how, as I've grown old decade by decade, I've interacted with the band at all these different junctures within their career, celebrating and cheering on that second wind that they got with *90125*, actually seeing the band for the first time live during that tour, and then touching down upon so many of the albums after that, as well as beginning to interview the band regularly through the 1990s and 2000s. In tandem with that, of course, I've been able to experience the band many more times live, and it's always a treat to witness such milestone music brought to life, in every instance to packed houses, at least every time that I've been there.

So, enough of my blather. Without further ado, come relive with me these times, using a format that really reminds us to think rigorously about time, and, through the addition of quotes from the players themselves and others... a word!

Martin Popoff

1

Pre-1970s

•••

As we begin our tale, timeline, time with a word, what do we learn about the members of Yes in their formative years?

Well, through fairly unremarkable childhoods, they all display an interest in, and a propensity for, music. Theories abound about how progressive rock is intrinsically British, whereas in America few bands of this ilk emerged from the late 1960s into the 1970s. One accepted theory is that Europe is the birthplace of classical music, whereas in America it is the nation's rich blues-based tradition that informs rock history. That supports the theory that 400 years of classical music is in the blood over there (or "here" if you are reading this in Europe!).

As well, arguably – and dependent on region – music education has always been said to be better in Europe than in America, more classically-based, more traditional in keeping with every facet of European life being more traditional. In any event, here come our soon-to-be heroes, Yes, receiving signals from centuries of classical music, the birth of The Beatles (proudly representing a taking over of this new music, an invasion), and then psychedelia, which, granted, was both home-grown and imported from San Francisco.

The big story pre-1970, of which Yes plays only a component part, is the establishment of a proto-progressive rock movement, or even the idea of a movement, necessarily welling up from the mind-expansion that was psychedelia. Following on is the establishment of a rock album tradition, as opposed to the 45 rpm domination, and, worse yet to the uninitiated, the concept album. Both can be laid at the door of psychedelic music, which was considered more serious artistic music, literally high-minded! When stoned, a band is prone to ponder and obsess on one topic. *Ergo*, a confluence of album and concept album came to be demonstrated by the likes of The Beatles, Frank Zappa &

The Mothers Of Invention, The Kinks, The Who, Pretty Things and The Moody Blues.

So where does Yes fit into all this? Well, there's definitely a psychedelic tinge, but there's also a strong group vocal element, where the band pick up on some of the more multi-vocal groups from the Haight-Ashbury scene, and down to Los Angeles. Due to Jon Anderson's tranquil influence, the band's psychedelia is soft, tender, less dark and druggy than, say, Steppenwolf, The Doors or Syd Barrett. Also, Anderson's strong vocal harmonies were to become a trademark of Yes immediately upon the release of their eponymously titled debut album in 1969.

There is also a demonstration of a group that has strong instrumental ambitions, and herein lies Yes's usefulness in the story of progressive rock, even before they became the crowning example of the nascent genre, which took off in earnest at the start of the new decade.

We must also note as part of the pre-1970s story, that the members of the first lineup of Yes–like the guys in Deep Purple and Led Zeppelin– had arrived there with some degree of a resumé. We can include late joiners Rick Wakeman and Steve Howe in this phenomenon as well, both of whom were quietly pushing the boundaries of their chosen instruments and for all the right reasons.

Bottom line, in terms of our story pre-1970, undoubtedly the main headline is that Yes had arrived with their debut album. On that record, as I say, one is confronted with a curious bouillabaisse of strong vocal work, instrumental discipline and good playing (but not wildly exploratory), new agey hippie lightness of being, a touch of psychedelia, a bit of fussy arrangement, bold tones, and a fair amount of drama. This was a band that was going places; that was a sentiment that could be gleaned simply from the seriousness in which the guys in the band addressed their career aspirations.

As we approach the end of the decade, it is hard not to view the closing four years of the 1960s as providing what is possibly the most creative period of musical and lyrical evolution that the rock 'n' roll world has ever witnessed. And, right at the end of the 1960s, there was little ol' Yes, with their own modest, but accomplished and creditable contribution, placing their thumbprint on the rapidly filling canvas, with an idiosyncratic sound that with retrospect can viewed as a rapidly discarded springboard to a wilder, more fantastic trip through an aural Eden that would satisfy the most acid-unlocked hippie of the era.

Yes had arrived with a polite wave, little aware that there was a ticking time bomb hiding behind their modest but likeable enough first record of comfortable conformity.

1944–1967

June 31, 1944. Artist William Roger Dean, is born in Ashford, Kent. When one "sees" Yes, a typical fan is as likely to picture one of Roger's fantastic worlds created for the band as much as live shots of the prog rockers themselves.

October 25, 1944. John Roy "Jon" Anderson, enters the world in Accrington, Lancashire, England; one of four children in the family. His father was a salesman and his mother worked in a cotton mill, and both were good ballroom dancers.

1946. *Autobiography Of A Yogi*, by Paramahansa Yoganada, is published by The Philosophical Library. A footnote on page 83 concerning the Shastric Scriptures will inspire Jon Anderson's lyrics for *Tales From Topographic Oceans* many years later, and thus set himself up for a subsequent lifetime of gentle ribbing over an album considered one of the most self-indulgent progressive rock farces of all time.

January 11, 1946. Anthony John "Tony Kaye" Selvidge, Leicester, England. Born into a musical family, Tony begins a lifelong study of the keyboards with piano lessons at the age of four. There's no indication on how soon he began attacking the keyboard with his elbows.

April 8, 1947. Stephen James Howe, Holloway, North London, England, the youngest of four children is born.

July 15, 1947. Peter William "Peter Banks" Brockbanks, born Barnet, north London.

March 4, 1948. Christopher Russell Edward "Chris" Squire, born Kingsbury, northwest London. His extensive experience as a trained choirboy through childhood will prove to be a career benefit later on, as will his early friendship with fellow songbird Andrew Pryce Jackman, who will become a musical collaborator in later years.

June 24, 1948. Patrick Philippe Moraz, born Morges, Switzerland.

May 17, 1949. William Scott "Bill" Bruford, born Sevenoaks, Kent, England.

May 18, 1949. Richard Christopher "Rick" Wakeman, born Perivale, Middlesex, England.

Time And A Word

June 14, 1949. Alan White, born Pelton, County Durham, England.

August 25, 1952. Geoffrey Downes, born Stockport, Cheshire, England.

January 13, 1954. Trevor Charles Rabin, born Johannesburg, South Africa.

1956. Rick Wakeman begins piano lessons.

1959. Jon Anderson leaves school at 15 and takes a series of odd jobs, beginning as a farm hand and soon driving a truck. His father becomes ill and it falls upon Jon and his older brother Tony to help support the family.

1959. Steve Howe receives, as a Christmas present, his first guitar, an f-hole acoustic. Steve hears, for the first time, artists who will become major inspirations such as Wes Montgomery and Chet Atkins.

1961. Steve acquires his first electric guitar, a solid body Guyatone; he is in his first group, with a regular gig playing Pentonville Prison twice a week to a captive audience. Meanwhile, Tony Kaye joins the Danny Rogers orchestra, playing four shows a week. Alan White is given a set of Ajax drums, replaced within three months by a set of silver Ludwigs. Alan's uncle was a drummer and his dad was a piano player, with Alan taking piano lessons from the age of six.

1962. Jon Anderson joins The Warriors, sharing lead vocals with his brother Tony. Drummer for the band is Ian Wallace, who joins King Crimson briefly in the early 1970s. The band cuts a single for Decca pairing "You Came Along" with "Don't Make Me Blue." Meanwhile, Alan White switches to drums from piano, and plays with his first band Downbeats.

Jon Anderson on his brother:
"Tony lives in the south of England now; he became a minister. But before, he was in the band... you remember that band that did the song 'Black Is Black', I want my baby back...? He went to join the Spanish band Los Bravos for a year, but he's changed direction and became interested in helping people and growing up with his family and became a priest."

Ian Wallace on turning down the Yes drum stool:
"The Warriors was my first foray into the dark nether regions of what is known as the music business. Jon Anderson was one of the singers in the band along with his older brother, Tony. After Tony quit, the band spent about 18 months playing clubs in Germany and Denmark, six sets a night, every night and nine on weekends. The remnants of The Warriors moved to London in 1968 and

tried to make it there. Six of us lived in one room in the same house as some of Yes. I actually did a gig with Yes when their drummer at the time got sick, and they offered me the gig, but I turned it down! I think I've remained friends with just about everyone I've worked with. Jon is definitely a good friend, but he tends to be rather elusive and I haven't seen or been in touch with him for some time."

1963. Rick Wakeman is in his first band, Atlantic Blues.

1964. Peter Banks, inspired first by Lonnie Donegan, then The Beatles and jazz guitarists like Wes Montgomery, is now past his first band The Nighthawks and into a new act called The Devil's Disciples, who cut a demo which is never commercially released.

1964. Steve gets himself a Gibson ES–175D, which will become a signature guitar for him. That same year, Steve makes his first recording, a cover of Chuck Berry's "Maybelline," with his Joe Meek-produced band The Syndicats. Two more singles, "Howling For My Baby" and "On The Horizon" follow, before Steve moves on to The In Crowd,

1964. Chris Squire is suspended from Haberdashers' Aske's Boys' School for his long hair. His dreams ignited by The Beatles, his first group The Selfs compete in a battle of the bands, only to be beaten by The Bo Street Runners.

1965. A young Roger Dean, after living all over the world with his family, is now back in the UK, and enrolls at the Royal College of Art.

1965. Tony Kaye adds to his resumé, having now played with Johnny Taylor's Star Combo, The Federals and Roy Orbison. Meanwhile, Alan–already gigging since the age of 13 and gaining accolades as "the youngest drummer in England"–wins a battle of the bands with his act The Blue Chips, name recently changed from The Downbeats.

1965. Chris Squire puts aside his Futurama bass and gets his first Rickenbacker 4001, an instrument only a year old in terms of its invention. Squire will be go on to become one of Rickenbacker's greatest ambassadors. He is now in his second group, The Syn (no relation to The Syndicats). Chris is soon joined by future Yes guitarist Peter Banks.

Peter Banks on meeting Chris Squire:
"I met Chris Squire on Denmark Street through a drummer friend that I knew named Martin Adelman. It turned out that Martin was the drummer in this band called The Syn, and Chris was the bassist in the group as well. As fate would have it, they just so happened to be looking for a guitar player. It all happened really

quickly. They said, 'Come into our manager's office,' which was also on Denmark Street. The Syn had another guitar player at the time named Jon Painter, and this was my first introduction to how cold the music business could be. Because I remember meeting the rest of the band, maybe two or three days later, and they said, 'We want to get rid of our guitar player, so why don't you come along and watch us play?' And that's exactly what I did. I went to see them on maybe three or four gigs, and even got to know the guitar player and his girlfriend. To be honest, he was a very nice guy. Yet the whole time I'm watching him, I full well knew that I was eventually going to replace him in The Syn."

April 1965. Parlophone issue a single by The In Crowd, pairing Otis Redding's "That's How Strong My Love Is" with "Things She Says." The single goes to #48 on the UK charts. Two more singles follow in the fall, "Stop, Wait a Minute"/"You're on Your Own" and "Why Must They Criticise"/"I Don't Mind," before the band change their name to Tomorrow.

1966. Steve's band Tomorrow play two songs, "Am I Glad To See You" and "Blow-up" in the movie *Blow-Up*.

1966. Rick Wakeman is in The Concordes, later called the Concord Quartet, soon acquiring his first electronic instrument, a Pianet. Meanwhile, down in South Africa, Trevor Rabin switches from piano to guitar and forms a group called Conglomeration.

1966. Bill Bruford is in a group called The Breed, followed by The Noise in 1967 and Savoy Brown in 1968, although he only plays three shows with the latter.

1967. Steve, still in Tomorrow, appears in a pie fight scene in a comedy about the Mod movement called *Smashing Time*. Trevor Rabin, meantime, has moved on from Conglomeration to Freedom's Children to Rabbitt.

May 1967. Tomorrow issue their first single, "My White Bicycle"/"Claramount Lake," on Parlophone. The A-side would become a minor hit for Nazareth in 1975. Meanwhile, the band is recording what will become their debut album with Mark P. Wirtz producing.

June 1, 1967. The Beatles' *Sgt. Pepper's Lonely Hearts Club Band* is issued; the album is considered one of the early examples of a concept album.

June 23, 1967. Chris Squire's and Peter Banks's group, The Syn (Mk I) issue, on Deram, "Created by Clive"/"Grounded." Chris likens The Syn very much to Yes, given its five-man lineup and emphasis on vocal harmonies.

August 1967. After a brief German tour, The Warriors call it a day in Frankfurt. Jon had been sole lead vocalist after the departure of his brother Tony back at the end of 1965.

Jon Anderson on making ends meet as a young rock 'n' roller:
"Thanks to working as a lorry driver, I found The Cavern. I was driving in Liverpool delivering sugar and flowers, and then I drove around the corner and saw The Cavern where The Beatles started, and about six years later I was playing there!"

August 5, 1967. Pink Floyd issue their debut album, *The Piper At The Gates Of Dawn*, and the progressive rock era is born, even though the band is essentially a psychedelic rock band at this point.

September 1967. Tomorrow issue their second single, "Revolution"/"Three Jolly Little Dwarves."

September 1, 1967. The Syn (Mk II) issue, again on Deram, their second single "Flowerman"/"14th Hour Technicolor Dream," in a picture sleeve. Chris cites The Syn supporting Jimi Hendrix at the Marquee as one of his pre-Yes career highlights.

September 21, 1967. The very first John Peel show session, features Steve Howe's band, Tomorrow.

Late 1967. Chris Squire has the mother of bad acid trips, which turns him into a recluse for a few months as he sorts his head out. The silver lining is that throughout the process of coming down, he woodsheds heavily with his bass guitar.

November 1967. Although many records could be said to be the first concept album for different reasons, *Days Of Future Past*, issued by The Moody Blues this month, is arguably the first concept album by a progressive rock band. Of note, Yes, although squarely a progressive rock band, rarely wrote in the concept album format, with 1974's *Tales From Topographic Oceans* being the only clear-cut example.

1968

1968. In this year, Steve Howe marries Jan, still his wife today; the couple will produce four children. Meantime, a 16-year-old Geoff Downes gets his first Hammond organ.

January 1968. Chris Squire forms Mabel Greer's Toyshop. Disappointed at failing to find a record deal, and simultaneously handicapped by Chris's LSD nightmare, and the fact that the band's lead singer wanted to hang it up, get married and get into the fashion business, The Syn cease operation at the end of 1967.

February 1968. Tomorrow issue their self-titled debut album.

March 1968. Parlophone issues a Jon Anderson demo as a single; the track, released under the pseudonym Hans Christian, is a cover of "Never My Love" by The Association.

March 1968. Chris Squire gets Peter Banks into Mabel Greer's Toyshop. Jon Anderson is soon in the group, but Banks doesn't last long and leaves to join Neat Change; Banks managing to record the B-side of a single with them during his six month stay. Whilst he is away, Clive Bailey takes over guitar duties.

Jon Anderson on copying:

"When I was in my first band, we copied The Beatles and The Rolling Stones, and then we copied The Beach Boys and Frank Zappa. There was that band called Vanilla Fudge, and we copied them a bit. But eventually, you start finding your own way."

Peter Banks on meeting Jon Anderson and Bill Bruford:

"I remember one gig where Mabel Greer's Toyshop played 'In The Midnight Hour' for an encore, which went on for about 30 minutes. Well, this little guy came up on stage and sang with us. It turns out this guy was none other than Jon Anderson. I didn't know Jon then, but Chris did, so he must've invited him up to sing with the group. Ironically, Bill Bruford had also sat in with Mabel Greer's Toyshop at a gig at the Rachel McMillan College in London. But I didn't really know Bill either. This particular gig is so often mentioned in 'Yes-lore.' I'm not really sure if I was there or not. It's hard to remember some things.

"One thing's for sure, Mabel Greer's Toyshop rehearsed a lot more than they gigged, which is not a good sign. We were not a band like The Syn. We were not touring up and down the country in a van. Mabel Greer never toured. We just played one or two gigs a week and that was about it. I finally had enough of that group after six months or so. Although I do believe they did continue for a while after I left. I then joined another band called the Neat Change, which is basically a Skinhead-type of group, the antithesis of Mabel Greer."

May 1968. A second Hans Christian single, called "(The Autobiography Of) Mississippi Hobo," is issued by Parlophone.

May 1968. Steve Howe is now in a band called Bodast, who garner interest from Deep Purple's US label Tetragrammaton, recording a number of tracks for a proposed debut album. But the company goes bankrupt before an album can be realized. Cast adrift, Steve joins The Nice (for a day!) and is rumoured for the Jethro Tull gig.

Early June 1968. Drummer for Mabel Greer's Toyshop, Bob Hagger, is replaced by Bill Bruford. Bruford, torn between his economic studies at Leeds University and a career in music, hitchhikes home to England with his drum set after a disastrous run in Italy with a band called The Noise. His ad in the *Melody Maker* looking for work is answered by Jon Anderson.

June 7, 1968. Bill Bruford plays his first show with Mabel Greer's Toyshop, at Deptford College, London.

Summer 1968. An attempt is made to pair Jon Anderson with the Gurvitz brothers' group, The Gun. A showcase gig takes place, but the favourable response to the show is dampened when Jon is sacked shortly after.

Jon Anderson on getting fired:
"They fired me! Adrian Gurvitz and the guys were really nice and we got on well. We'd only practised for three weeks before a show at Middle Earth, but we went down well. Then we played the Marquee for free with The Who, which I thought was wonderful, just to get seen. But afterwards they said, 'Where's the money for the petrol?' Of course, there wasn't any. They got very uptight and a week later, I saw they advertised for a show and they'd forgotten to tell me!"

July 1968. Mabel Greer's Toyshop invite Tony Kaye, recently of Bittersweet and Winston's Fumbs, to join the group. Peter Banks has returned by this point after his six month defection to Neat Change. The guys—in order of arrival to the ranks: Chris Squire, Jon Anderson, Bill Bruford, Peter Banks, Tony Kaye—are now set on acquiring a new name, frontrunners being Life and Yes. A handful of gigs take place throughout July although these are not considered official Yes gigs.

Peter Banks on how Yes got their name:
"It was me who came up with the name Yes. Actually, a couple of years before, around the time of The Syn, I had the name floating around. I always liked one word names and Yes was short and sweet—it looked big on posters. Since it was only three letters, it would get printed bigger, like The Who. The name must've stuck with Chris, because he and Jon decided to call the group that at the beginning. Believe it or not, the name was supposed to be only temporary. The group figured we'd come up with a better name later—that was the idea. Like all names, at first, it sounded a little silly and a little pretentious. Yet after six months, it kind of stuck, and nobody came up with something better, so Yes was it."

August 3, 1968. The guys play their first show as Yes at a campsite: East Mersey Youth Camp in Essex, followed by a show on the 5th at the Marquee in London.

September 16, 1968. Trial by fire as Yes play a gig in place of the last-minute no-show Sly & The Family Stone at Blaise's club. Going on at 1:00 a.m., the band win over the surprised crowd, which includes the likes of Eric Clapton, Pete Townshend and Jimi Hendrix. This show is also where the band met their first manager Roy Flynn, who is also in charge of the venue. Flynn now takes over from existing manager Jack Barrie and quickly proves his mettle, securing the band better gigs and culminating in getting them in with the prestigious Atlantic label.

Chris Squire recalls this landmark gig:

"There was somebody there who suggested to the club manager that they get us, because we lived real close to the club and had all our equipment readily available. I was actually in bed at the time! We got organized and went out and played. There were a lot of stars there at the time. The members of the Beatles were there. At the end of the night, the manager of the club was so relieved that he offered to manage us. It probably wasn't the greatest thing that ever happened to him in his life [*laughs*]."

October 1968. Gun (previously The Gun) issue their cult classic debut album. Not only is it the band Jon Anderson might have fronted, but their album cover would be Yes artist Roger Dean's first jacket job. Roger also worked on early covers for Atomic Rooster and Babe Ruth.

November 26, 1968. Cream play their farewell concert, at the Royal Albert Hall. Support comes from Rory Gallagher's band Taste and openers Yes, who are allocated a 30-minute set. Prior to the gig, Bill Bruford actually quits the band and decamps to Leeds University. After a disastrous gig with a very drunk replacement drummer, Yes beg Bill to come back, which he does.

1969

1969. Rick Wakeman drops out of the Royal College of Music after a year, to immerse himself in all things rock. Rick takes umbrage at the term "drop-out:" as it "implies failing exams etc. and being asked to leave. I passed all my exams but left mid-term of the course as I felt that the openings that had appeared for me within the music industry were too good to miss. Sometimes you don't have to finish a course in order to finish your own course."

Geoff Downes on early prog rock being very much about keyboard players:

"That post-San Francisco, post-hippie period, there was a lot of reaction toward doing pop music in less conventional ways. People were experimenting with other styles, incorporating classical music and jazz elements. Instrumentally it

started to develop. Rather than just a singer and a backing band, bands started to feature guitar players and keyboard players. Rock keyboard players came to the fore, people like Keith Emerson with The Nice, and Rick Wakeman and his early stuff. You had bands like Procol Harum, bands that suddenly had keyboards as a feature, rather than just sitting in the corner accompanying the singer.

"Britain was probably the leader in that field, with these artsy bands that suddenly started experimenting in the studio and live with these strange sounds. At the time we didn't really call it progressive, which is after the fact. We used to call it underground music; that was how we described it. Technology-wise, you had Hammond organs that had their own Leslie cabinets, but then there were Mellotrons, so you had a keyboard player who could be the orchestra, and then synthesizers. So, all of a sudden a keyboard guy could play lead lines as well, rather than just being a guy sitting around an acoustic or electric piano."

Spring 1969. Yes begin work on their debut album at Advision, a new 16-track studio in Bond Street, London. Paul Clay produces.

Peter Banks on getting a record deal:
"We did have a few labels interested in us, certainly. We also had Robert Stigwood very interested in the band, and he was managing Clapton and the Bee Gees. But Yes ended up signing with Atlantic Records. Ahmet Ertegun, the president of Atlantic, came over and watched us perform. And Roy Flynn engineered a very modest deal with Atlantic. The idea was that we were the second white English band to sign with them, the first being Led Zeppelin. And Atlantic said to us, 'What we've done for Led Zeppelin, we're going to do for Yes!' You know, the usual record company line. Of course, this never happened and the first album received virtually no promotion whatsoever—that definitely wasn't the original plan."

May 25, 1969. Yes play a quality multi-band bill, along with Procol Harum, Soft Machine, Third Ear Band and Blossom Toes.

June 1969. Session musician Rick Wakeman, known around town as "One Take Wakeman," plays Mellotron on David Bowie's "Space Oddity."

Rick Wakeman on working with Bowie:

"I had done a session for Tony Visconti with a band called Junior's Eyes and had played the Mellotron. Tony produced David Bowie and they wanted to use the Mellotron and I was the only guy that Tony knew who knew how to play it! So I got the job and became great friends with David and have done quite a lot with him over the years. I learned more from David Bowie than anybody else in the studio as regards professionalism and how to work."

June 21, 1969. After playing regularly in late 1968, and all through 1969, Yes play their first show outside of the UK, in Antwerp, Belgium, followed a week later by a second mainland European date in Amsterdam.

July 12, 1969. Yes play the 12 Hours Of Happiness Concert, in Nottingham, with The Nice, King Crimson, Junior's Eyes, Edgar Broughton Band, Idle Race, Status Quo and Caravan.

July 18 – 19, 1969. Yes play Ireland for the first time, the three-date tour reduced to two because of lack of power at the third scheduled show at a Cork football pitch. The bill was Yes, then The Bonzo Dog Doo-Dah Band, then headliner The Nice, with the 18th being Belfast and the 19th, Dublin.

July 25, 1969. Yes issue their self-titled debut album, accompanied by a UK-only single pairing "Sweetness" with "Something's Coming." More of an idealistic, fussy, well-recorded pop album, *Yes* makes resplendent use of Jon's uncommon alto voice, adding it to the record's many trademark harmonies, an extension of the band's appreciation for the stacked melodies prevalent in bands from LA and San Francisco at the time. The album is produced by Paul Clay and the band, and includes a Byrds cover, "I See You," a Beatles cover, "Every Little Thing" and a song from the band's Mabel Greer's Toyshop days called "Beyond And Before."

Peter Banks on the first album:

"I was bitterly disappointed with the sound. I think the rest of the band felt the same. We'd been gigging constantly, rehearsing constantly; none of us really felt the first album truly represented what Yes was capable of doing. I used to tape most of our early gigs on my little cassette machine and some of the live versions of the songs just blow away the studio ones. So as far as the actual sound goes, there was a sense of disappointment, because we sounded a lot smaller.

"I mean, in retrospect, it's not a bad album. I believe a lot of blame definitely goes to the producer. For instance, if we had gotten Paul McCartney or Pink Floyd's producer, it obviously would've sounded much better. But everything sounded very compressed—there was quite a bit of compression used. And we did have the engineer keep telling us to turn down, which really got on our nerves. Then when he'd leave the room, we would turn up again—very childish games like that. I think we were just a little intimidated by the environment. And certainly the engineer and producer were intimidated by us."

Bill Bruford's take on the first album:

"Yes was jazz and rock, with me swinging along behind Peter Banks. Somebody in the studio told me you could hear different instruments and levels in your headphones, so I played most of it with deafening Peter Banks and just a squeaky cymbal for three days."

August 4, 1969. Steve Howe's son Dylan is born; Dylan will much later collaborate with dad on his solo works, as will Steve's other son Virgil, born in 1975. Steve and Jan also have two daughters, Georgia (born 1982) and Stephanie (born 1986).

August 9, 1969. The 9th Annual Jazz, Blues And Pop Festival in Sussex, England finds Yes playing with The Who, Chicken Shack, Fat Mattress, Aynsley Dunbar's Retaliation, The Spirit Of John Morgan, The Groundhogs, King Crimson, Idle Race and others.

August 20 - September 7, 1969. Yes play Germany and the Netherlands, their first sustained set of dates outside the UK. Atlantic renege on their promise to send the band to the US. The band plays alongside the likes of Soft Machine, The Nice and the blues boom version of Fleetwood Mac.

Peter Banks on Tony Kaye:

"Tony Kaye, 'the old bard of rock' as I used to call him, was great. He was a very rhythmic player, and certainly a soulful player. He was a real 'rock' keyboard player in every sense of the word. Tony would fill in any gaps. What we played together was seldom discussed. I never knew what chords he was playing. I would just find my own inversions of what he was playing and fit around it. In the beginning, Tony would claim he had a Hammond organ, pretty much for the same reasons Bill claimed he had Premier drums, but in reality, he had a disguised Vox Continental. Six months after he joined Yes, Tony did finally get a Hammond. I believe we first rented one for him, because I remember hauling this massive thing up and down the small staircase of the place we used to rehearse in."

October 1969. Yes's debut album is released in the US. Also this month, the band get a second UK single release with "Looking

Around"/"Everydays" while the first US single,"Sweetness"/"Every Little Thing" is issued three months later.

October 9, 1969. Yes play a festival date in Essen, Germany, alongside Fleetwood Mac, Spooky Tooth, Pretty Things, Keef Hartley, Warm Dust, Free and Hard Meat.

October 10, 1969. King Crimson issue their acclaimed debut album, *In The Court Of The Crimson King*.

Peter Banks remembers King Crimson:

"Another major reason for discontentment was because the first King Crimson album had also just been released, which knocked us completely sideways. King Crimson were formed after Yes. I knew Robert Fripp, because he used to come down to watch Yes play at the Marquee. What I remember about Fripp was this guy with a kind of Afro hairdo wearing a monk's cloak, which was either black or brown, had a cord around the waist and a hood up. And he used to talk to me about guitars and such; he was a very likable guy. I had no idea that he played guitar, not a clue, until we saw Crimson play their second or third gig. We were absolutely stunned! At the time we thought Yes was a pretty cool band, and there were no other groups that could touch us. And I remember standing at the bar, and not touching my drink throughout Crimson's entire set. They were just dynamite. I was totally dumbfounded. And when their first album came out, it was so much better than ours. It kind of blew our thunder completely. Also, their album did very well, in contrast to ours, which didn't. Yes was not happy."

November 1969 - January 1970. Yes work on their second album, again at Advision Studios, London, with producer Tony Colton.

Peter Banks on the second album:

"Eddie Offord did the engineering, and did an incredible job considering what he had to put up with. There's an interesting story about how we ended up with Eddie Offord as the engineer. I remember Bill and I were listening to John McLaughlin's first solo album, called *Extrapolation*. I think I played it for Bill, and he was totally knocked out by the drum sound, particularly the bass sound, because the bass was just an acoustic bass, but it was so far up in the mix. Certainly no one in the jazz field had ever recorded jazz like that. So Bill and I wondered, 'Who produced this?' Well, lo and behold, the album was produced by Eddie Offord. We both thought, 'Who the hell is this guy?' Ironically, it turned out that Eddie worked at Advision Studios! So Eddie just kind of came along with the studio.

"I believe *Extrapolation* was the first album he had ever produced. And Bill and I just loved it. Bill and I went into this second album very much with the idea of the *Extrapolation* album, with Yes sounding like that, especially in the bass drum department. Of course, it turned out very differently. Eddie Offord was a real character. He had great ears, fantastic ears! He was very proficient, but not particularly technical. And he was very good at all the tricks in the studio. I've never seen anybody on a mixing board like Eddie before. He was very cool, and used to get very stoned and sometimes became incomprehensible. He and Jon took an instant bonding, and there would be lots of intense conversations at four in the morning, leaning on the faders. It was that type of atmosphere. It's really a shame that he didn't produce the second Yes record; Tony Colton, the producer, on the other hand was a whole different package. Let's face it, he hated me—it's as simple as that."

November 26 - December 2, 1969. Yes play five dates in Switzerland. November 30th finds the band on a bill with Deep Purple, Brian Auger Trinity, Manfred Mann, Free, Atomic Rooster, Liverpool Scene and Village.

Peter Banks on Chris Squire:

"Chris Squire was the slow one, always. Chris was very solid in the bass department; he had a very unique sound. Chris was also the one who would think things over carefully; he was never impetuous. He was very slow and methodical—painfully slow in everything. Chris was the same as he had always been in the other bands we were in together. I mean, it would take two hours to get out of bed, and another hour to have breakfast and so on—nothing had changed. He and Bill Bruford made a real powerhouse rhythm monster cooking in the boiler room. Chris used to think of his bass as a second lead guitar. At times it meant that he and I would be at the top of the neck, the consequence of which meant all the bottom end of the group would disappear, frustrating the hell out of Bill. This kind of friction would sometimes work to our advantage."

December 12, 1969. The Plastic Ono Band, featuring John Lennon and Yoko Ono, issue a live album called *Live Peace In Toronto 1969*. The band's drummer is Alan White, who plays with Lennon on and off over a two-year period. Pre-Yes, Alan also played with Billy Fury And The Gamblers, Ginger Baker's Airforce, Balls, Bell & Arc (supporting The Who in the US), Happy Magazine (later called Griffin), and for a year-and-a-half, Alan Price.

2

1970s

•••

The 1970s, for Yes, is of course the story of an improbable band of nerdy types operating collectively at a surreal level, in a music industry that resembles not one wit the one we have today. The band begins the decade stuttering, not happy with their label, not getting anywhere with *Time And A Word*. Enter eccentric ignorer of accepted tonal values Steve Howe on guitar, and the possibilities begin to expand two- and three- and four-fold. *The Yes Album* is such a conundrum, it triumphs. People begin talking about this strange band of holdover hippies, rescuing then bending psychedelia in a scholarly manner. All wiry and lanky, extended and ethereal, the band's songs break all the rules, and sends nascent progressive rock fans out to exciting new territories. Each member of the band stands out with distinctive contributions, but it is Tony Kaye with his forceful Hammond work that distinguishes the band, broadly speaking, at the crossroads between *The Yes Album* and what came after.

The next plot twist, through the bloody-minded insistence represented by four landmark albums, the centre shifts for the definition of prog rock, to the place where Yes reside. To be sure, there would be other fiefdoms, but when the collective rock subconscious thinks prog rock without additional qualifiers or descriptives, the answer is always Yes. The essence of what prog means began with *The Yes Album* but is underscored with 1971's *Fragile*, when another enabler of the fantastical joins the band, hotshot keyboardist about town, Mr. Rick Wakeman. A song pulsating upon the bed of Bill Bruford's and Chris Squire's ingenious rhythm track called "Roundabout" is edited down for single consumption, and Yes is off to the races, infecting, informing.

In the UK, the rock music of the 1970s consists of nascent glam, strong openers for heavy metal, still much retrograde rock 'n' roll,

HAROLD DAVISON & MARQUEE-BLOCK PRESENT

IN CONCERT
QUEEN ELIZABETH HALL - LONDON
(Adjacent to the Royal Festival Hall)
THIS SATURDAY, 21st MARCH, 7.45 p.m.
"Yes" will be joined this evening by the twenty-piece orchestra, who accompany them on certain tracks of their new Album, "Time and a Word", to be released shortly on Atlantic Records.

Tickets: 8/-, 10/-, 14/-, 17/-, 21/-
Available from Royal Festival Hall Box Office, all usual agents and Harold Davison Ltd., 235-241 Regent Street, London, W.1.

and in general, the continuing category known vaguely as album rock. But there's also now a subset of that called symphonic rock, art rock, progressive rock or even jazz rock, which is essentially a dressing up of underground rock, carrying on from Cream through the poorly selling—save for Heep and Sabbath—Vertigo Records ethic. It's a murky melange of music that, on paper, shouldn't sell, but weirdly does so anyway.

Going from strength to strength, Yes return with an even more challenging record than *The Yes Album* or *Fragile* in the shape of *Close To The Edge*, distinguished for its side-long title track of swirling, masterful, giddy music-making. Maximum credit really goes to the rock audience for embracing records like this and sending them platinum in the United States. Indeed, arguably, *Close To The Edge* just might be the most complex, opaque and faculty-demanding album ever to go platinum, so you've got to tip your hat to those one million Americans, surely most of whom are not musicians.

Now, it must be said of many of these bands in the 1970s, Yes included, that even though they weren't turning in double and triple platinum albums, once you were at this level in this decade, you basically had a stage show as big as anybody else's and you were putting that sound and vision technology into venues as big as anybody else got. In other words, the great leveller at the top was the insane amount of tickets you could sell as you crisscrossed North America and Europe. So, we talk about bands like Black Sabbath and Deep Purple and Yes, and even Jethro Tull and ELP, being in the same top class in the 1970s and they were. Loads of press, playing hockey barns... the only slight pullback was that they weren't necessarily selling as many records as Led Zeppelin or toward the end of the decade, Eagles or Fleetwood Mac. And maybe they weren't playing stadiums as opposed to the arenas graced by Zeppelin and the Stones, although as you read on, you will see Yes do climb to those dizzy heights on occasions.

But Yes, had other things on their mind as well, including inventing punk rock. Through their preposterously indulgent noodling, inscrutably hippie-fried and spiritual *Tales From Topographic Oceans* album from the winter of 1973, a quiet revolt had begun, whereby the rock audience was becoming not so much fed-up *en masse*, but fragmented, with more than enough still patronizing rock bombast in droves, but also a sizable amount revolting at the rock star excess, the self-importance, and the sheer expense all-around of the extreme progressive lunacy that Yes were the high priests of. *Tales From Topographic Oceans*, not much more mainstream than a record financed by the Krishnas or the Moonies, became a lightning rod, a signifier that hippies must take their depleting numbers off the streets once and for all, and pixie-dance into field and forest where they belong.

But I steadfastly wanted to qualify there. We all know that the story of progressive rock being stomped by punk rock is a lazy shorthand trope, and statistically, in the wallet, it doesn't quite bear out as true. Case in point: while not a single punk album sold in any numbers, our heroes merrily rebounded, crafting *Tales From Topographic Ponds*, otherwise known as *Relayer*, basically one record's worth of exactly the same thing, if a little tougher and to the point. Now, we're not into the punk era yet at this point, but the idea that Yes can bounce back from the critical trouncing of *Tales* with more of the same, and survive, is demonstrating legs for prog. This was high-minded music, and it's a continuing credit to record buyers at the time that the album didn't sink without a trace.

It is additional testimony to the band's ingrained placement in rock culture, that, like Kiss in 1978, they would be so bold as to each and all crank out solo albums at the same time—though none troubled the charts much. However, again, testimony to their reach, the band's technology-encased shaman, Rick Wakeman, had found himself a career as cranker-outer of solo albums just as convoluted as *Tales*, and getting miles of column inches for it, as well as gold records in the US— for a brief spell there, Wakeman was essentially the biggest publisher of history textbooks on tape.

However, back to work, post-*Relayer*, Yes was smart enough or restless enough or impatient enough to try something new when it came time for them to answer for their sweet an' sour, hard rocking jazz fusion album with the snake on the cover. Rick Wakeman had returned on keyboards, and brought with him the chemistry he had taken away, as well as his sociability and joviality, and the result was a confident, ebullient triumph of a record called *Going For The One*. As a result, Yes would still fly high, ever-present in the press, treated with a degree of respect (even though they would never particularly get across to the likes of *Rolling Stone* and *Creem*), and more importantly, continue to expand the minds of millions of fans per year, all during the sullen hot summer of the Pistols and The Clash in 1977.

Its follow-up, *Tormato*, arrived in late 1978, and guess what? Punk rock was already declared dead (apparently because The Clash had signed to CBS). But that didn't stop Yes from turning in a record of short, urgent sounds, recorded with screech, even though the effect was accidental. King of the delete bins at the time due to over-shipment, *Tormato* was nonetheless a commercial success even if, at this point, there was indeed a growing piling-on from the press and fans that progressive rock had finally run its course.

To sum up for this quintessential 1970s band, it's no surprise, and it's common knowledge, that the band's reputation, most of what it will be remembered for, is their bold and brave and commercially rewarding participation through an entire decade known for dozens of huge, respected, now legendary bands. In other words, Yes, competed on a grand scale with the best of them, all through the decade, save perhaps for its very first year and its very last, still gathering its sea legs in 1970, and in need of a reboot by 1979.

1970

1970. This year, Jon Anderson marries Jennifer; their marriage would last 25 years and produce three children. Also in 1970, Rick Wakeman marries for the first time. Although he divorces Roz Woolford in 1980, the union produces three children: sons Oliver, Adam and Benjamin; the couple also raised stepdaughter Amanda.

January 30, 1970. A particularly tasty bill finds Yes playing Lanchester Polytechnic, Coventry, with Atomic Rooster, Free and Mott The Hoople.

February 19–24, 1970. Yes play Scandinavian dates with The Edgar Broughton Band, following upon three shows earlier in the month with The Nice.

March 21, 1970. Yes play a rushed, haphazard second set of a concert with orchestra, at Queen Elizabeth Theatre, conducted by Tony Cox. The orchestra consisted of students from the Royal School of Music.

Peter Banks was against orchestra being used for the album, and he was anti doing this type of gig, an idea of Jon's.

April 1970. Rick Wakeman joins The Strawbs.

April 18, 1970. Peter Banks plays his last gig with Yes, after which Steve Howe joins as his replacement; Robert Fripp having turned the gig down. With much tension between Banks and producer Tony Colton, it had been pretty much decided during the close of the sessions for the album, interspersed with steady gigging, that Peter would have to go.

Peter Banks on getting his marching orders:

"I got fired from Yes after a gig at Luton College. I don't think it was a particularly bad gig, and I don't think it was a particularly great one. After the show in the dressing room, I was given the news. Jon was the one broke it to me, and Chris was there also. Actually, Tony and Bill didn't even know about it until that day, which I found out later. Jon said to me, 'I think it would be better for you and the band if you left. And the reason is...' At that point I went crazy and yelled, 'Don't give me any fucking reasons!' I didn't want to know. I guess I was kind of in a state of shock.

"And so I just packed up my little gig bag. The worst thing was that I couldn't even storm off and leave, which would've been the sensible thing to do, because we all drove to the gig in the same car. So I had to hang around and drive back with them to London, or I'd have been stuck there. The drive home was very uncomfortable. I didn't say anything and nobody else did either, because I was obviously very upset. I was extremely angry! Frankly, I think if anybody would've said something, I probably would've punched them. I made that totally clear. It was a total shock to me, a complete surprise. I had no idea at all that I was going to be fired from the band that I loved! And as I found out later, neither did Bill or Tony."

Steve Howe on his audition:

"When I went for the audition for Yes it was quite a straightforward thing. I had been putting my face around saying, 'I am not doing anything right now.' That was about the most I have ever been without a group when I wanted to be in a group. Chris called and said, 'We have been seeing you play and you have been doing great things. Come and see what it is like to play with us.' It was that first day that I heard in Jon and Chris tremendous originality, capability, style and technique. Bill was just awesome. When Bill played I was like, 'I think I'm going to like this!'"

May 5, 1970. Yes issue the title track from their forthcoming album, *Time And A Word*, backed with "The Prophet," as an advance UK-only single.

June 20, 1970. Yes issue a UK single pairing "Sweet Dreams" with "Dear Father."

July 11, 1970. Progressive folkies Strawbs issue a live album *called Just A Collection Of Antiques And Curios*; it is a coming out party of sorts for future Yes keyboardist Rick Wakeman, who had nonetheless first played with the Strawbs as a session musician on their *Dragonfly* album from earlier in the year.

Rick Wakeman on leaving The Strawbs:

"Strawbs were going through a transition that I personally wasn't into at the time. I always felt that Strawbs revolved around the writing of Dave Cousins and that was what made Strawbs sound like they did. We did an album called *From The Witchwood* which contained some great songs but only half of which I would call Strawbs music. This upset me as I felt the band was meandering as regards to material. As it turned out, it all worked out well as I left to join Yes where I felt I could really add my weight in the keyboard orchestral department and Strawbs went on to have their biggest selling singles and albums; so everybody was happy. Dave and I are still close friends."

July 17, 1970 – July 31, 1971. Yes embark on regular tour dates (first in support of *Time And A Word*), punctuated by recording sessions for their forthcoming third album. A recording of the band's performance of "The Clap," at the first show at the Lyceum Theatre, London will be included on that third album, to be titled *The Yes Album*. The first show of this tour show marks Steve Howe's first gig with the band, Yes supporting Iron Butterfly in January and February of '71. Support for much of the back half comes from Jonathan Swift.

July 24, 1970. Yes issue, in the UK, their second album, *Time And A Word*. The album reaches #45 in the UK, but would not chart in the US, upon release five months later. A highlight, with its unusual but hooky chord changes for Yes, would be "Sweet Dreams," a song co-written by Jon and his teenage band mate David Foster, the song becoming a live favourite. Like the debut, the album includes two covers, a rendition of Buffalo Springfield's 1967 song "Everydays" and Richie Havens' 1968 song "No Opportunity Necessary, No Experience Needed."

Steve Howe on *Time And A Word*:

"When I was asked to join Yes in 1970, the record that they had just finished was with the guitarist Peter Banks. And Tony Colton, the producer, had a team of people—Eddie Offord was one of his friends. Tony Colton produced very well, I must say. He produced a guy, Tony Cox, the arranger on *Time And A Word*. Anyway, when I joined, I learned some of *Time And A Word* and we walked on stage and played it without the orchestral arrangements, and as time went by and we recorded things like *The Yes Album, Fragile, Close To The*

Edge, which were like three monumental, important albums for Yes that took a long time.

"But after a while, I looked back on *Time And A Word*—the record I wasn't on—and I started to love it. This was a kind of embryonic Yes, and lo and behold, they took the orchestra on as well. What happened in that era of Yes, they were learning certain techniques, certain stylistic trademarks, that would hang. And I believe that much of what Yes has done was hinted at and put onto a blueprint in the album *Time And A Word*. It's a remarkable album. It has all the key ingredients of what Yes does. It has big intros, it has obscure, quite original guitar. It doesn't fall into, 'This is a blues guitarist; this is a rock guitarist.' You know, Peter is very tasteful in what he does.

"And of course, you've got the power of Chris with Bill Bruford, who is surely is one of the most inventive drummers I can think of. Bill, subtly and without notice I must say, nobody has ever said it to me and I'm saying it to you, Bill was part of the embryonic style and makeup of Yes. And the way he did things greatly affected the way we did them. Therefore, Bill was as much a part as Jon was in formulating what Yes is.

"So I happen to like *Time And A Word*; I think it's a sensational record in the Yes story, and the fact that I'm not on it allows me to say what the hell I like about it. If I was on it, it would sound like a big stroke [*laughs*]. 'I'm great on this album!' But I'm not on this album—it's by the group I'm in. But to me, it's when the blueprint, the basic foundation of Yes was created. And when they do that line in, I think it's 'Everydays,' [*sings it*], that to me epitomizes everything that Yes set out to do. There's no sense of time, you don't know where you are, and you've got this line. And I think Yes, in a way, had been trying to re-create the musicality of *Time And A Word*, *Fragile*, *Close To The Edge* and *The Yes Album*, because it's a very high musicality, a very intense, very... I don't want to say arduous, but it was well constructed and no stone was left unturned."

Peter Banks on *Time And A Word*:
"My perception of that whole album is very subjective, because I was having definite problems with the producer. Everything I played on there was subject to much scrutiny. And when the producer asked me if I could play a bit like Jimmy Page, whose guitar playing I loathed, I just overreacted and went crazy! For me, at the time, that was probably the worst comparison that could've been made. So all these memories kind of cloud my perception of what actually happened at the time.

"Once again, King Crimson and The Nice were both influences on us. Also, Stravinsky and Holst, who we just used to flat-out steal from! So all of these artists were the main influences of Yes that I can think of. We all had different tastes in music; there's no question there. Chris Squire would probably say Sly & The

Family Stone, because he liked the bass playing in that group. Of course, Bill was into Art Blakey and the other jazz artists. All of these diverse musical influences were what made Yes so unique. We would try most ideas first, then accept or reject. Sometimes, last week's bad mistake became this week's good idea."

Bill Bruford discusses his jazz influences:
"Jazz and rock are quite different. Rock is generally slow and loud. Jazz, generally speaking, is fast and light. Rock, generally speaking, is played pretty much all the way through with one pattern. Jazz, as you know, is improvised. In other words, they couldn't be more different. All the great jazz drummers I know play quite quietly and are trying to play quieter. Most of the rock drummers play loud and are trying to play louder. Everything is probably about as different as it can get. Jazz tends to take place in small, intimate rooms where the speed of the playing and the excitement of it can translate well to 300 to 500 people, that kind of number.

"Rock of course takes place in stadiums where, if you are in the back of the hall, you need to wait a week before you hear anything. I grew up with jazz as a kid. From 13 to 18, 19, it had been the love of my life. And I knew how to play jazz better than I knew how to play rock when I joined Yes. Not that any of us thought much about rock or jazz. We just kind of started playing. If you asked me at the time and forced me, I would've said that I thought Yes was going to be a jazz group. I didn't know it was going to be a rock group. That didn't matter. It just changed direction a bit."

Fall 1970. Yes work on what will become their third album, again at Advision Studios, after shifting locales from impoverished writing sessions at a farm house in Devon. The band by now have cut their losses with Roy Flynn and hired Brian Lane as their new manager, who Chris had met through his hairdresser.

September 21, 1970. Yes issue "Sweet Dreams," a second and last single from *Time And A Word*.

November 1970. *Time And A Word*, sees American release, with different cover art, dominated by a band shot with new guitarist Steve Howe included, even though he wasn't on the record, of course.

November 13, 1970. Yes get in a head-on collision, with the gravest injury being a broken foot for Tony Kaye. Not only does the Hammond expert perform subsequent gigs in a cast, he is photographed as such in the band shot to be used for the cover of *The Yes Album*.

December 11, 1970. King Crimson issue their third album, *Lizard*; Jon Anderson guests on the side-long title track.

1971

January 8, 1971. Yes begin an extensive tour of mainland Europe supporting Iron Butterfly. The bands get along great, jamming into the night. Yes is hugely impressed with the American band's modern and sophisticated PA system and vow to get one of their own. They wind up buying Iron Butterfly's, as the band is breaking up. Yes management and Atlantic's Phil Carson conspires to finance the equipment, but in the process, Yes have to cede some of their publishing monies to their management company.

January 16, 1971. Future Yes vocalist Jon Davison, is born.

Early 1971. Patrick Moraz's progressive rock band Mainhorse issue their only album, an eponymously-titled record, on Polydor.

Early 1971. Osibisa issue their debut self-titled album. An as yet undiscovered Roger Dean is the cover artist of choice, Dean also illustrating the band's follow-up, *Woyaya*, issued the same year, in his signature style. It is his Osibisa work that Yes saw, prompting a call to Roger from Steve.

March 5, 1971. "Your Move" is issued as a US single from *The Yes Album*, backed with "The Clap." The single reaches #40 on the charts.

Jon Anderson, on learning to play an instrument later in life:
"I didn't really start until I was 27, 28, when I started playing piano and guitar at home. But it was very lame at the start, and then I met Vangelis who was a mentor for me. I used to watch what he played and how he played. Then I got home and tried to be a 'sort of Vangelis.' It's impossible, but I was trying to imitate his work and learn more about technology. And now I have a very beautiful studio; I have some very fine equipment, so I can compose every day, some symphony or some other music. Over the years you grow into your own style."

March 19, 1971. Yes issue their third record, *The Yes Album*. The band hang onto their Atlantic deal when Phil Carson convinces Ahmet Ertegun to rescind his notice to drop Yes from the label. The album reaches #40 in the US and #4 in the UK, a lofty position that Chris Squire attributes to a British postal strike meaning that sales figures are limited to the Virgin store in London, where the band's fan base is strongest.

Jon Anderson reveals what made *The Yes Album* so different from *Time And A Word*:
"It's Steve Howe. No doubt about it. It was Steve Howe joining the band and coming up with a plethora of musical ideas, chords, stylistic guitar playing,

classical guitar playing, jazz guitar playing, rock guitar playing. We connected right away and started writing. I hadn't really had a strong writing relationship with Peter Banks, even though we got on OK. But I was writing more with Chris at that time on the first two albums.

"And when Steve came, all of a sudden I had a guy who could understand what I was talking about [*laughs*]. Because, you know, I was... as Bill Bruford once said [*laughs*], 'Jon's definitely living on another planet.' And Rick coined it best; he said, 'Jon's the only guy I know trying to save this world while living on another one.' These are classic lines. And they actually ring true now. Because I'd be listening to Stravinsky one day and then go and work with the band. I'd been listening to 'Rites Of Spring' and go work with the band. I'd be listening to Sibelius and go and work with the band, and thinking, well, why don't we do something as inventive and as wild and as drastically different?"

Tony Kaye on *The Yes Album* producer Eddie Offord:
"Eddie was the catalyst and the crazy energy in the studio that Yes needed at that time, and was instrumental, along with the band he loved, in creating what became the Yes sound. He encouraged the band to stretch out sonically and musically in ways we had never achieved before. It was our dream to come and play in America and *The Yes Album* gave us that opportunity. To be able to support Jethro Tull and Alice Cooper in big arena shows was for us, an amazing and unreal experience. I loved the US so much, I stayed."

March 19, 1971. Progressive rock crafters Jethro Tull issue what will be their most critically acclaimed and commercially successful album, *Aqualung* (which currently sits at triple platinum). One of the album's more prominent and heavy tracks is "Locomotive Breath," which Trevor Rabin's band Rabbitt covered back in South Africa, scoring a local #1 hit.

Mid-1971. Strawbs issue *From The Witchwood*, the first and only Strawbs studio album to feature Rick Wakeman before his departure for Yes in July of 1971, pleading poverty in light of the high cost of maintaining a Hammond. By this point, Rick has discovered the Minimoog and plays a number of high profile sessions.

June 24 – July 24, 1971. Yes mount their first North American tour, playing 27 dates in the US and Canada. Yes supports the like-minded Jethro Tull, and do not have to cart their new PA system overseas for the dates. However, a new and compact system was created for the tour by Roy Clair, improved by the fact that the band had along with them Eddie Offord as soundman, who occasionally had to be rescued by Roy due to Eddie's on the road drugging.

Jon Anderson on being musically adventurous:

"It's just adventurous music. Rock is fantastic, but I also like folk and all sorts of music. With Yes, in the beginning, we played pop music—The Beatles, Frank Zappa, The Beatles—and it was an extension of that experience, where you're going to do rock music but adventurous, not basic, [music] working from the structure, like symphonic structure, where a lot is going on, and instrumentation. So, we expanded on that; we expanded our musical thinking. Then I did that with my solo work and my work with Vangelis, doing different things, writing for dance theatre, working with Kitaro and others—it's all experiments in music."

Bill Bruford on touring:

"I would love to be the spontaneous comic for you and have all those stories at my fingertips, but I'm afraid anything I might recount would be fairly dull from your point of view. I find pretty much the whole business of being a musician more or less absurd, to one degree or another, with more or less irritations, and more or less successes of one sort or another. It is permanently exhausting.

"Yes, on a daily basis, it can be very, very funny. But unless you have a very well developed sense of the absurd, you won't last for more than about 30 minutes in the music industry. Do I have specific funny things, whereby people are shooting fire extinguishers or throwing TVs out the bedroom window? No."

Late July 1971. With rehearsals for the band's next album floundering, it is decided that they need a new keyboardist, and Jon Anderson and Chris Squire ask Tony Kaye to leave the band, even if the main problem had been essentially a personality clash between the hard-partying Tony and the more mild-mannered Steve. After a late night phone call from Chris, Rick Wakeman checks the band out at one of their sessions, and decides to throw in his lot with Yes, at the expense of an offer to join David Bowie's Spiders From Mars. History has framed the switch as one where Tony, although classically trained, brought the wrong sort of classical to the band, as well as too much of a straight blues technique. The band is instantly productive, knocking out three of *Fragile*'s anchor tracks in the first three days.

Rick Wakeman on the first late night call to arms:

"I couldn't believe it. I covered me ear holes up and Rose, my wife, picked up the phone. I could hear the conversation. 'He's only just come in. He hasn't been back for three days; you know, he's really tired.' I was awake by then and let me tell you, I was furious! 'Gimme that phone.' 'Who's that?!' And this voice said, 'Oh, hello. It's Chris Squire from Yes.' It's three in the morning, mind you, and he said, 'How are you?' I said, 'You phone me up at three in the morning to ask how I am?!'"

Chris Squire on Rick:

"Rick brought a style to the band that was flashier and more solo-inspired. Tony Kaye, I suppose, you would call more of a rhythm keyboard player, as opposed to a lead keyboard player. Rick had a lot of lead chops, which was great for *Fragile*, which was a very rushed affair. But it went pretty smoothly, and we came up with a good album at the end of the day. I suppose Rick's humour helped a bit there."

July 31, 1971. Tony Kaye plays his last gig with Yes, in London, before returning years later.

September 9, 1971. John Lennon issues his *Imagine* album, featuring drummer Alan White. White is also one of many session musicians on George Harrison's album from the previous year, *All Things Must Pass*.

September 14, 1971 – March 27, 1972. Yes mount the Fragile Tour, which blankets the UK and the US, with only select mainland European dates. In December of 1971, support comes from Humble Pie. November 31 - December 18, 1971, Yes undertake their second ever US tour after their summer tour earlier in the year. After a handful of European dates into the new year, the band return to the States in February and March of 1972, where the band play dates with Black Sabbath and Wild Turkey in the west of the country.

Black Sabbath's Bill Ward on Yes:

"Great band, they're the best. They've left some very high quality music. If you're a student of music, then go listen to Yes, because the quality and the level of musicianship is brilliant, and it comes together very well. And Jon's lyrics are very pleasing because it's coming from a strong place and he's talking about humanness, which is what makes the world turn around. So Yes is a very important band, brilliant. On that tour, we were the headliners. Kinda strange to say that, but yeah, we were the headliners. Good tour; we had Rick Wakeman with us all the time. Nice guy, great musician—that's why he ended up on so many of our records. We were always with Rick. He'd travel with us; he'd be on our bus or he'd be on our plane. 'Oh, Rick Wakeman again [*laughs*].'"

October 1, 1971. Cat Stevens issues his *Teaser And The Firecat* album. One of three smash hits on the record is "Morning Has Broken," which features an uncredited Rick Wakeman playing the iconic piano part.

Rick Wakeman's debt to David Bowie and Cat Stevens:

"I was very fortunate to play on probably two of the most recognizable piano pieces—'Morning Has Broken' and 'Life On Mars'—and to arrange both of those. Now, the interesting thing is, if it hadn't been for Cat Stevens wanting to do 'Morning Has Broken' and David writing 'Life On Mars,' then it wouldn't have helped people to recognize the way I play. So I have a great debt of gratitude to both David Bowie and to Yusuf Islam, or Cat Stevens, a great gratitude. And it was an amazing time! It was an amazing period of time."

November 26, 1971. Yes issue, in the UK, their fourth album, *Fragile*. The album would be recorded over the space of a month, at Advision, with Rick later lamenting that the sessions for *Fragile* and its follow-up, *Close To The Edge*, would mark the only times the band would ever sit in a room together and bang out their parts. On the strength of the "Roundabout" single (an edit from the album version; b/w "Long Distance Runaround"), the album would go double platinum in the US and silver in the UK. Roger Dean's fantastic and ecology-minded illustration for the front cover would summarily reverse what was becoming one of rock's worst run of album jackets! As well, Roger offers a half-formed version of one of the most recognizable band logos of all time. Atlantic's Phil Carson had his eye on Roger for Yes from the beginning, but *Fragile* turned out to be the first time that band and painter would collaborate.

Chris Squire on the "Roundabout" single:

"Remember, this was very much the era of the album being the important part. The single thing was secondary, really, in that era. All of us were a bit surprised that Atlantic Records wanted to cut down 'Roundabout' to make it more palatable for radio, to make it a kind of digestible piece of music. We went along with it, but we weren't really happy with the edit, which was done with some Atlantic engineer in New York. We didn't think it was a very good edit, but it went out anyway, and of course, now lots of people have heard it [*laughs*]. Ultimately it was a good thing, but we weren't really focused on singles."

Jon Anderson recalls the benefits of the "Roundabout" edit:
"It was very simple, basically. When we put together the *Fragile* album, that was the real testing ground for us as a band. We had written, together, 'Heart Of The Sunrise' and 'Starship Trooper' and these are long-form pieces, you know? Especially 'Heart Of The Sunrise;' very complicated piece. And it's one of those things, if you'd have been in the studio when we did it, there I was with a very, very simple song idea, and Chris and Steve and Bill were doing this sort of aggressive phrasing. And I just walk over and say, 'Can you do that in another key?' and they did. And, 'Can you do it in another key?' and they did. And I said, 'Great, because that could be the beginning, and then the song will come.' And that's how it worked. I'd be listening to what people were doing and performing, and sort of drag it into the complex idea. And that was the concept of making music.

"So at that time, as it happened, we toured in America, with the *Fragile* album. See, *Fragile* and *Close To The Edge* were actually done in the same year, which is quite a trip. Musically speaking, it's an incredible amount of music, and I think it's because we were very connected. We were very much in harmony. And what you had was, we started playing around America and Canada, and we were starting to play universities. And the local radio stations, the university radio stations, were actually working with FM for the first time, which is a higher frequency. And actually, didn't have many advertisements in their daily projection of music. So when we went to these radio stations, they would play the whole of 'Roundabout,' which was kind of wonderful to us, because that's how it was created.

"But, 'Roundabout' was also edited down to a five-minute single, without us knowing. And it was a big surprise to hear it on the radio. And of course, we were very musically zealous and said, 'Oh, why did you get the big scissors out and do that?' But of course, it became a very big hit record, and that's why we sold a million records. It wasn't because of the long-form pieces. 'Roundabout' made us into a commercial entity, which was very interesting, because you had, say, a million people buying the record, and they would come and see the show, and go, what the heck is this? [*laughs*]. Expecting us to do ten versions of 'Roundabout,' or that kind of song, kind of a nice and dancy and poppy kind of song, which is cool. But that wasn't all we were. And so that's why we gained these legions of fans, who were very connected to what we were doing. And the reason was that we were connected to what we were doing. We weren't doing it just to be rock stars."

Rick Wakeman's views on "Roundabout:"

"I think Steve was playing the chordal riff and I was looking for something to play and tried a few things out. You know when something is right, and luckily something came up that was right! *Fragile* was a wonderful album to record. The record company left us alone. The management left us alone. In fact everybody left us alone to produce what we wanted. That was a wonderful time. It happened on *Close To The Edge* as well. It doesn't happen too much these days. And it was the first time working with Roger Dean. Steve discovered Roger, I believe, and introduced him and his work to us. We were all mightily impressed and Roger became a really important part of the Yes family."

Bill Bruford ponders the question of band democracy:

"*The Yes Album* I don't remember so much about. We were still in our Beatles phase I think, writing Beatles-influenced songs, on that album. But *Fragile*, that was a bit of a misconception, in a way. 'Heart Of The Sunrise' was great, 'Roundabout' was great, but the general mood within the band was one of frustration. And I remember, distinctly, suggesting that we all—any one of us—could write music for the group and should so do, and everybody should be given one track with which to use the talents of the group, write something for the group, and orchestrate it the way they wanted to. That fell into a big mistake and turned into a solo track by Howe, a solo track by Wakeman, and I think Jon and I were the only ones who managed to write something for the group."

December 17, 1971. Rick Wakeman plays on the late David Bowie's fourth album, *Hunky Dory*, which is release on this day. "I was very lucky with that album; I'd worked with David on 'Space Oddity' and I did 'Memory Of A Free Festival' and 'Wild Eyed Boy From Freecloud' with him, and then he called me 'round his house and said, 'I want to play you some songs,' and he played me 'Life On Mars?' on this battered 12-string, that phenomenal song, and my jaw dropped. He said, 'On the album, I want it to come from the piano, not from the acoustic guitar. So I want you to make some notes, learn the song and then play it almost as a piano solo, and I will get the band and everybody to work around what you do,' which was wonderful. Some people have said, 'You must've worked really hard to do that arrangement,' but it was actually very easy 'cause everybody had to work around me."

1972

1972. Geoff Downes is enrolled at the Leeds College of Music this year. On the side, he's got a band called She's French.

January 1972. Progressive rockers, Flash, featuring Peter Banks (and Tony Kaye as guest), issue their self-titled debut.

Peter Banks finds life after Yes:

"I felt my playing was better than what I did on the Yes albums. Obviously, I felt better because I had people who were prepared to compromise with their way of doing things, which was not always the way with Yes. Thinking back on it now, when people said it sounded like Yes, I hated that. I went out of my way not to make it sound like Yes. I guess there are similarities, probably through the way the songs were arranged. The fact that I was the original guitarist with Yes would obviously be apparent on the first Flash album. At the time I took it very badly. I didn't even want to do any interviews with anyone who mentioned Yes. I was young and pretty arrogant. My stance was, 'Hey, that's old history— nothing to do with me.'"

January 4, 1972. *Fragile* is released in the US, where the album will peak at #4, while rising to #7 in the UK.

February 1 & 2 1972. Between UK and American tour dates, Yes nip into Advision to begin laying down tracks for what will become *Close To The Edge*. Fatefully, the US tour dates after this studio visit would pair Yes with King Crimson.

March 10, 1972. Yes receive their first certification with *Fragile* going gold, three months after release. Lead single from the album, "Roundabout," peaks at #13 on Billboard. The song was inspired by the "40 or so" roundabouts the band had encountered winding their way one time from Aberdeen to Glasgow. Meanwhile, on the same day, Jethro Tull issue their revered *Thick As A Brick* concept album: Gerald Bostock lives!

Chris Squire on *Fragile*:

"We were just doing what came naturally at the time. *Fragile* was one of those albums where we had very little time in which to do the whole project. And that's why it ended up being an album with four songs on it, and then the solo tracks filled in the other part of it. And that was mainly because of time. But fortunately, what we did do, is turned it into one of our best-selling albums."

March 27, 1972. On the last day of the American Yes/King Crimson dates, in Boston, Bill checks in with Robert again about joining King Crimson. Robert tells Bill he is good enough for the gig

May – June, 1972. In May, Yes conduct more rehearsals for their forthcoming *Close To The Edge* album, working at the Una Billings School of Dance in Shepherd's Bush. Come June, the band was back at Advision for the serious graft of recording, spending the entire month crafting what will arguably be their greatest work, even though relations were tense within the band, with Bill Bruford especially unhappy as the band does more writing on the spot than is usually advisable.

June 1972. Atlantic issues a sampler album called *The Age Of Atlantic*. Yes is included with a 10:30 version of Simon & Garfunkel's "America." The track is subsequently edited down and released as a US single, backed with "Total Mass Retain," a piece of "Close To The Edge." The full-length version of "America" is included on the 1975 compilation *Yesterdays*.

July 19, 1972. Bill Bruford quits Yes, telling the story that manager Brian Lane makes him pay $10,000 to leave, with Bill also coughing up half his royalties on the *Close To The Edge* album to incoming drummer Alan White, as well as ceding to White the spiffy new set of drum cases Bill had just bought.

Rick on Bill's jumping ship:
"Sadness at the end of it all. It always puzzled us as to why he didn't leave before the album was recorded. If he knew he was leaving, he could have given us a chance to bed somebody new in. It did put a dampener on the final few days."

Steve Howe's reaction:
"The worst thing about *Close To The Edge* is that at the end of it, Bill said, 'I'm leaving' [*laughs*]. And I was totally devastated. I mean, I couldn't believe that Bill had even been thinking of it. I love Bill very much; he's a friend of mine. But I couldn't believe it. I mean, he knows I was obviously so shocked. I was almost... well, I was upset, because I didn't want Bill to leave. The fact that he wanted to go with Fripp also tended to insult me more, because he was a guitarist. It was a bit like me deciding to go with Aynsley Dunbar, or I was gonna join a band with Stewart Copeland. 'Bill, I'm gonna join a band with Stewart Copeland—goodbye!' And Bill said to me, 'I'm gonna join a band, and it's called King Crimson,' and I knew that was Robert Fripp.

"But I also understood and respected greatly Bill's musicality, and his desire to learn about music, which is why he went to Fripp. He wanted to learn more about improvising, more about free music. And he considered *Close To The Edge* actually quite commercial [*laughs*]. Well, I mean, in record sales it has to be. It has to have been seen in some way as being commercial. But commercial because it's uncommercial, more than it's commercial because it repeats the main line 25 times."

Jon Anderson's reaction:

"I was devastated when Bill said he was leaving, because I thought we'd really, together, made one of the most wonderful adventurous pieces. I would never have believed that we could do the *Close To The Edge* album, that kind of music. So I was on cloud #9 and I quickly descended [*laughs*], to cloud #2, when he said he was leaving. And he went to join King Crimson. And I thought, well, can't you get off on being in Yes and get the same energy? And he said, 'Nope. I just can't; it's not free enough for me.' So it was really tough."

Bill Bruford on whether Yes was a creatively healthy environment:

"Not particularly. Well, you say 'healthy' and 'creative' as if the two were kind of related. There's no necessary relationship between those two things. Sometimes things are intensely unhealthy but extremely creative, and very bad for your health. I found on the whole that both Crimson and Yes were quite difficult and we didn't achieve anything without some blood on the floor from somebody or another. Yes was an added difficulty because we were four or five people from all over the country with very different backgrounds and very different musical abilities. And sometimes there was the linguistic problem where we couldn't understand each other verbally, because of the different accents and so forth. So it's a bit like a guy from New Orleans and a guy from Alaska and a guy from Hollywood and a guy from Kansas City forming a group. It was a little like that. And it caused a lot of mayhem and also a lot of interest. You get those abrasive moments which give you creative flight. But that's not necessarily healthy and it's not necessarily going to be fun.

"I have no interest in working with King Crimson or Yes again, I think. That for me was very much the first, you know, 25 years of my career that suited the 20th century. I'm happy with that and I just spent quite a long time finding my way back to jazz. Now I have a state-of-the-art jazz group, which, you know, gets four stars in *Downbeat* and has some of the finest players in my country. It's portable, it's light, it's quick, it's fun. I've been known to have fun in Earthworks. I've had more fun probably than in any other group I've been in. So the idea of going back and knocking out a big four/four in a stadium somewhere is probably unlikely."

July 27, 1972. Alan White meets with Anderson and Squire, and agrees to join Yes. Alan had been a frustrated sideman playing with Joe Cocker at the time, but more importantly, he was Eddie Offord's roommate and close friend, which had prompted the odd visit to Advision for a look-in even before Bill Bruford had left the band.

Alan White on joining Yes:

"That was a great period of my life, a great stepping stone up to playing with a band like Yes. I was so young and naive at that time. I was like 20, 21 years old, and I was playing with people like that and doing sessions all around London, but the time was past almost before I knew what was happening. You have to pinch yourself on down the line to let yourself know you've been part of history like that."

Chris Squire's new partner in the rhythm section:
"Alan and I have been playing for what, nearly 40 years, since 1972, and it goes without saying that we know how to play with each other and turn it into a successful rhythm section. Alan, when he came in, was quite a different drummer from the drummer on the first four Yes albums, Bill Bruford, or should I actually say the first five Yes albums. Alan was a very different kind of drummer to Bill, and at the time of the transition, he wasn't exactly compatible for a while, because Alan wasn't really from the school of jazz rock that Bill was from, and so a lot of Bill's parts were hard for Alan. But after a while he learned and personalized them, and then that became standard for him. On the live *Yessongs* album, there's drumming from both Alan and Bill on it. If you listen to that, you can hear the difference between the two drummers. So it's great for me to have had the experience of working with two great drummers."

Jon Anderson on Alan White:
"We went to rehearsals trying to figure out what to do, and Alan White walked through the door. It was like Christmas had arrived. It was like, Alan White, he played with John Lennon! Come on! And Alan is one of the most lovely guys in the world. He was best man at my wedding, whatever, 20, 21 years ago. I was always connected to Alan on a different level, because he's just the sweetest guy. And boy, can he play. He can seriously play. He's an aggressive player. Where Bill was, you know, convinced that jazz fusion was his world. And jazz fusion for me, not too sure. I wanted to delve into deeper power, more power playing, if you like. And Alan sort of fitted the bill. We went on tour, and he learned the whole show in a couple of weeks, and then there he was on stage, driving the band like crazy. He just added another dimension."

Steve Howe on Alan:
"Bill was replaced by the perfect solution, which was Alan. He brought his solid robust drama. He saw what we hope any member of Yes will see and that is that Yes is a great vehicle if you keep your head screwed on. If you play and you develop your own parts and your own landscape for Yes—Alan did that. I still carry a bit of the Bill Bruford flame because we still play so much of his music. I mention it because I don't think anyone else does. I don't think that you can forget an originator."

Alan's drumming style:
"One attitude I have towards playing, is that when I was young—I guess it's because I'm a Gemini—I liked lots of different kinds of music, from classical to jazz, big band, fusion, R&B and rock 'n' roll—I was a big Weather Report fan

from when I was 18. So I try to incorporate that all into one style, but I want to always play with a lot of feel. One of my philosophies in playing, though, is just to play what is necessary for the songs. And wherever there is a possibility to try and do something different—we play things in fives and sevens, and it's pretty complex—that makes for some interesting drum playing beneath the melodies. There's so many people that play so many different ways. I like the Steve Smiths of the world, Lenny White; some of the fusion guys I loved a lot, and I use things from them within my style. Andy Newmark, Steve Gadd—all those guys influenced me from a distance in different ways."

July 30, 1972 – April 22, 1973. Yes conduct their Close To The Edge Tour, with new drummer Alan White. Support for the first three months comes from Eagles. In April, support comes from Poco, like Eagles, country rockers.

Bill Bruford's verdict on Alan:
"Alan plays very differently from me; he is good at steaming on all four. Very good timekeeper. Maybe he didn't do the fancy bits I did, but we are radically different. And I think when Alan came, it was a change. I think that now he has worked his own style into the group. It was quite a lucrative job, but I wasn't doing my best after *Edge*. There was very much a feeling that we'd cracked it and become famous. Later, all that became self-congratulatory, which I didn't really like."

Jon Anderson on playing the new album's centrepiece live:
"Every time we played 'Close To The Edge,' it was always, how did we do this? How did we put this together? [*laughs*]. And I remember when we were creating it, I was very interested in and had been listening to a lot of electronic music, particularly Walter Carlos, who had done this beautiful album, *Sonic Seasonings*. So the introduction and the centrepiece—especially the centrepiece—was this sort of spaced-out, nothingness of nothing, and then out of that will come a song. And the guys in the band would sort of look at me quizzically and say, 'Are you sure you want to keep going with this?' I said, 'Yeah, because out of that calmness, that gentle song period, we're gonna really go crazy, and make some really wild music.' Because we, up to that point, we'd been doing the song over, and then the bridge over, and then the main sort of chorus part, and we'd done it two or three times, and it was time to relax go and go into this deep space time.

"And to perform that on stage with dry ice and everything, the audience, for 20 minutes, would actually be spellbound. And that was the incredible thing—we didn't ask them to be quiet. We were too busy making the music, so we were sort of committed to getting through the music. But we'd finish the music and realize that the audience, especially in the middle section was so quiet, and you could hear a pin drop for 20 minutes, and then all of a sudden the audience would go crazy at the end. And I always remember performing it at the Maple Leaf Gardens. It was like unbelievable, the energy after the event of performance, you know?"

September 13, 1972. Yes issue their fifth album, *Close To The Edge*, produced by Eddie Offord. The album would peak at #3 in the US, and #4 in the UK, with the lone single from the record, "And You And I" being Chris's main songwriting contribution to the Jon- and Steve-dominated album. The title track, considered by many the greatest prog composition of all time, was initiated by Steve as a song about living along the river Thames; Howe was impressed with Jon's overhaul of it to make it more mystical and universal. Roger Dean's gatefold artwork of waterfalls enhanced the effect in a multimedia sense, but Dean's biggest breakthrough is the inaugural flight of the band's iconic logo, the product of 20 hours' worth of tinkering on the part of Roger, who was dismayed that it wasn't reproduced in stamped silver foil as originally requested.

Steve Howe, looking at Martin Popoff's copy of *Close To The Edge*:
"Eddie Offord. The guy in the right top-hand corner. He was no mean... he wasn't just there for the ride. Eddie, as it says, production: Yes, stroke, Eddie Offord. Eddie Offord was one of the guys who could take his dream, that he wanted to live out, and adopt it to Yes, and squash Yes together in an assemblance of balance, which I think, we've not known since. We've unfortunately lost his creative work. Basically, what I'm saying is, when you get five musicians together, they all want to play stuff at once [*laughs*]. It's not easy to balance. And Eddie had a terrific way of squashing and limiting and compressing things. So this is the apex for Eddie; this is the moment where Eddie and the band were synchronized.

"*Fragile* was like the warm-up to this. And *Close To The Edge* was the fruition of our work. Look, after all, he made *Time And A Word* as well. So this is a remarkable album; it has a remarkable drummer on it. Says, 'percussion' [*laughs*]; I like that—Bill Bruford: percussion. Bill helped invent the Yes sound before I came along and before Alan White came in. Bill is a musician. He's not just a drummer. He writes tunes, and some of the stuff that we play on this album, much of the stuff we play in this album, was inspired by Bill.

"So I hold this album high in my estimation. And the results we've had from it are amazing, in the longevity we've been able to play this material. Last night we played 'Khatru' and 'Close To The Edge,' so we keep going back to this. This was a very steep time in musical history for us, with the way that we recorded "Close To The Edge," carrying on from "Roundabout" and "Heart Of The Sunrise," where we started playing longer and longer tracks. And this is also a great piece of Roger Dean, where it came together, not only the first time you saw the continuing Yes logo, the bubble logo, and you've got the whole space to do this amazing sort of drippy, droopy water island."

Jon Anderson on "Close To The Edge:"

"'Close To The Edge' is realization. I'd actually been reading books at that time by Herman Hesse, which was *Journey To The East, Siddhartha*, and these are very enlightening books for me because there wasn't anything in scriptures that I tended to appreciate as much as what Herman Hesse was writing about, which was the understanding that we are collectively one on this planet. This is sort of a broad statement here, but he was saying that the journey to the east is a realization that God can be found anywhere, everywhere. Because God is all that is.

"And in a sense that grew upon me. So when I was singing, 'Close to the edge, round by the corner.' Actually, Steve wrote the lyric, 'close to the edge,' in a sort of song to me, singing to me. He said, 'I just started this song this morning, "Close to the edge, round by the corner."' And I sang, 'Down by the end, down by the river' because in *Siddhartha*, the river was the sort of the pinnacle of the book, where he realized that the river is like the soul. All of the rivers meet in the same ocean. So all the souls meet the same divine spirit of God, what we call God or whatever you want to call it. But it's the idea that we collectively, worldwide, we all are connected as one.

"And when you start writing 'A seasoned witch could call you from the depths of your disgrace,' which is what I wrote, that's a line relating to the fact that your soul consciousness, your higher self, will bring you to a realization. So I wrote it in a different sort of rhythmic fashion. There'll always be your higher self, grabbing hold of you from your point of confusion and disgrace of life, or why am I here, what am I doing? But your higher self will call you and say, 'Hey, no worries. Everything is OK. Nothing matters. You're living this experience. It's important to grow.' And that's what life's all about. You know, you get up, you get down. The whole idea is the constant flow of realization. It was always close to the edge of realization—for me, anyway.

"One other thing, with Steve, it's like, the middle of 'Close To The Edge,' you have this song, 'two million people barely satisfy.' 'I get up I get down.' And that's me singing to his chords. So the next day, we were going through the song again, and then I just heard him using the same chords, singing another song. I said, 'What's that?' He said, 'Well, before I played you these chords, I'd actually written this other song, "In her white lace, she can clearly see the lady looking..."' And I said, 'Wow, why don't we just put them together?' So that's what we did. We stuck them together with super glue. And it's kind of magical. You have two songs, moving together, creating that little section of 'Close To The Edge.' And that's one of the reasons it worked."

Bill Bruford on *Close To The Edge*:

"*Close To The Edge* was a really nice album. I think we got lucky. We were sailing. It was kind of being written while it was being recorded. It was one of those things where the bits fell luckily where they fell, and it made that perfect side of an album, and a lovely form for a record. So even though it's probably laughed at now, *Close To The Edge* was, and in 20 years and in 30 years, will stand out as one of the great records of that particular year."

Rick Wakeman's favourite *Close To The Edge* moment:

"For me it's the church organ bits leading into the Hammond solo. As far as a keyboard player is concerned it's manna from heaven to be able to do something like this on record."

October 1972. "And You And I" is issued in the US as a single, the first two parts split between a side each—the single reaches #42 in the charts.

Jon Anderson on changing drummers mid-stream:

"It probably came as a shock to Bill that we found a replacement so easily. We are happy with the outcome and we hope Bill will be happy. All artists have a lost period after doing intense work. The ideas are drained out of you and frustration seeps in. It was the same thing when Tony left, and we thought that Rick could do a better job in bringing new ideas. I don't think it's as hard, fitting in a drummer as it would be a new instrumentalist. The instrumentalists are soloists in Yes, and the drummer is the root."

October 30, 1972: Close To The Edge is certified gold, virtually upon release.

Chris Squire on doing a long song:

"When we came to *Close To The Edge*, we were attempting to do the first album with a 20-minute long piece of music, which back in the days of vinyl, was about the length of time you could do and maintain the sound quality. And so that album is known for that, where we pulled out the long-form music, which we became famous for. But I don't think it stands out particularly from other albums we made, other than the long-form pieces. Not really anybody else was doing it, although I have to tip my hat to The Who, because they had done their sort of rock opera thing, which we loosely based our idea on that concept. *Close To The Edge* is still very enjoyable to play, all three of those songs, actually, and people really have a fond memory of that album, which is why it's so successful in a live situation."

Jon Anderson on spirituality and "Close To The Edge:"

"When I was writing 'Close To The Edge' with Steve, I was reading a lot about spirituality and how it stretches across the entire world. There's a connection, like all rivers lead to the same ocean. So I thought, you know, 'Close To The Edge, down by the river.' And it's like people say "'Close To The Edge' is about disaster," but no, it's about realization! We're on this journey and the only reason we live is to find the divine. To find God from within. You can be out there with your car and big TV and marriage and kids and money, or no money, or whatever, but the only reason we live is to find contentment and a spiritual connection with Earth Mother. And that's what I sing about. I sing about it on different levels; I try to jump from one experience to another experience, and balance it out."

November 1972. Flash issue their second album, *In The Can*, rush-finished after the band returned from their first US tour, September 18, 1972.

Author review:

This post-Yes Peter Banks vehicle was a not-to-be-ridiculed marriage between pop and progressive, Flash also adding elements of Wishbone Ash-like leads and faint proto-metal from years gone by. But mainly, what we have here is complex, involved song structures not over-laden with chops, sorta like soundtrack or stage music, passage leading to passage to passage, each part on its own not all that remarkable. Sort of Tull, Genesis, Gentle Giant and moldy Yes all mushed together, *In The Can* is a disciplined enough hippie excursion, even lightening up for a 1:50 drum solo called 'Stop That Banging.' Vocalist Colin Carter is perhaps a bit of an old '60s ham, but one can become endeared. All in all, *In The Can* shows its age, sounding not unlike Banks-era Yes stretched out to prog extremes.

December 1972. Chris Squire buys a home called New Pipers (in Virginia Water, Surrey), which the band will take advantage of for recording purposes. Also in 1972, he marries Nikki, entering into his first of three marriages. Chris tells the story how he went from renting a flat to buying a mansion with no steps in-between; similarly, his first car was a Bentley.

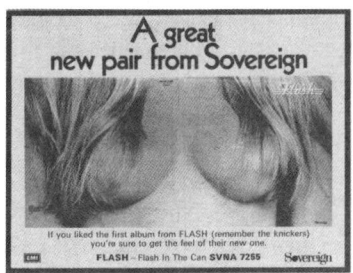

1973

1973. In this year, Roy Flynn, manager of the band through the *Time And A Word* era, settles out of court with subsequent management company Hemdale (personified by Brian Lane) for $150,000, in payment for his considerable investment keeping the band afloat in the lean years.

January 23, 1973. Rick Wakeman issues his first of what will become over 100 solo albums, *The Six Wives Of Henry VIII*—a 1971 covers record called *Piano Vibrations* is alternately considered the first, but not by Rick and many Yes fans. The album reaches #30 on Billboard and goes gold. Guesting on the record are Yes members Steve Howe, Chris Squire, Bill Bruford and Alan White. "Catherine Of Aragon" turns out to be pretty much a Yes track *sans* Jon Anderson.

Rick Wakeman on his songwriting, particularly on piano:
"I can thank David Bowie very much, because David told me many years ago to write everything on the piano. He said, 'If you write it on the piano and it works as a piece of music, you can do anything with it.' He writes everything on a really horrible old 12-string guitar, and he says, 'If it sounds good on this, then I know it will sound good whatever I do; it can only get better and better and better.' And so everything that I've ever written, I've done on the piano, and the great thing about that is that you can't get any more minimalistic than when you're sitting at the piano."

Author review:
One of the key Wakeman records from the man's vast catalogue of approximately a hundred titles, *The Six Wives* is a pleasant enough marriage of progressive rock and renaissance classical, with Wakeman overflowing with every sort of keyboard sound from then-modern synth to pipe organ. Reinforcing each daunting track is a coterie of players, most notable performances coming from the bass players and drummers, both guitars and vocals (used instrumentally) left merely textural, as keyboards, bass and drums propel most tracks to blustery, dreamy conclusions. The record is designed to instrumentally evoke the temperament of the six wives, each partitioned to a track, each supported on the back cover with a short paragraph of biography. Picture instrumental Yes or Jethro Tull super-dosed with keyboards and you'll pretty much arrive at this melancholy, often mysterious and depressing affair. However. it laid the groundwork for Wakeman's future pioneering of new age music.

March 8 - 27, 1973. Yes play dates for the first time in Japan and Australia, notching 11 shows.

Jon Anderson on the band's power in the early 1970s:
"I think the band at that time was in harmony to the max. It was like, we knew we were good at what we did. Whether people liked it or not wasn't the point. We just knew we were good. And we performed with real passion and real commitment to being who we were. We just had this harmony. And during the course of that period of time, some of the great stage sessions happened where we were at times pretty loose, a little bit adventurous. The concept of the band was to structure your music so you knew it heart by heart, note by note. You knew exactly what

you were going to play, what you were going to perform. And the rest was the joy of performing it as damn tight as possible, as clear as possible, but with incredible passion and making it sound obviously better than the record."

March 17, 1973. Better late than never, *The Yes Album* is certified gold.

March 23, 1973. Robert Fripp totally revamps King Crimson's lineup for *Larks' Tongues In Aspic*. The band's new drummer is Bill Bruford, who will be with the band through its break-up in September the following year, then rejoining for the band's reunion in the 1980s.

Bill Bruford likes improvising with King Crimson:
"Great fun and very exciting and nobody told us we couldn't really do that. We perceived of ourselves as a kind of improvising rock group really, in a European sense. In other words, this wasn't Eric Clapton-styled improvising on the blues pentatonic scale. It was improvising more with timbre and sound and power, and often with less familiar scales, whole tone scales for example and so forth. And Robert, he has a dark side certainly, and that resonated within the band."

May 18, 1973. Yes issue their first live album, a triple LP set called *Yessongs*, which goes to #7 on the British charts and #12 in the US.

Roger Dean on working with Yes:
"The images for Yes are a bit of a conflict. The ones that worked best for me were the *Yessongs* ones, and they were the only ones I did without being totally involved with the band. *Fragile* was a real long drawn-out struggle; it went on for months and months, talking and drawing and talking, compromise and balances of opinion and things like that. I think on *Fragile*, the struggle shows too much. It shows less and less with each successive album. *Topographic Oceans*, which has more compromises in it, it shows much less. I've managed to cope with it."

July 1973. Badger issue their debut album, *One Live Badger*, which features a Roger Dean cover and a pop-up cardboard badger when you open up the gatefold sleeve. The band features ex-Yes, keyboardist Tony Kaye, and David Foster, who had worked with Jon Anderson in The Warriors as bassist. Tony's original name for his new band was Angel Dust until cooler heads prevailed.

July 9, 1973. Jethro Tull pre-empt Yes with their own *Tales From Topographic Oceans* (of sorts!). The similarly spiritually questing *A Passion Play* contains one song split over two sides. As would be the experience with *Tales*, some fans and most critics revolt.

Late summer – early autumn 1973. Yes work at Morgan Studios, north London, on the material for their forthcoming sixth album. The band

had gotten favourable financial terms to use the place, plus Morgan had been outfitted with the first 24-track equipment in England. Brian Lane, because Jon had wanted to record the album in the country or maybe even outdoors in a forest at night, decided to dress the working environment up to look like a farm, complete with hay bales, white picket fence and cardboard cut-out of a cow.

Fall 1973. Flash issue their third album, *Out Of Our Hands*, just before breaking up in November. Peter Banks's first solo album *Two Sides Of Peter Banks* is also issued this year.

September 1973. *Melody Maker* mounts an awards ceremony celebrating the winners of their 1973 Pop Poll Awards, which is dominated this year by Yes.

November 16, 1973 – April 23, 1974. Yes execute their Tales From Topographic Oceans Tour, a North American and European jaunt only. February and March finds John Martyn supporting the band in the US. Yes bring an elaborate fibreglass, steel and lights set, designed by Roger Dean and his brother Martyn, to the venues–much more than they would be able to use back home in these bigger arenas.

Journalist and Yes author Chris Welch analyses *Topographic Oceans* live:
A disturbing night for a Yes fan at London's Rainbow, when the group unveiled their new work, *Tales From Topographic Oceans*. For despite the applause that followed, despite the laudatory cries of "fantastic" from those around me, my own feelings were of having been drowned in the Topographic Ocean. The new music gave the impression at least of being one long embellishment, with no other foundation. A series of meticulously rehearsed sections, assembled and dovetailed together, it was like playing by numbers. Where was the sparkling individuality of the players?

November 19, 1973. Emerson, Lake & Palmer issue their critically acclaimed fourth studio album *Brain Salad Surgery*. Every record this band releases in the 1970s is certified gold, save for one live album. ELP and King Crimson were positioned in the minds of prog fans as the wilder and darker of the big prog acts, with Genesis as more plush and melodic, and Yes—with the counterpoint between Howe and Squire on one side and Wakeman and Anderson on the other—somewhat mediators at the midpoint, joined there arguably by Jethro Tull.

November 28, 29, 1973. Yes play the Manchester Free Hall. At one of the shows, Rick, having had a few beers, yells to his keyboard tech John Cleary stationed beneath the keyboards in case of breakdowns, that once the show is over, they'd head out for a curry. John misreads him and shows up 20 minutes later with a chicken curry plus sides, which Rick proceeds to park on his keyboard, tucking in. The famous episode represents in Yes lore a couple things: first, Rick being a meat-eater against a bunch of vegetarians, but second, his lackadaisical attitude toward his job—a justified accusation at this juncture, as Rick has already given his notice that he will be leaving the band after the current tour obligations.

December 14, 1973. Yes issue, in the UK, their sixth studio album, the double LP concept album *Tales From Topographic Oceans*. The album is produced by Eddie Offord, who has now produced four studio albums for the band, as well as engineering on *Time And A Word*. The sprawling album, with one track on each of its four sides, is summarily ridiculed by critics and the industry, in large part due to its meandering music, but also its almost religious cult-like lyrical musings. Nonetheless, the record ships gold rising to #6 on the Billboard charts.

Steve Howe defends *Tales From Topographic Oceans*:
"*Topographic* was our indulgence. Most people think of it as that, but it was a musical indulgence where we didn't see why we couldn't have more time

than we had on the last record. And that's not really a failing. But yeah, we did that because we really did have space. We had the writing power, we had the arrangement power, to go beyond the size of *Close To The Edge*. But I don't think size is really it. I think it was just that we dreamed up this concept about the four sides, and had the music to fulfil it. And all we needed was the group's enthusiasm, which wasn't there all the time. Jon and I did have some uphill struggles with the other three guys in the band, who weren't always convinced we were doing the right thing. We somehow convinced them, for better or worse.

"*Topographic* is just our exuberant, over-the-top record, that I guess, you'd have to like Yes quite a lot. But I'd like to point out one thing: when it came out, of course, the press slagged it like mad; Rick left the band, virtually, because all his friends said they hated it so much, and that was really dumb. I've got a review of *Fragile* from the *Melody Maker* which slagged *Fragile* totally. Not wishing to demean your trade, your business, but sometimes reviewers go too far. And, well, they tried to kill *Fragile*. It didn't work. They tried to kill *Tales...* It didn't work. Because a year later this record was being heralded by Yes fans as a masterpiece. I'm not saying it is a masterpiece, but it's certainly a lot of Yes music."

Rick Wakeman's mixed views on *Tales...*:
"You see, what people sometimes forget, is that while I'm in the band, I'm a fan as well. You can be in the band and be a fan of the band as well. All the times I've not been in the band, I've been a fan of the band. And, as a fan, I think I'm as entitled as anybody else to say I love that album, that's quite good or oh, I don't like that. And *Topographic Oceans*, there would have never been a problem with it if the CD had been around. The problem was, we had a little bit too much material for a single album, and not enough material for a double album.

"So you do one of two things. You either say, OK, we'll make a nice single album, or you expand. And we went down the expansion route, but we didn't have the material. So there was padding for days to get a track to each side. And a lot of the padding was junk. And I'll stand by that 'til this day. If the CD had been around, we would have had probably 50 minutes, maybe an hour. One of the tracks might have been 10, one of them might have been 20, one of them might have been 14. But they would have had their natural length, not, oh, let's bash away here and do something to make it longer. How long is that? 14? Oh, we need another four minutes. Bash away a bit longer. There was too much padding, and I know where the padding is and it pains me every time I heard it.

"But it was back in those days when, you go back into the '70s, everything was black and white. So I said what I thought, and when I said something was very black, others said it was very white. Back then we weren't in a mature situation where

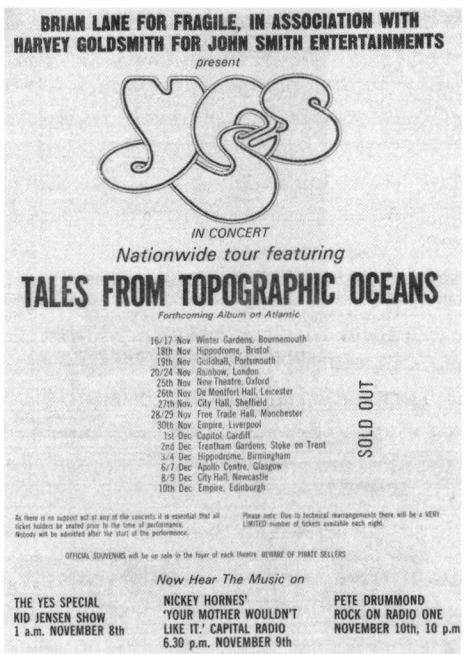

we could sit and say, 'Hold on a minute, let's talk about this.' So, to me it was black and white; I hated it. But the truth, in the cold light of day, there are some beautiful things on there. 'Ritual (Nous Sommes Du Soleil)' is beautiful. There are some really, really nice bits and pieces on there, and a lot of junk. Interestingly enough, now everybody else pretty much feels the same way, and say, 'Yes, there's some great stuff on there but, oh boy, did we really do that? We really shouldn't have done that.'

"And when we came to do 'Ritual' for the '04 tour, we revisited it. I mean, completely revisited it. It still sounds like 'Ritual,' but it's tightened up; it's tighter, slightly different arrangement, got rid of a few things that weren't necessary. It's 100 times better than on the album. But that's why I don't like the album, because basically, it was music to fit the constraints of vinyl. And that's never how music should be written. It's really funny, because when we did 'Revealing' for the first part of the last tour, again, we revisited it and played it 100 times better than it ever was on the record. When we finished the first leg of the tour, we always have private votes on what we should keep and what we should keep out. On the second leg of the tour, the vote was four to one to get rid of it, and I was the only one who voted to keep it, which is quite funny, for somebody who actually hated the album. But 'Ritual,' I wasn't sure we could make work, but we have made it work, and it's really, really good. That happens with a lot of Yes stuff. Some of it works better onstage and some of it's better on the record, for some reason."

Time And A Word

Writer Chris Welch on *Tales...*:
Brilliant in patches, but often taking far too long to make its various points, and curiously lacking in warmth or personal expression. If this review sounds like a series of carping complaints in the face of marvellous musicianship and obvious sincerity, I can only say that the music is more of a worry and test of endurance than a transport of delight. But doubtless *Topographic* will give many pleasure, and the band should be congratulated on setting themselves such high standards. I just wish they'd make it easy on themselves. The strain is becoming unbearable.

Journalist Steve Clarke's view:
The colour and excitement which Yes usually get down on record is entirely missing. Wakeman almost exclusively sticks to Moogs and Mellotrons, opting for piano a couple of times and organ once. Far too often, the music seems to lack positive construction, just losing itself in a wash of synthetic sounds. Steve Howe's guitar playing adopts the same tonal colour as Wakeman's keyboards, and comes over as boring. A great disappointment, and I only hope that Yes return to real songs on which they demonstrate fully their excellent musicianship.

Future Yes multi-instrumentalist Billy Sherwood:
"The funny thing about *Close To The Edge*: that was the first record I ever listened to by Yes. My brother and Jimmy Haun, who was the guitar player for Circa for a while, they were five years older than me. When I was a kid, I was listening to Earth, Wind & Fire, Ohio Players, and funk stuff, Rufus and Chaka Khan, and I was loving that stuff. And they said, 'You've got to hear this band called Yes.' And they played me *Close To The Edge*, and I just... I couldn't believe how bad it was! [*laughs*]. I hated it. And they were like, 'What?!' And I just said, 'I don't get this at all. I'm sorry.'

"And then a couple of weeks later, all of a sudden, I kind of wanted to hear it again. To figure out what was it about it that was putting me off. And I started listening to it again and again and again, and before you know it, every other band went by the wayside. And Yes became my favourite. And then *Tales From Topographic Oceans* came out, and it was like, there's no better band than this. This is the coolest band ever. That's my favourite, and most sort of emotionally attached record, because it's the first one I ever got totally immersed in.

"And I went backwards and got into *Fragile* and *Close To The Edge*, *The Yes Album*, *Time And A Word* and all that stuff, started understanding who the other players were, and I always dug it all. That's the one thing that, for me, I enjoyed every lineup that has been in Yes. You know, for a lot of people, that's upsetting [*laughs*], because they're just, this is the best version, that's the best version! Forget about this other one. For me it's all just music, and who was there was there, and they contributed, and let's hear it. It all has a different sound and a different phase, but there's always a continuity going on through Yes music.

46

But *Tales* and then *Relayer* and *Going For The One*, there was a period there when that's all I wanted to listen to over and over."

Author review of *Tales...*:

Call this one the black hole of Yes experiences, the band dissipating, expanding, exploding and imploding all at once, Jon Anderson blowing out a lifetime of spiritual restlessness over four sides of alternately agonizing and purifying progressive rock lunacy. As Jon's foreword to the lyrics explain, the record's four sonic labyrinths correspond to the four part Shastric scriptures.

All told, *Tales From Topographic Oceans* succeeds in creating at least strong, complicated suggestions of its many motives. But talk about walking into the "prog rock sucks" trap. You couldn't get much more hippie-tripped than all this claptrap.

Of course, non-fans practically threw up at the mere mention of this record (after they stopped laughing hysterically that is). Fans quickly and permanently divided into camps of praisers and detractors. Rick Wakeman was severely perturbed at the whole high-falutin', high times concept (eventually leaving the band in disgust), and Yes blinked nary an eye at playing the whole enchilada live.

If you can push aside the overbearing Yogi-ness of the thing, *Tales* actually contains some fairly accessible music. Side one gives us the most connectable stuff, the band writing a fairly level-headed multi-part composition. I mean, that chorus is almost catchy. Side two once more offers a million things, but the overall tone is quite melodic, pleasant and mellow, even madrigal-like unto Jethro Tull, albeit very old Jethro Tull. Steve Howe, in particular, gets to express himself, offering a number of guitar sounds, but again, rarely veering too crazy.

But one begins to tire of all the channel-surfing as the track winds to an end. The record begins to feel like a coterie of engaging players on a relaxing but aimless stroll, no real work on anyone's mind, but for this reason, no egos. Side three was the whacked-out one, perhaps betraying the actual personality of the record and the band during this tense era, sounding like flopped and floundering fish trying to make it as an ELP covers band, completely gelatinous despite jarring little robot bursts from Jon. Quite bizarre.

If *Tales* is the revisitation record for the bored Yes fan, then side three is the final frontier. The slinky music and warped rhythms are supposed to evoke thoughts of ancient societies, in sync with the near hieroglyphic lyrical thread, but what emerges is simply a wondrous example of how far from the commercial 1970s music could be allowed to wander. Nice extended solo excursion from Steve and his ever thoughtful acoustic guitar, after which Jon chimes in with the track's most logic-grounded segment.

So three sides gone, and the same sort of one-level fuss-about of it all continues, each track featuring much loitered creation of environment or backdrop without a whole lot of personal projection. This is a subdued record through and through, even when a majority are trying to muster aggression, a happenstance which may have to do with Offord's liquid, treble-soft production.

Side four offers no solutions although a certain hazy hope pervades Anderson's lyric. The music is just too languished and insufferably relentless in its somewhat trashy advance unto resolution. But after a heavy-ish cornucopic miasma of fast music, resolution most certainly arrives, in the closing percussive jam, where each member had been given a drummer's toy to bash (Sepultura does it better!). After this, Jon sings a mildly moving bit of love balladeering, a moment that is as personable as parts of side one, and then after a bit more jiggling and doodling, it's all over.

Quite the baffling bunch of sonics by any measure, *Tales* is nevertheless a necessary record to the Yes saga, the point to which the band had to go, to snap back on track, to provide contrast to more urgent material, and as previously supposed, to provide a lush jungle for the fan who has grown tired of the cultivated landscaping which he visits often and unfearfully.

1974

1974. Tony Kaye and Badger issue their first studio album (and last album), *White Lady*. Saxophonist Eddie Harris issues *E.H. In The U.K.* The album is recorded at Morgan Studios with a bevy of prominent English rockers, including Jeff Beck and Ian Paice. Chris Squire cites the album as the favourite guest slot of his career, playing on a couple of tracks with Alan White, Tony Kaye, Albert Lee and Steve Winwood.

January 1974. Yes issue a UK single pairing "Roundabout" (live) with "And You And I" (live).

Eddie Offord on Jon Anderson:
"The spontaneous member of the band, Jon writes or co-writes all the songs and lyrics for Yes, and has a lot of nice ideas for arrangements, although he hasn't got any talent for playing an instrument. He's very spiritual. Chris and Jon are like the yin and yang. They balance each other out."

January 9, 1974: *Tales From Topographic Oceans* is released in the US, attaining gold certification a month later.

Chris Squire comparing Bill Bruford with Alan White:
"Bill was with Yes from the ground up from the first album, and we had a great relationship in terms of how and what we did. We really didn't plan it. He just played like he played, which was a jazz-influenced style of drumming. And I had my Who influence, if you like, and somehow or other the two fit together in a peculiar way that became a sound. We had quite a fluid relationship, actually, from

John Smith productions presents

RICK WAKEMAN

Performing

"JOURNEY TO THE
CENTRE OF THE EARTH"

Accompanied by

FULL ORCHESTRA
AND CHOIR

Narrator   Conductor
DAVID HEMMINGS   DAVID MEASHAM

LEO SAYER
PROCOL HARUM

Plus **GRYPHON**
WALLY THE **WINKIES**

SATURDAY, JULY 27th

Noon to 8 p.m.
DOORS OPEN AT 11 A.M.
TICKETS WILL BE ON SALE ON THE DAY
TICKETS £2.75 (inc. VAT) in advance
£3.00 (inc. VAT) on the day
ADVANCE TICKET AGENCIES
from all branches of
HARLEQUIN RECORD SHOPS
(01-492 3063)

LONDON THEATRE BOOKINGS   MR. FOX RECORDS
(01-439 3371)   (01-688 0975)
96 SHAFTESBURY AVE., LONDON, W.1   34 STATION RD., WEST CROYDON

what I remember. I mean, Bill was pretty outspoken. I welcomed that; it's good to have someone who has a clear idea of what he wants, and knows what he wants to play. It all seemed quite natural to me, what Bill was doing. We definitely came up with a few things together that have stood the test of time. And when Bill left, after *Close To The Edge*, Alan came in, and he was almost 180° different as a drummer from Bill. Alan had serious rock staples under his belt, like playing on *Imagine* and the George Harrison album, at the time. And so he came from a very different school. But at the end of the day, playing with both drummers was a great education for me, because their styles were so different. But fortunately, my style seemed to fit in with both of them."

Alan White on the band's long-form music during this period:

"It became the norm—yeah, rebels [*laughs*]. There was so much musical talent in the band at the time that we wanted to try to find a new avenue. I don't think there's many people that can can emulate some of that stuff because it's pretty difficult to play. We just went down our own avenue and created our own style even more. This band came from more of a musical space, saying, 'Let's test ourselves out, as long as we're making something that looks like the future.'"

February 18, 20, 1974. Yes play two shows at Madison Square Garden, sponsored by *Melody Maker* magazine. The sold-out shows gross about $260,000, the reporting of which got the magazine in a bit of hot water.

May 9, 1974. Rick Wakeman issues his second solo album, *Journey To The Centre Of The Earth*, which, like the debut, goes gold. The concept album also goes gold in the UK and garners a Grammy nomination.

Author review:

Ol' Rick, the Svengali of super serious silliness is at it again, going well beyond the call of duty, constructing an elaborate concept record complete with symphony, narration and lots of acid-placid pictures. This one's based on the Jules Verne story, Wakeman concentrating on a scant few themes, a) the beginning of the journey from Germany to Iceland, b) a little metaphysical recollection of a life gone by,

c) a bizarre battle between two sea monsters (including an eight-page booklet which shows them atop a couple of frosty pints!); and d) a depiction of the destination, or forest, which the included photos would have us believe looks like the inside of a mouth.

Musically, it's all a little much (like that fall-down-laughing Deep Purple thing), a classical record with rock passages and lots of Wakeman synthesizer worming around the place. There's very few lyrics, but the narration fills in the gaps. That is if you care. Wakeman breaking all the rules of restraint, leap-frogging prog into the Tap zone. But hey, the goofy music fan of the day liked it, propelling the record to #1 on the UK charts, and aiding in Rick's decision to leave Yes after an unpleasant sail on *Topographic Oceans*.

May 18, 1974. Rick, on the phone from his home in Devon, tells Brian Lane that he is indeed quitting the band, confirmed in his decision by the material he was hearing coming out of the *Relayer* sessions. Moments later he gets a call from A&M's Terry O'Neil telling him that his new solo album had just hit #1 on the British charts.

Rick Wakeman accentuating the positive in 1973:

"I've worked with plenty of bands, but Yes is just incredible. The band's main composer is Jon Anderson, and he's just so gifted at it that it's right we do mostly his stuff. I work primarily as an arranger in the group; that's the capacity I served on *Close To The Edge*, which I was much more comfortable working on than *Fragile*. It was really strange, since they asked me to join the group and the next day they were in the studio to record *Fragile*, with me playing parts they had written that I'd never even seen before."

And talks about his least favourite moment too:

"Tales From Topographic Oceans Tour. It's very hard to play music that you are not into. You can play the notes, but there is so much more to music than playing notes."

July 1974. Rick is admitted to hospital after a minor heart attack.

August 1974. After auditioning Greek synthesizer magician Vangelis Papathanassiou for a couple of weeks, the band put Patrick Moraz through his paces. He is from post-Nice band Refugee and plays to the guys in Chris Squire's barn, using Vangelis's keyboards—he gets the gig.

Vangelis Papathanassiou quashes the idea of joining Yes:

"To me, there are only two types of music—honest music and dishonest music. Now, when I listen to Yes's music, I am conscious of the fact that it is occidental music. It is very English in its nature. Now I am not like that. I'm not saying I'm an oriental, but Greece has such a rich heritage and there are certain similarities between some ethnic Greek music and Chinese music. It would be very difficult for me to play with any band. I wouldn't like to have my music limited by the abilities of one particular group of people."

Patrick Moraz recalls his audition:

"I remember it very well. It was a Wednesday afternoon, and what I saw was incredible. There was a trailer lined up with vegetarian food, an army of roadies, amazing monitor systems. I mean, Refugee was selling out 3000-seat halls in England, but this was a whole new plateau. We introduced each other, had some tea, and then they played what was to become 'Sound Chaser' on *Relayer*— just the middle part, because I would write the introduction later. I was totally overwhelmed, because they played so fast and so precisely and so well."

August 1974. Canadian hard rockers Bachman-Turner Overdrive issue their third album, *Not Fragile*.

Randy Bachman on *"Not Fragile:"*

"'Not Fragile' is a great track because Fred Turner wrote that and it was the antithesis of the Yes album, which is called *Fragile*, which was such intricate playing. I'm not putting down Yes, because I really like them and their sound; they had some good hits. But the *Fragile* album is like the ultimate, you know, almost being too much, almost too cluttered. Obviously this was before the heavy metal speed guys, but there was a lot of stuff to ingest in your brain when all you wanted to do is enjoy the music. So Fred came up with this absolutely simple, mindless but headbanging riff [*sings it*], to scream and sing over. And the thing about that was that anybody can pick up the guitar and play 'Not Fragile.' Nobody could go play the *Fragile* album by Yes; that was the difference. One was the LCD, the lowest common denominator that always ran through the band. That's what BTO was, the lowest common denominator. You don't want the guy who's 40, who's been studying guitar for 30 years, to buy your record, to learn your riff. You want the 13-year-old kid who can't play to buy your record to learn your riff, and you want him to be able to learn and play the riff because then he'll keep playing your records and keep buying them. I learned that long ago."

August – October 1974. The band work on what will become *Relayer*, at New Pipers, Chris Squire's home using Eddie Offord's mobile equipment, with mixing to take place at Advision.

Patrick Moraz remembers how he joined Yes:

"Personal contact with Jon Anderson, which had been arranged by my very good friend Ray Gomez, guitarist extraordinaire, also by Chris Welch, the main journalist for the music paper *Melody Maker* and also through a request by Brian Lane, Yes's manager at that time. Then through the request by the whole group. Apparently, it was a unanimous decision and the invitation came quite instantly. The day after I played with them for the very first time, I got a call telling me I was in the band as an equal member, and my presence was being requested immediately! Personally, I wasn't sure I wanted to get into Yes at the time because I was doing film scores—I was working on two movies at the same time, one with my friend Gerard Depardieu—and I was still under professional commitment with Refugee. Although we were on the verge of splitting up Refugee, we still had some concerts to do, promoting our first and only album *Refugee*, which had entered at #28 in the *Melody Maker* British music charts a few weeks earlier and was still climbing."

Steve Howe on *Relayer*:

"*Relayer*—and this is almost the same for *Topographic*—it's a very stylistically definitive record. Because we invented it right there and then. We worked out how to make 20-minute tracks that we took three days to record. We wouldn't stay in there for three days, but when we came back the next day, we carried on with the song. It was a quest, it was a mission, it was a concept."

October 6, 1974. King Crimson issue their seminal *Red* album, simultaneously with Robert Fripp announcing that the band is breaking up. Bill Bruford is fine with it, up for whatever comes next.

November 18, 1974. Yes rivals Genesis issue a concept double album, an answer to *Topographic Oceans*, called *The Lamb Lies Down On Broadway*. Unlike the Yes record, however, history views *Lamb* as a classic, maybe the band's greatest triumph, and indeed the record most cited as a rival to *Close To The Edge* as greatest prog rock album of all time.

November 28, 1974. Yes issue, in the UK, their seventh studio album, *Relayer*. It is a dense, jazzy, opaque album for the band, but not as inscrutable as its preposterous predecessor. The record peaks at #4 in the UK and #5 in the US, despite its challenges. As well, the album goes gold in the US within a month, which speaks favourably of the record buying public's willingness to support complicated progressive rock. Roger Dean offers one of his most monochromatic covers, the idea inspired by Tolkien, with the scene representing a potential Garden of Eden, hence the presence of the snake.

Steve Howe on containing Patrick Moraz:

"*Relayer* was almost as hard as *Topographic*, even though it was only a single album. It was a tough album to make. It was, once again, conceptualized to the nth degree. Patrick Moraz joined us, and we had to kind of contain him as well as push him and let him lead occasionally. We had to contain him because in a way, that wheel on the Minimoog, the wheel on that synth, was one of the sounds he liked most. And we didn't want him to touch the wheel and make that vibrato. So in the way the guitar wasn't playing blues and therefore wasn't playing vibrato, we also didn't want the group to suddenly sound like, you know, Chick Corea And Return To Forever. We didn't really want it to sound extremely jazzy or extremely fusion, because we wanted to keep our identity. So one of the charming things was keeping Patrick under control. He had a lot of breadth to his writing, but sometimes he said he wanted to get more jazzy. And we kind of went, 'Hmmm, yeah, eh;' we didn't always agree. So in a way, *Topographic* and *Relayer* were as experimental as *Close To The Edge*. More so, in a way, because at least *Close To The Edge* had more of a stable lineup."

Patrick Moraz on *Relayer*:
"When we started to record *Relayer*, some of the music had already been written and rehearsed by Chris, Jon, Steve and Alan. I contributed as much as I could to the overall picture of the pieces. However, it is a fact that Steve used quite a lot

of tracks for his many overdubs everywhere on the album, except when there is no guitar at all, which is a rare occasion. We all participated in the compositions and the final arrangements, even if most of the 'songs' were originally composed somewhat more by Jon, and Steve in some instances. I liked to work with Jon and Chris, especially. Alan was always contributing some very good rhythmic ideas. I also worked quite a lot with Steve during the whole time I was in Yes."

Rick Wakeman on *Relayer*:
"*Relayer* is a funny thing. When I left after *Topographic Oceans*, I just couldn't get it musically. I thought, you've got to give and take. No point in being part of something you can't give to. When I heard *Relayer*—I was actually asked to review it for the BBC—I said, 'Look, if I say I like it, you'll say that's because they're your friends. And if I say I don't like it, then you'll say, well that's because you're not there anymore.' And I played it, and I didn't like it. But I was really pleased that I didn't like it. It was far too jazzy and freeform, which I didn't like. And I said it's not my cup of tea, but I'm really pleased that it sounds like this. And the guy scratched his head and said 'Why?' And I said, 'Well, if I had heard something that was melodic, that was full of Yes thematic things and melody, I would be really pissed-off. Because I left the band, because I felt it was heading this route. And on hearing this album, I said, there isn't anything I could have offered to this album, absolutely nothing I could offer to any one of these pieces at all. So I'm really pleased. I'm pleased I made the right decision to leave the band when I did.'"

Jon Anderson stands at "The Gates Of Delirium":
"I actually wrote that on the piano and then brought it to the band. I had this crazy idea and just gave it to them and they understood me. That's why I worked on Yes's music. I didn't want to be a pop star; I wanted to make some great music, and I think we have over the last 40 years."

Alan White on *Relayer*:
"There are a lot of periods where Chris and myself had a very adventurous time in the studio, let's put it that way. *Topographic Oceans* had a lot of very strange percussive and bass work on it, but *Relayer* was also very inventive, with songs like 'Sound Chaser' and 'Gates Of Delirium.' Basically it was because we were constructing music as a five-piece. Pieces weren't constructed before we entered the situation, so some of the music was structured around the rhythm section."

November 8, 1974 – August 23, 1975. Yes fulfil the dates of their Relayer Tour, with Gryphon supporting on the front half and Ace picking up in mid-May. Over Moraz's time with the band, his live rig would expand from five keyboards in 1974, to 14 in 1975 and in his final year, 24 instruments necessarily arranged on two levels.

Howe on "To Be Over" and *Relayer*:

"I have voted that one as one of my favourite tracks and *Relayer* one of my favourite albums. The sleeve is one of my favourite sleeves. It was a very combustible time. We had already achieved our first major big stepping stone. We got to playing the 20-minute style piece and we were in this enormous landscape where we could do things like that. We did *Topographic*. We had not even absorbed all of the criticism from when we changed keyboard players and we still went in and did another 20 minute piece. We did an album almost identical to *Close To The Edge* in structure. I think it is a really exciting format for Yes."

Journalist Ed Sciaky:

Relayer is reassuring. The production, by Yes and near-member Eddie Offord, is flawless and astounding. The role of Moraz's keyboards is naturally subdued from Wakeman's, but so is that of Jon Anderson's essential vocals. The result is greater individual importance of Steve Howe's brilliant guitar work, Chris Squire's foreground bass lines and Alan White's powerful drumming, leads to the most unified blend of musicians Yes has yet produced, playing music that's melodic, cohesive and concise. *Relayer* is exactly the album Yes needed to survive the crises, convince sceptics, and at the same time, further the enchantment of believers.

1975

1975. Trevor Rabin issues his first album, *Boys Will Be Boys*, with his band Rabbitt. The record will be moderately distributed in North America, more so than 1976's *A Croak And A Grunt In The Night*.

Trevor Rabin, on moving to the US because of A&R guru John Kalodner:

"He is one of the best A&R people that I've ever met, even though, at the end of the day, he dropped me. There is nobody like him in the business anymore; he is a true genius. Rabbitt had saturated the South African market and we needed to try to break elsewhere. Management had a very different way of thinking on how we should do that and it really screwed it up. It led to me leaving. I am happy to say that the guys in Rabbitt are still close."

January 8, 1975. A portion of "The Gates Of Delirium" called "Soon" is issued as a UK single from *Relayer*, backed with "Sound Chaser."

Jon Anderson on "Soon:"

"It's a very difficult song that you're singing to God and saying, 'Come over here. What's happened? You know we want some light.' We're asking the Divine to show some light in this world, as we need a reason to be here. And, of course, over the years I have more light every day. I think we all have the same spirituality deep inside and we grow to learn more about it all the time, and we

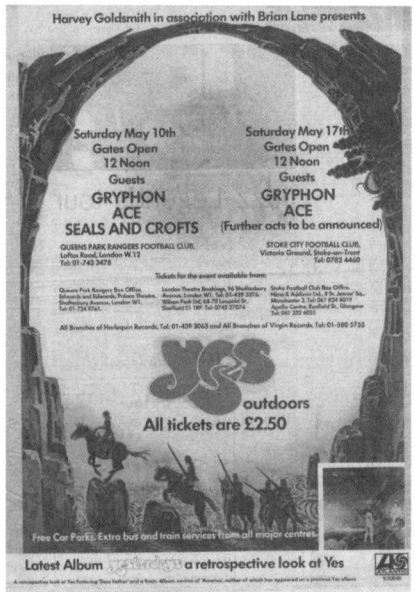

Beginnings, Steve Howe's solo album. Available on Atlantic Records and Tapes.

try very hard to become better people as we grow. We search all the time for the truth. We learn more about the world and we can't have thoughts like, 'We are better than them' or 'They are not good enough for God.' This is a very bad way of thinking, you know?"

Steve Howe defends the band's predilection for epics:
"That is one of the things that I am most proud of with Yes. In the mid-'70s we used to say that we were purposely un-commercial. Atlantic really did want us to have hits. We had 'Roundabout' which was a very deserving kind of hit because it so encapsulated the style of Yes. We just haven't written enough songs like that but we should. It gave us a foot in the door with Atlantic. On *Close To The Edge* they asked, 'What's the single?' but we really didn't have one. They were quite happy that we sold millions of albums so they were not ready to kick us out the door! There was a marvellous leverage for originality and lack of commerciality. We had people in America that were playing this on the radio. We were one of the only bands to do that. That was based on our reputation."

Alan White on *Relayer*:
"*Relayer* was a totally experimental period as far as playing drums go. Not that *Topographic* wasn't; *Topographic* had a lot of intricate bass and drums, with the rhythm section being adventurous in trying to find new rhythms, with a lot of direction and ethnic music in the background. *Relayer* was an extension of that, but obviously down the road a bit, after we'd been playing that for a while. I

find songs like 'Sound Chaser' very exciting. Nobody was doing anything quite like that at the time, where songs sped up and slowed down three or four times within the course of a song, that kind of experimentation. And I remember recording some of the percussion on 'Gates Of Delirium;' Jon Anderson and myself used to stop in a scrap yard every day, and pick up pieces of car, and we made a kind of framework of pieces of cars in the studio that we could bang on [*laughs*]. We'd go through the car scrap yard, and find springs and pieces of metal. So some of the percussion on that is actually us playing pieces of cars in the studio, making big clanking noises."

February – September 1975. Chris Squire works on material for his first solo album at Virginia Water, Surrey Sound Studios and Morgan Studios. Yes alumnus Bill Bruford along with Patrick Moraz contribute to the sessions.

February 28, 1975. Yes issue a compilation of songs mostly from their first two albums, called *Yesterdays*. The album reaches #27 in the UK and #17 in the US.

April 1975. Rick Wakeman continues his winning streak, landing his third RIAA-certified gold album in a row with *The Myths And Legends Of King Arthur And The Knights Of The Round Table*.

Rick Wakeman shares his heart attack experiences:

"Three actually and the third was not very minor! I wrote the album while in hospital. It's a parallel musical autobiography. I was told I would not be able to play live again and should retire. There is much of me in that album, personally. The main theme is probably the best I have managed to produce."

May 23 – 25, 1975. Alan White records the material for what will be his first solo album.

May 30, 31, June 1, 1975. Rick Wakeman's latest concept album, *The Myths And Legends Of King Arthur...* is presented as a skating pageant, at Wembley Empire Pool.

Unknown writer for *New Musical Express*, April 5, 1975:

It is planned as a colourful spectacle, involving lavish costumes and a huge castle setting, with the ice representing the moat. Seventeen skaters will be taking part and Wakeman will make his entrance on a white horse. Supporting Wakeman musically will be the 48-piece English Chamber Choir, the eight-piece Nottingham Festival Singers and his group, the English Rock Ensemble. Narrator, as on the album, is Royal Shakespeare Company actor Terry Taplin and the musical director is David Meacham. Another innovation will be the special "Sound in Around" system, which involves the PA being suspended from the roof.

Time And A Word

October 31, 1975. Steve Howe issues his first solo album, *Beginnings*. Included on it is current Yes drummer Alan White and past drummer Bill Bruford, along with Patrick Moraz. The album reaches #22 on the UK charts and #65 in the US.

Patrick Moraz on his contribution to *Beginnings*:

"In the very early part of 1975 we somehow had discussed the idea of each and every one of us doing a solo album. Steve asked me if I wanted to take part in his own *Beginnings* album. I said, 'Sure I would love to!' Then he gave me a tape with a few notes on it and asked me if I could arrange and orchestrate it like Vivaldi. I said I would do my best and I worked on it for about three weeks. When I came to play him the demo and show him all the work I had done with the piece, 'Beginnings,' he loved it immediately and he told me that we would record it. And we did. I also played the harpsichord on some other tunes with him on the album. I also conducted the chamber orchestra for the recording sessions. Of course, my arrangement sounded nothing like Vivaldi, but it had its own personality and uniqueness to it.

"Steve—I remember the moment very well—was kind of in shock and at the same time very happily surprised that I had come up with the whole arrangement like that and wanted to use it immediately, without any changes. We recorded the whole session with Steve on acoustic guitar. Along with my final harpsichord parts, I conducted the orchestra, while he eventually re-recorded his guitar parts at a later date. The video was taped also at a later date."

Steve Howe on Patrick Moraz on *Beginnings*:

"Patrick Moraz went on to play some remarkable things on my album, *Beginnings*. He really surprised me when I heard 'Will O' The Wisp' and other songs that he played on. And then to the second album, there's the amazing Mellotron and keyboard work and piano work he did on 'All's A Chord'—really remarkable."

Author review of *Beginnings*:

Steve Howe's first solo record is wonderfully predictable, Steve proving his inherent, comfortable Yes-ness with an airy, idealistic, dreamy display of hippie music that surely any Yes fan could appreciate. The overall sound is benevolent and homey, close, countrified and folksy, Steve playing most guitar and bass, and singing every track in his somewhat fragile but warm style. It's a voice that is not without eccentricity and flat notes, but the minstrel-like DIY good intention of it all erases any thoughts of critical malice.

Most tracks mix effortlessly many acoustic and electric guitar textures, side one closer "Lost Symphony" adding an arresting horn pattern to what is the bravest, most ambitious and perhaps lasting track on the record. Side two opener "Beginnings" features Steve treading ethereal footsteps through an eight-piece orchestra, whereas "Ram" tender-picks to trilogy with "The Clap" and "Mood For A Day" as a light-hearted Dixie rag extraordinaire.

Many of the other tracks are quite busy, falling just this side of prog, more like complicated folk rock, Steve making good use of Alan White's blocky exuberance and, to a lesser extent, the sticks of David Oberle and Bill Bruford, whose two tracks are fairly straight-forward, even if closer "Break Away From It All" is the rockiest thing on the record.

But one listens to this record not for progressive brilliance, but for Howe's particular idealism, bolstered by his fluid if edgy, very painterly guitar tones. Eddie Offord's homespun recording values also help the cause, the seasoned sonic sculptor of Yes providing grounded and objective separation between instruments, and an overall home-baked humanity to the project. As with the best of Yes, *Beginnings* takes the discerning listener to meadows of contemplation, any bluster more than doubly paid off by soothing warm melodies, and a timeless lyrical invitation to relax."

November 7, 1975. Not to be outdone, Chris Squire issues his first solo album, in the UK, called *Fish Out Of Water*, with US release to follow December 30th. The album reaches #25 on the UK charts and #69 in the US. Fish is Chris's nickname, derived from the fact that the notorious slow-moving Squire spends a long time in the bathtub and in the shower, which was a particular irritant back when Yes had their own communal band house at 50A Munster Road, Fulham, in which all the band and their girlfriends lived, save for Tony Kaye who lived in Chelsea.

Chris Squire on his solo album:
"I enjoyed doing that album. At the time I was working with Andrew Jackman, who'd been a friend of mine since I was a teenager. And he was a great arranger and even helped co-write some of the material. Unfortunately, he's no longer with us. So that was a fantastic experience, that whole orchestral molding of that album and the ideas that we put into it. And his brother, Gregory, was the engineer on it, and, in fact, Greg Jackman is still around these days making hits. Very exciting time; it was made in my first home studio in my house in England. So there were a lot of good vibes around that album."

1976

1976. John Wetton, Rick Wakeman and Bill Bruford float the idea of forming a band called British Bulldog. Harvest Records reissue Tomorrow's one and only album, from 1968, *Tomorrow*.

February 1976. Illinois' Starcastle issue their self-titled debut, on Epic. The band would crank out four records through 1978. Their claim

to fame? An astonishing recreation of Yes's classic sound; Starcastle attempting and achieving such a bald-faced tribute to Yes, that not even any of the myriad neo-neo-prog bands of the 1990s would ever dare try to trump them.

Rick Wakeman on Starcastle and "borrowing" other people's music:
"I haven't heard them. If they're good musicians, perhaps they'll develop a style of their own. Everybody plays other people's music when they start. I remember Keith [Emerson] pinched half of Jimmy Smith's licks for some Nice records."

March 1976. Alan White issues his first solo album, *Ramshackled*, with members of the Alan Price Set. Jon Anderson and Steve Howe guest on "Spring-Song Of Innocence." The album fails to chart in the US, but reaches #41 in the UK.

Author review of *Ramshackled*:
Alan White lets fly with perhaps the most churlish, eccentric and blender-made of the batched solo records clustered in and around 1976. I mean, not like he does much here, writing nothing, and letting one of his earlier, non-recording bands define the record, White doing... well, who knows? In any event, "his" record is a cyclone of weird musics, not so much prog, just off-kilter, similar soul tones to Peter Hammill, Steve Hillage and Ian Anderson colliding with American over-profusions like Chicago, Santana, Steely Dan and even Zappa.

So this warm, likeable and unrestrained mish-mash of musical elements becomes a healthy, super-dated curio shop, not really all about drums, but about everybody packed into a VW bus. Reminds me of the spirit behind Ian Gillan Band, Gillan Glover, Ian Gillan, and for that matter Roger Glover's *Mask*, a yearning to be free of definition. So there's a baked dozen energy levels here, from the Jimbo mojo Zappa of "Everybody" to the orchestrated hippie wash of "Darkness", brass everywhere in such a '60s sort of Herb Alpert way.

Indeed, all sorts of '60s sounds bong through this record, "Ooooh Baby" combining Tom Jones with Richie Havens, "Giddy" doing a sort of CSNY thing. But the whole pop, fruity, brass-adelic hippie chumble becomes a total lark given that White's stamp is near non-existent, indeed the myriad of percussion flavours resulting in no central persona whatsoever. Closes with a nice Yes-type all-is-well-in-Eden number called 'Spring-Song Of Innocence,' lead vocals by Jon Anderson, slippery axe work by Steve Howe. Original vinyl featured fancy embossed album cover (undermined by casual graphics), including sleeve with pictures and painting and colourful felt pen lyrics on separate sheet. A cornball oddball to be sure.

April 1976. Alan White's solo album coughs up a UK-only single, in "Oooh! Baby (Go to Pieces)"/"One Way Rag."

April 1, 1976. Rush issue their landmark fourth album *2112*, which eventually sells triple platinum. Like Yes, Canada's famed prog rockers are known for long-form pieces but not particularly full concept albums. *2112* wins on both counts with one side being a concept, the other side not.

May 28 – August 23, 1976. Yes embark on the 1976 Solo Albums Tour, on which a small amount of solo material from the somewhat concurrent spate of solo albums from the guys is massaged into the set. Support for the front half comes from Pousette-Dart Band. Gentle Giant support in July.

Chris Squire's influences:
"Different people have different ideas: people compare me to Jimi Hendrix in some ways. I used to like Jimi Hendrix's bass playing very much [*laughing*] so I'm sure I borrowed some ideas of his for the bass. But then again, I had a great many influences in my career, like Paul McCartney and Bill Wyman and, of course, the late great John Entwistle and Jack Bruce. And of course, all the members of Yes that have been coming and leaving and coming back: I've learnt a lot from all those musicians too, from their influences onto Yes, which has given Yes maybe a different look every time we changed somebody. So that's been a big learning curve for me."

June 1976. Patrick Moraz, as part of the plan for each of the members of the band to construct and issue a solo album, releases *I* or *i*, popularly known as *The Story Of I*.

Time And A Word

Patrick Moraz discusses his first solo album:
"*The Story Of I* is an allegory about life and beyond. It takes place in an environment which implies the notion of virtuality. However, if the games are artificially monitored and use technologies which go beyond what is understood nowadays as digital and virtual, the emotions are very real, and the feelings are definitely human. The inspiration for *The Story Of I* came to me during the course of an elevator ride in a newly-built hotel in America. The idea implanted itself in a flash. It immediately became clear that it was an allegory about life itself. What came to me was a way to present an abstract and spiritual train of thought under the guise of a concrete story, a kind of sci-fi story with plenty of symbolic narratives and figurative twists, with its own rites, games and rules as well as endless interactive situations. Always with a hopeful goal, however, with eternal light in sight, a sort of modern times search for the ever-elusive Holy Grail.

"For a first 'concept' album, the task was formidable and proved even more so as time passed. However, as the original idea was firmly rooted, the development of the whole work grew virtually at an exponential rate. All the elements came into place at the right time, even if over a period of a few months. I should have said 'almost at the right time.' A few timing problems and conflicting schedules presented themselves towards the end of the recording and at mixing time. Even the emblem came to me like an 'apparition,' during one of the most spiritual visionary encounters I have ever had.

"In regards to approaching the recording of *Story Of I*, like any of my other recordings, first and foremost there was always a different feeling and different emotions. All the senses are alert. Even some sense of humour is indispensable! Being able to go to the depth of my thoughts. Different states of consciousness, different levels of awareness, also various mechanisms of creativity, spontaneity, improvisation and composing in real time, cognitive memory, playing (or not) with other musicians, interacting with other people, psycho-acoustics, instruments, technology, geographical location, atmospheric conditions and so forth. By 'composing in real time' I mean that *The Story Of I* was composed, arranged, orchestrated, recorded and produced over a period of more than four months."

Author review of *The Story Of I*:
Of all the batched solo releases, Patrick Moraz certainly captured the spirit of progressive rock most splendiferously, constructing this frightfully elaborate, chops-driven musical *tour de force*, adding an imaginative fantasy tale to match. Everybody plays their pants off here, turning *i* (or *The Story of I*, or *The Rtist 4merly Known As I!*) into a prog jazz fusion world music extravaganza worth hours of deliberation.

Performances of note would include Moraz, of course, but heck, his band often runs away with the show, the fluid runs of bassist Jeff Berlin sliding

effortlessly under Ray Gomez's sinister licks, furtive percussion giants Mouzon and Newmark defining a sort of busy finesse, recalling U.K., Zappa and, oddly enough, Ian Gillan Band work.

The story line has something to do with the ascension of self through plateaus of emotion (true love triumphing as the only emotion that separates those who die from those who "vanish into the skies," all taking place in a "hotel" on a jungle plateau, while all the world watches through special broadcast). Reinforcing the fantastic imagery is the record's very flavourful percussion display, like I say, these two great drummers putting on a clinic, while The Percussionists of Rio De Janeiro fill up the spaces with a myriad of exotics.

Moraz's array of synth skronks definitely date the album, but there's no denying the massive amount of work that has gone into this thing. Worshippers of craft and other progressive ideological cornerstones will have a field day, the listener invited vortex-like into Moraz's lush jungle of sounds. And, of course, those who already snigger at Yes will break full belly-laughs at this most meddlesome of concept projects.

June 3, 1976. In a tribute to the resurgence of Beatlemania, Yes encore at the Omni in Atlanta with a rendition of "I'm Down," cooked up one day in rehearsal with no real intention of ever playing it in front of a crowd.

June 12, 1976. Yes play JFK Stadium in Philadelphia to a crowd of 110,000, followed the next night by a show at RFK in Washington, DC. Through the summer, the band play to 1.2 million fans, who witness an elaborate mechanical lights and laser show.

Chris Squire on the JFK gig:

"JFK was the biggest gig the band has ever done. It was a fantastic place to play, it really was. It's so beautifully laid-out, and it was really one of the best sounds that I've ever experienced in an open-air gig. You just have to be adjusted to doing it, really. We had a PA that was equivalent to 14 ordinary systems, and it was on three levels on each side of the stage. It was really lovely."

July 24, 1976. Jon Anderson issues his first solo album, *Olias Of Sunhillow*, on Atlantic, which vaults to #8 in the UK and #47 in the US.

Jon Anderson dismisses drugs:

"In general, there's no way you can get to the truth about life through drugs or magic, things like that. It's within you. It's there, it's resting, and you can bring it to life, any time you want."

Author review of *Olias Of Sunhillow*:

It is no wonder that Jon Anderson digs into this idea of solo flight with such relish. Always the spaciest of Yes astronauts, Anderson shows us fantasy like no Yes before or since. *Olias Of Sunhillow* is a considerably complex tale that originates with Roger Dean's *Fragile* and *Yessongs* artwork (thanks go to Dean "for planting the seed"). Taking this idea of planetary break-up and rejuvenation of the pieces as a literary base, Anderson weaves a tale draped in filmy new age poetics, a story of a band of three mystical beings with distinct but complementary powers, who conjure from nature, nurture and song a great ship (the Moorglade Mover), to rescue the four tribes of Sunhillow, and transport them to Earth where their races will continue. True to heroic form Olias, Ranyart, and Qoquag, having accomplished their mission ascend and vaporize into the sun, becoming one with the universe, powers ever present.

Religious connotations to the story are numerous (the Trinity, Exodus, Moses, the Ark, the Flood), but Anderson cloaks the scene in so much fanciful science fiction that the tale stands useful and engaging on its own. One must read the gatefold (plus extra leaf) to get the whole story, as the lyrics tend to be quite song-shaped, opaque and succinct.

Musically, the record remains light and exotic. Anderson sings and plays everything on it, layering and texturing with simple parts that together form a close-knit, new age orchestra. One can almost envision a dozen white-frocked Jons hitting and strumming various medieval instruments around a huge bonfire. The madrigal vision is definitely apt, as all remains timeless, music and lyric existing in a vacuum, fable transcending, unfolding with deeper and deeper shades of meaning with each attentive experience.

Truly light, airy, yet ambitious of plot, *Olias* is the personified, human face of progressive rock, the actualization of an art rock artifact using vocal and word as its main vehicle, expanding frontiers through human sound, while relaxing other tones, in loving construction of a lush but understated garden bed on which to build the plot-heavy storyline. The force, motion and energy of *Olias*'s wave-whipped, beam-bound journey exists within a contemplative, soft-rhythmed throb, one which counters and synergizes until all is well on the new blue planet. On a more practical level, the record is a rousing reassurance that a Yes with Jon Anderson at the helm will forever be a cloud-lofted seeker of truth.

October 1976. Jon Anderson's album yields a single in "Flight Of The Moorglade"/"To The Runner."

Early October 1976. Yes begin work on what will become *Going For The One* at Mountain Studios in Montreux, Switzerland, producing themselves, with John Timperley engineering, assisted by David Richards. As they are arriving, Emerson, Lake & Palmer are just leaving, having recorded *Works Volume 1* and *Works Volume 2* at the same venue. A planned quick four weeks would soon stretch to seven months. A tense and irritable Steve is calmed by his new hobby, transcendental meditation. Meanwhile, band and crew let off steam racing and often crashing cars while zooming around Lake Geneva.

November 1976. Rumours fly of a new supergroup in the making, featuring John Wetton, Bill Bruford and Rick Wakeman. A jam takes place, but nobody has the appetite to turn it into a touring act and plans are scrapped.

November 1976. Patrick Moraz is fired from the band, as Yes are dissatisfied with his sound and work ethic at the sessions for the next studio album. Rick Wakeman returns as keyboardist, lured in as a session player, then asked to do the tour, before being talked into rejoining full time. The reunion is eased by the fact that Rick very much likes the immediacy and brevity of the material the band has been cooking up after the space and time excursions of *Tales...* and *Relayer*.

Patrick Moraz's side of the story:

"We had written, together, quite a lot of the material which ended up on *Going For The One*, like 'Awaken,' 'Wonderous Stories,' or even 'Parallels,' which were as much part my composition as anyone else in the band at that time. I also came up, during the two previous years prior to the recording of *Going For The One*, with a lot of ideas and contributions to the band and its sound. The fact that I was not credited as a writer of the songs does not mean I did not compose for the group. As a member of the band, I composed as much as I could, as much as I was 'allowed' to compose by the others.

"Unfortunately, I was forced to leave. And even though, at the time, the split was not made to appear acrimonious, I suffered extremely and extensively. To be 'asked to leave' so suddenly put me in a lot of turmoil and disturbance. The fact is, I was never compensated for anything. I never ever got paid for any of my tour participation in the extremely successful and extensive tour of 1976, which comprised about 65 concerts, many of them in front of sold-out audiences of more than 100,000 people. After all, as a member of the band, I was entitled to a 20% cut from what the band was getting. I don't like to dwell on negatives, however. I can tell you that I had absolutely no desire to want to leave Yes, at the time, in November of 1976. We had just finished the biggest tour Yes had ever done, the Bicentennial Tour, a huge, extremely successful tour for Yes.

"Somehow it had been decided that we would go and record, in my own country, Switzerland, what became the album *Going For The One*, which we had extensively composed, developed and rehearsed during the course of 1976, and even before that. There was no reason in the world for me to want to leave the band! Also, I understood, much later, that Rick was already in town, with his own crew, when I was still in the group, and I was still part of Yes. In addition, it was an extremely complicated and difficult situation for me to be stranded, on the street, with my baby daughter who was only one month old and her mother, without any transport or money, in the cold winter of Switzerland. Then with the fight for survival to stay alive, it all became surreal."

Rick Wakeman, in late 1977, on his much improved relations with Jon Anderson:
"We've found out we're after the same thing, and we've gotten to know each other on a friendship and musical level better. The irony is that Jon and I now realize that we're after the same thing, but it's just that with our different musical upbringings and backgrounds, we're trying for it in a different way. So what we've done is spend an awful lot of time together and become bosom friends now. Jon will take his harp, and we will go into a church somewhere and we'll sit down for four or five hours and record everything we play."

1977

1977. This is the year that Geoff Downes and Trevor Horn form pioneering electronic post-punk band The Buggles. The band's manager is Brian Lane, who, of course, also manages Yes.

Geoff Downes on his prog pedigree, despite forming The Buggles:
"Round about the time that *Close To The Edge* came out, I had just started at music college. So I was very much into Yes at that point. I really liked *Time And A Word*, *The Yes Album*, *Close To The Edge*, *Fragile*; those were very much albums I listened to in that period in music college. But by '76, '77, I started to work more towards different types of music. I did a lot of session work in London

doing mainly disco and dance stuff, and that's how I met Trevor Horn, because there was quite a well-known disco singer called Tina Charles at the time, and he got together with them, and I auditioned for the band, and that's how we got together. So at that point, we were into more mainstream pop stuff, more to do with the fact that we were making a living out of it, than we were going to make a living playing music that we particularly liked. It was more the fact that we were doing stuff that was keeping us alive."

January 2, 1977. Patrick Moraz gets busy on his next solo album, slated for an April release.

Early 1977. Tony Kaye resurfaces in Swan Song Records supergroup Detective, who issue a self-titled record followed by *It Takes One To Know One* later in the same year. The band features ex-Silverhead vocalist Michael Des Barres, who marries super-groupie Miss Pamela later in the year.

April 8, 1977. The Clash issue their angry and groundbreaking self-titled debut. Yes suddenly looks like a luxury item.

July 7, 1977. Yes, issue their eighth studio album, *Going For The One*. The album, late in the shops by seven months, reaches #1 in the UK, and peaks at #8 in the US, on the strength of singles "Wonderous Stories" and "Going For The One" suggesting that the demise of prog has been grossly exaggerated despite punk's onslaught. The album achieves gold certification in the US within a month of release. For cover art, the band go for a modern approach, eschewing fantastical illustration for a sleek sleeve by Hipgnosis, who will be on board for the follow-up as well.

Rick Wakeman on *Going For The One*:
"We both, me and the band, did a different journey around an egg to arrive at *Going For The One*, which was great. I suppose if you have to pick pieces that are highlights for me, it would have to be 'Awaken.' I still think that's a Yes anthem. If anybody ever asks me, what is Yes all about? I say, well, if you listen to 'Awaken,' that gives you a pretty good clue."

Steve Howe on "Awaken":
"'Awaken' is really an Anderson/Howe song, but because the guys did a great job on arranging it, we included them in on the arrangement. They didn't actually write the song but we put their names on the song and that's because you can't kind of give and take away at the same time. If you're going to give credit to somebody, then you have to give it to them, and it rewards them. On the other hand, sometimes it does sort of mystify the actual writer credit. Jon and I always assumed that 'Awaken' would say Anderson/Howe, and it doesn't."

Time And A Word

Chris Squire talks about Jon Anderson's world view:

"Of course, Jon Anderson was responsible for a lot of those lyrics. I'm not going to say that a lot of them didn't mean very much, because Jon's philosophy was more about how things sounded. So, it was more the sound of the vocal that he was trying to always write for, as opposed to the actual logical sense of the lyric [*laughs*]. And so, for years, of course, I was singing harmonies with sentences that didn't mean a thing, really, but sounded good [*laughs*]. Yes's philosophy, by the name alone, was always to have a positive influence. We weren't as concerned with the dark side of rock 'n' roll as a lot of artists are. And a lot of people like that. Yes always had that philosophy of hope and a brighter future."

Alan White on Jon's world view:

"A lot of the older material was driven, in that sense, by Jon, with his exploration of spiritualism and surreal situations, and using his voice like an instrument more than anything, within the whole mixture, where he let the audience translate what it meant. Because it could conjure up a lot of different things. Yes had that mystique about it, right from the early days. But the message of the band is, just we keep on going, trying to create music that no one else is playing. You can always tell a Yes song on the radio."

Author review of *Going For The One*:

Yes signal a new era with bold new graphics. Gone is the swirly escapism of Roger Dean; in its place, a new accelerated, late-'70s escapism through the clean lines of Hipgnosis, who combine slick, futuristic geometric urban angles with a man in his birthday suit, perhaps urgently propelling the band forward, while simultaneously embracing roots. Whatever the case, *Going For The One* becomes a splendidly well-written, instantly likeable progressive rock record, a balance rarely attained by anyone, a balance Yes has known on their three great records from years earlier, *The Yes Album*, *Fragile* and *Close To The Edge*.

The album's kick-off track is indeed a kick, Yes surprising everyone with a rousing, jaunty bit of Foghat boogie. When the shameless Americanizing evaporates, soaring, sun-dappled cathedrals spring from the soil; Yes inventing perhaps the most compelling short track of their career, replete with vocals from (the circus of) heaven, heaps o' Howe slide, and well, rock 'n' roll! Firmly ensconced as a concert fave, "Going For The One" is a lusty lead track indeed, announcing that the bewildered wilderness of *Tales From Topographic Oceans* and *Relayer* has been energetically clear-cut to make room for beefy cattle.

Next up, with "Turn Of The Century," things became more ethereal and light, Jon adapting the *La Boheme* tale of a sculptor molding his love for his departed soul mate into his work. Steve and Jon trade textures throughout the touching first half, the track building, first with bass and peaceful keyboard washes, then with more effortlessly integrated strata of the same, adding Alan's timpani and soft cymbal crashes. A gorgeous, deceptively full-bodied track, the ultimate demonstration of dynamic sonic layering.

And, in crashes "Parallels," Wakeman droning forth with powerful church organ chords from St. Martin's Church in Montreux, on what is a rousing Chris Squire composition, again filled with texture of a very different sort. Wakeman's organ virtually acts as bass guitar, as Squire straddles bass patterns to soloing, and Howe exclusively colours as soloist. Indeed riff and bass both seem to be hallowed domain of Wakeman, as Jon belts out an uncharacteristically lucid tale of betterment over the mistaken identities of his band mates. It's a rocker for sure, and is as much as a metaphor as "Going For The One" for the revival of good feeling the band was experiencing at the time (plus Wakeman gets to belt out a solo eventually!).

Side two opens with yet another Yes classic of a more benign stripe, "Wonderous Stories" being perhaps the most beautiful Yes composition of the quiet sort, an angelic acoustic bit of frolic, whose deceptive, simple arrangement bears many hard-won treasures. Anderson is truly dramatic in his presentation of this tale reaching back into times classical, renaissance, and wonderous [*sic*]. Like "Turn Of The Century," its build is subversive and effortless, Alan White's percussion truly that, percussion that accents and shades, all the while Wakeman slowly filling up all until the heaven-sent environs is achieved come climactic round by Jon and Jon and Jon.

Closing the show is "Awaken," an involved composition that harkens back to any kitchen sink Yes prog monster one can imagine. All aspects of this very difficult track are bewildering, from Jon's supposed lyrical sources (timeless song cycles, Rembrandt, classical music, *Topographic Oceans*), to Wakeman's recording of his pipe organ parts over Switzerland's sonically super-efficient phone lines.

The deposed Patrick Moraz, who was very instrumental in the writing of the album as a whole, feels most slighted by his being uncredited here on 'Awaken,' the piece on the record he felt was most his. And given that his contributions were surgically but somewhat subconsciously removed, the track does sound a little forced, a little too eventful and segued. But those wishing to hear a superhuman Yes labyrinth for 1977 found themselves floored or at least satiated.

All told, *Going For The One* is a fun record, reversing the furrowed seriousness of the last two slabs of pain. Switzerland helped, but so did the return of Wakeman, who added oddball spice to the sessions. Once he was back as full collaborator and Yes member, his ideas proved paramount. Keyboards of many stripes are all over this record, yet a raw, rock 'n' roll guitars and vocals record is what springs to mind first. Yes as sonic deceptors par excellence.

July 30 – December 6, 1977. Yes mount their Going For The One Tour, with Donovan as support.

Alan White on *Going For The One*:

"A memorable experience for everybody in the band. It was a period when Rick came back to the band, and we were all excited about that, and we just enjoyed living in Switzerland together. I think we were there six, seven, eight months, in the winter. We'd turn up at the studio every day, and everybody had fun creating this wonderful album. And it's a great album to play on stage, particularly 'Awaken.' The song itself, 'Going For The One,' a lot of people, really, really love that song. And 'Turn Of The Century' is one of the more difficult pieces for us to play on stage, and that's a song I did with Jon Anderson. You've really got to be on top to play that on stage. A lot of the parts don't have any time signatures, so you have to listen really intently to what the other guys are playing."

Journalist John Swenson:

As the band continued to run through the possible program readouts, less and less creative energy became available and Yes sank into cosmic torpor. *Going For The One* reverses this process in a fascinating move that ties them even more closely to Zeppelin. By letting the Chris Squire-Alan White rhythm section construct a bottom for Howe's guitar, and by using Wakeman's unquestionable keyboard talent intelligently, *Going For The One* takes the right step toward downplaying Anderson's conceptual stranglehold on the band. Entropy can work to your advantage. You just have to be selective about where the energy is taken from.

September 1977. "Wonderous Stories"/ "Parallels" is issued in the UK as 7", 12" and blue 12" vinyl single form, reaching #7 in the charts. The American version of "Wonderous Stories" is backed with an abbreviated "Awaken." As well, "Wonderous Stories," presented in fairly rudimentary live format, stands as the band's first single track production video.

Jon Anderson, in 1977, on *Going For The One*:
"This album is a kind of celebration. Over the last two or three years, we've been experimenting a lot, and we're happy to have been given that chance. Any musician should be given the chance to extend his horizons and luckily we've been successful enough to do so. We think of this as a more eventful album. We've come back to a happier medium. It's something we felt we wanted to do. If we wanted another *Tales...* concept, we would've gone in that direction, but we needed to relax for a while—a little more laughing and jive."

Rick Wakeman, in 1977, on *Going For The One*:
"The new album bears no resemblance to the last couple of albums—it's all songs again. It's a rock 'n' roll song album. In the same way that I had to leave— because I couldn't bear playing anymore— in order to find out that these were the people I wanted to play with, we now happen to think we make pretty good music together."

Steve Howe, in 1977, on the same album:
"It takes discussion, strictness and ambition! Ambition is one of the heaviest driving forces. It's not a matter of aggression, but freedom to comment about what's going on. There was a fair bit of go and aggression in the music I was first involved in, with The In Crowd and Tomorrow. In those groups, we wanted to tear the people apart! And Yes were doing that too, in their early days. Because of our achievements later, we began to go off at a tangent and become mellow. 'Going For The One' on the album was a rebirth of that fire."

October 27, 1977: The Sex Pistols issue their incendiary one and only studio album, *Never Mind The Bollocks, Here's The Sex Pistols*. It seems that punk rock's main beef is with the likes of Emerson, Lake & Palmer and Yes, the latter coming in for particular scorn due to the bombast and excess of their *Tales From Topographic Oceans* album.

Alan White's views on punk:
"Yes is a band that is set in its way and not influenced by anything around it. The punk movement at that time... the way we were looking at it, it was a fad. But at the same time, I liked the more adventurous punk stuff, although not so much the basic stuff."

November 1977: *"Going For The One"/ "Awaken" (abbreviated) is issued in the UK as a single, in 7" and 12" form, subsequently charting at #24.*

1978

1978. Trevor Rabin moves to England from his native South Africa. The following year he marries Shelley. Still married to this day, the couple have one child. Meanwhile, same year, Trevor's 1977 South African release *Beginnings* is re-issued as *Trevor Rabin*.

Trevor Rabin on his pathway toward music:

"I have never had a job. I have never worked in a record store, or anywhere. I really have never had a job. My dad, who was a wonderful man, was a wonderful musician. He was the first chair in the Johannesburg Symphony Orchestra. He put himself through college to become a lawyer by playing fiddle at a hotel for years. He would walk five miles there and then play the fiddle. He was a really good lawyer and he was very involved in the anti-apartheid movement.

"My brother, who was a great violinist, followed in his footsteps and became a lawyer. By the time I was 16, I was making a good living doing session work. I said to my dad when I was 16, 'I guess I should really decide what area of law I should get into.' My dad said, 'You've got to be a musician.' Usually, parents are the other way.

"I had played in bands for years and I wanted to continue to play in bands but my desire was to be a conductor. I learned from Walter Mony and I learned all of these fabulous pieces of music. One day, after years of hard work, I was talking to my dad and he said, 'Look, you don't have to be a conductor to be a musician. Your gift, for my ears, is your guitar playing. You need to be a guitar player.' He never told me to do music and then have something to fall back on. In fact, he was the opposite. He told me that if I ever wanted to do something else then I always had my music to fall back on.

"Stephen Biko was a militant protester against the government. He was killed in detention. He became a hero in England and he is in the South African Apartheid Museum. He is a real hero. Growing up during apartheid, a lot of white kids were opposed to the way things were. I grew up knowing what an evil it was. My entire family was the same way. At age 19 I was with a band called Freedom's Children and I wrote a song called 'Wake Up State Of Fear.' It was not received well by the government. Management came up to me a couple of times and told me that there were some Secret Service at our shows. I hated the system so much that I was very involved with that. I eventually moved, but it had nothing to do with politics."

Author review of *Trevor Rabin*:

Trevor Rabin's first post-Rabbitt run exploded with energy, combining bright, brash histrionic arrangements with songs that crossed Queen with ELO, all sheened and shined with the compressed pop values of post-punk new wave. So songs like

90-minute Radio Special-Sunday, Nov. 26, 1978

Recorded live on their current tour

For the name of the King Biscuit Flower Hour station nearest you, plus details on this and other upcoming shows from DIR, write to: The Blast, Box RS, 445 Park Avenue, New York, N.Y. 10022. In Canada: John Rourke (416) 929-3155.

a DIR Broadcasting Production

"Finding Me A Way Back Home," "All I Want Is Your Love," and "Fantasy" were celebrations of hope, sort of like a heavy Cars. If there's one thing lacking here, it's groove, each track lurching and thumping as if Rabin really was the drummer and not a great one at that. Sugary sweet and loud as a crowd, *Trevor Rabin* displays in hair-raising, shake-booty fashion the dynamic energy and pop sensibility Rabin would bring to Yes, not to mention his penchant for the power chord and stadium rock guitar solo. Even a band as distinct and travelled as Yes couldn't help but be transformed by the marriage.

January 20, 1978. Patrick Moraz issues his second album, *Out In The Sun*. Many more solo albums follow, but of note is Moraz's 13-year run with prog pioneers The Moody Blues.

February – June 1978. Yes work at Advision Studios on material for their ninth album. Self-producing again, the band work with engineers Geoff Young and Nigel Luby.

Rick Wakeman on *Tormato*:

"A 'could have been' album for me is *Tormato*, which had some great tracks on it, like 'Arriving UFO.' But the production on that record was just abysmal. I mean, you could have produced it better by throwing it in a food mixer. Basically, it was just awful. If I was given the chance, to be given the masters of that album I'd go away and remix it and redo it. Because amongst that record is some classic stuff. One of the great things about Yes is light and shade, and that album doesn't have any, because none of us could agree on who the producer was. None of us could agree on who the engineer was. So there were five producers and five engineers—and five of us. So there were 15 pairs of hands on the faders. And in the end, all that happens is it gets more and more and more and more and more and more compressed, and you just have a compressed album. And that's the tragedy about that album, because there are some really, really good tracks on there, but it doesn't have that great light and shade that it should do. And I think if we could revisit and remix it, there's the potential for some cracking tracks there."

Alan White's take on *Tormato*:

"*Tormato* was a strange time for me in the life of Yes. We used to come to the studio every day and we were kind of lost with the music and where it was going. And it took a long time to work some of those songs into what they are. There are still a couple I'm not sure about, but 'Silent Wings Of Freedom' is absolutely fantastic. So it was very extreme."

March 1978. Prog supergroup U.K. issue their first of three albums, two studio and one live. Drummer on the debut is Bill Bruford. Also in the band are John Wetton, Eddie Jobson and Allan Holdsworth.

August 1978. Bill Bruford issues his first solo album, *Feels Good To Me*. It, along with *One Of A Kind* from 1979, are considerably embraced by prog music fans, further underscoring Bruford's particular and singular percussion style while also helping establish Allan Holdsworth and Jeff Berlin as eminent members of the prog rock family.

Bill Bruford reveals his impatience with gear talk:

"Let's not spend too long on drums. Drums I have no great love of particularly. Drumming and drummers, yes I do; music, I do. Drums themselves and cymbals are mass-produced instruments of perfectly suitable quality and I have no special tricks or techniques at all. I put the drumheads on same as anybody else does and hit them. It may be that I hit them in a slightly different place than other people, or in the musical space, or maybe it's that I tune them slightly different, but basically there's nothing to it. But everything is in the control of sticks—that's how you play a drum set—and the greater control you have of the drum set, the more wonderful an instrument it will be. So my instrument is quite traditional but they are laid out in quite an unusual fashion, namely flat, tympani-style."

Author review of *Feels Good To Me*:

Light, airy, energetic, swift... these are all words that can describe Bill Bruford's zesty form of electric jazz. *Feels Good To Me* benefits from the man's tireless osmosis of the love of music, Bill finally tying all those influences in one big bundle and singing it to the world. The drumming is of course, buoyant, fresh and personal, Bruford working in nicely the tonalities of tuned toms, working a three-way magic with the fluid runs of guitarist Allan Holdsworth and the pert phrasings of Berklee [music college] newcomer Jeff Berlin, who can sound like a flugelhorn, even as Bill adds flugelhorn to the band.

The record's cool melodies are a two-part force between Bill, who writes tortuously on piano, and Dave Stewart who adds the heft when Bill loses track. But it is really the similarity of creative intellect between Bruford, Holdsworth and Berlin that defines this classy, cruising, jet-set sound. Topping the band's popped jazz lilt is the occasional but memorable vocals of Annette Peacock, who paints more than she sings, counterbalancing a buzzing hive of melodies with pensive, wandering tones.

And the whole thing is captured with crystal clarity, tracks like lead scorcher "Beelzebub" really thriving through one perfectly hi-fidelity mix. No doubt about it, Bill can groove, cook and create in a commercial instrumental vein, all without sacrificing spontaneity. One compelling introduction to jazz for those who would normally run in the opposite direction with Godspeed.

August 28, 1978 – June 30, 1979. Yes mount the extensive Tormato Tour, taking in much of the US and Canada. The band play "in the round," pioneering the concept, and earned a Golden Ticket Award for over $1 million in concert receipts.

September 22, 1978. Yes issue *Tormato*, which is widely considered a creative disappointment. The album nonetheless goes platinum within a couple of months. Issued as a single in the UK this month is "Don't Kill The Whale"/ "Abilene," which charts at #36. The production video created for the track is the band's first to move beyond simple live montage work. A video filmed for *Tormato* track "Madrigal" raises the bar higher yet.

Steve Howe on *Tormato*:
"I'm not really a defender of *Tormato*, no. I think the weaknesses in that record are the first time we really had trouble in tone, in quality of sound—that was there. But this is because the group was starting to produce ourselves, each other and ourselves. It was a difficult time for me. It's particularly nice when Rick and I aren't competing, with me on an electric guitar and him on a synthesizer. Because right at that time, that was when the guitar and synthesizer sounds weren't mixing well. He was playing a thing called a Polymoog which he loved to bits, and he had his Birotron or something. He loved all those things, which we did as well. But in particular the Polymoog was very destructive towards guitar. I would play something and he would play something, and they would kind of cancel each other out. That was one of the weaknesses.

"But I would say we were different. We were finding ourselves in a different place. Some of the band wanted to be somewhere else. You know, they wanted to be somewhere comfortable and warm and easy. And some of the band wanted to stay in England, and work in London. That's what we'd always done. That's where we had written *Close To The Edge*, *Fragile*, *The Yes Album*. You don't go to Marrakesh to write those [*laughs*]. So at the time, I wanted to stay with that kind of reality. But also, we weren't working with Eddie and we'd moved studios and for a while we didn't know what our records sounded like.

"And like I say, the Polymoog and things like this, created utter hell for me. I've never liked it. But then again, you've got 'Madrigal,' which is Rick on a harpsichord, and 'Release, Release' has some merits, I must say, as well as 'Silent Wings Of Freedom.' I don't think it's a crap album. I just think it's a troublesome tonal album. Some of the trouble we had there, getting along, agreeing about geography, became a bit of a problem with Yes. Where are we going to work, where are we going to write, where are we going to record? Because guys were starting to leave the country and going to America; or Europe was really appealing. We did one record, *Going For The One*, in Europe and it cost $1 million. The next time someone said, 'Let's go to Europe and make a record,' we said, 'Yeah, do you want to spend $1 million making a record again?' I mean, you could make a record in those days for $300,000, a good record. But if you spend one million, what you've done is pay for skiing lessons, Swiss chalets, rental cars, and everything you ever wanted shipped over to Switzerland at the group's expense.

"But I think there were reasons why *Tormato* was the testing place. Because we did have our time working in England, we had to try to respect people who didn't want to stay in England, didn't want to pay English tax; all these problems were getting so claustrophobic. That's why after that we went to Paris and started another record, which we never finished, with Roy Thomas Baker. Alan broke his foot while we were recording in Paris [in 1979, roller skating with Richard Branson!] It was kind of a messy time [*laughs*]."

Alan White on how the sleeve art came about:
"We couldn't decide on an album cover for *Tormato*, and Po, the guy who ran Hipgnosis, he got really bored one day and was just looking at the art in his office, I guess, and he was eating lunch, and just threw a tomato at it. It's actually *Tormato* with an 'r' in it, because it's all centered around the tors in England—tor is an old, old, English word for rocky hill."

Rick Wakeman, countering that it was he who threw the tomato:
"We had paid a fortune for the artwork, which when we were shown it, we all agreed we had been ripped-off. It was a pile of brown smelly stuff. I picked up a tomato and threw it at it. The album was meant to be called *Yestor* but was hastily changed to *Tormato*. The tragedy about that album is that it had probably the worst

cover of any Yes album and contained some great music. Sadly, the production of the album was poor, very poor."

Author review of *Tormato*:

Even as *Going For The One* was still fresh, Yes had it in mind to crank out another record very soon. By September of 1978, *Tormato* had arrived, the band invigorated (perhaps too decisively), opting for their most succinct tracks ever, the single record comprising eight or nine tracks, depending on how one counts.

In the harsh light of history, and in many opinions at the time, *Tormato* is seen as a bit forced, hysterical, choppy, brash and jammy. Plus there's the matter of Anderson's lyrical hippie tendencies spiralling out of control. Obviously the man has always backstroked among the clouds, it's just that amongst such paradoxically sparse clamour, his musings approach rant. The band itself admits the record lacks direction, that relationships were strained, and that the record was rushed, rehearsed under the pressures of studio sessions, the resulting product lacking in production tone.

All in all, it seems a scrap yard of brief Yes ideas and fleeting thoughts crammed together until a song barely escapes with its life. Such is the case with nightmarish opener "Future Times/Rejoice," which seems to lurch along to the pain of an all too exposed Alan White non-groove. "Don't Kill The Whale" found the band boldly political, somewhat unintentionally, even scoring a bit of a hit with the song, following a greater smash status for "Wonderous Stories" a year earlier which had broken a drought that led all the way back to "Roundabout." But again, the track was a chop-block of tribal drums and braying, whale-squeal synthesizer—Steve felt in competition with Rick's tones throughout the record—despite Anderson's lyric being comparatively lucid and brief.

"Madrigal" was a welcome toning-down, Jon and Rick quite spontaneously putting together an actual madrigal, an old-English-folk-after-dinner-song. The lyric makes sure to tie in Jon's and Rick's UFO obsessions, amongst Jon's dissipated but quite beautiful and imagistic blatherings.

Then another jarring occurs, with an almost light gothic metal, "Release Release" skipping nimbly but hard rockin', Jon playing front man on a lyric about as scatterbrained and verbose as his canon gets. Power, anarchy and positive vibes swirl until the head swells with responsibility. And then there's a contrived drum solo shoved in the middle, Alan playing an average series of rawk tom fills over fake crowd sounds. Quite illogical, as Spock might say.

And speaking of Spock, "Arriving UFO" opens side two. Once again, we have a spirited, high energy rocker full of production holes, low on cohesion as all five players seem to be cramming in their licks, no one wishing to commit to timekeeping, bedrocking or chording. But "Circus Of Heaven" is in my opinion, *Tormato*'s finest hour, Jon singing/reciting a soaring, fanciful poem over a celestial reggae anchored by Squire's playful basswork. Alan stays back with bass drum timekeeping and tinkly crotales, Steve and Rick continue their duel but tastefully, and Jon's son Damien cameos a couple lines of disappointment at this heaven for adults.

Squire's "Onward" arrives next, a simple ballad which again should have flowed more lushly than it did. Steve's staccato picking lends continuity to Rick's quite uncontinuous synth bass pattern. Chris's lyric is a simple love ode, quite a contrast to Jon's metaphysical labyrinths elsewhere on the record. Closing the show is another exposed, powerless, but jazzy rock-hopper, "On The Silent Wings Of Freedom" adding to the scant but arguably existent core characteristic of this ultimately sour, cold record. For perhaps the fifth time on the record, a track is dominated by bass and drum interplay, leaving Steve and Rick to dive-bomb each other with bits of effluent. This longest track on the record, very inappropriately, contains the least backbone.

So, all in all, despite the fresh aggressive, pert and pertinent nature of *Tormato*, it seemed that Yes was too frayed and edgy to pull off their heavier aspirations. If the material is allowed to stand, then the sparse, mid-rangy production must be faulted, many of these songs needing multiple additional layers of simple playing to achieve their intended trajectory (that is unless jazzy and conversational is what the band's intentions actually were). The novel "in the round" stage set-up that was utilized on the record's tour had the band somewhat happier and more enthusiastic again, even to the point of working on an ultimately shelved live record for 1979.

November 1978. The US single from *Tormato* is "Release Release"/"Don't Kill The Whale;" it fails to chart.

Journalist Michael Davis on *Tormato*:

Jon Anderson's still hot on the trail of innocence, trundling down Mystical Ways, through Celestial Seasons, chirping his pre-testicular vocals for all to hear. Every time Steve Howe finds a rock 'n' roll riff in his Les Paul, he makes it gargle milk and honey, then tickles it to death. Rick Wakeman's found a Birotron (a beer-guzzling Mellotron, didn't ya know) to keep him company. Chris Squire's discovered a bigger bass sound through harmonizers, and Alan White's gone the opposite route with his finely-tuned buddies, the Crotales.

Late 1978. Patrick Moraz issues *Patrick Moraz*.

Patrick Moraz on *Patrick Moraz*:

"My third album, entitled simply *Patrick Moraz* (a wish of the record company, at the time), uses the concept of 'primitivism and civilization.' The harmony of the primitives, the struggle for survival, the arrival of the machine world, the impact of the robotization on the human world, the aliens' arrival and help to save the human race, the hope and the potential co-existence of those worlds, on planet Earth. Originally entitled *Primitivization*, a neologism I created at the time, the entire album was conceived as a ballet and features acoustic trans-cultural percussion as well as acoustic keyboards and electronic synthesizers, vocoders and the human voice."

1979

May 1, 1979. Jon Anderson performs his first solo show, also playing this year in July at the Montreux Jazz Festival.

October 1979. Yes, somewhat unwillingly, travel to Paris to work on a new album, with producer Roy Thomas Baker, fresh off drunken sessions with Foreigner as they wobbled through their *Head Games* album. A rift occurred, with Jon and Rick ostensibly liking the softer, more ethereal material, and Steve, Chris and Alan wanting to rock harder, causing Jon and Rick to become fairly absent at the sessions. Compositions worked on during this period include "Richard," "Tango," "In The Tower," "Everybody Loves You," "Friend Of A Friend," and "The Flower Girl."

Alan White on his foot fracture caused by a roller skating mishap:
"We worked with Roy before, in Paris, in the late '70s, working on an album that kind of stopped halfway through. I actually had a hairline fracture in my ankle. It was my bass drum foot. We were only halfway through the album, so the album got kind of canned [*laughs*]."

November 1979. Steve Howe issues his elegant second solo record, *The Steve Howe Album*, complete with gatefold and Roger Dean artwork. Guesting on the record are Yes alumni Bill Bruford and Patrick Moraz, plus Alan White.

Late December 1979. After a frustrating commute between Paris and London, the band move everything back to Britain. Jon takes off to Barbados, on the pretence of writing more lyrics for the album. Yes break up, but will soon reconfigure. Along with the tension at the Paris sessions, also contributing to disintegrating relations is the fact that the band has scattered in terms of home locations, with Alan in LA nursing his ankle. Rick set up as a tax exile in Switzerland, and the others still in Britain. Yes briefly consider continuing as a three-piece with Chris as lead vocalist, given the quality of the material they had been cooking up when Jon and Rick weren't around.

Steve Howe on Jon Anderson:
"In the time he was away, we were supposed to get together with Rick. He was going to fly in from Switzerland, rehearse with us for a week, then go home

again. We were supposed to do the backing tracks separately, and he was going to record his keyboard parts afterwards. Nobody liked the idea very much. It was getting more and more fake. [Jon] was really just hanging in. He was fading into the background. The more nothing happened with him, the more the rest of us carried on working every day."

Rick Wakeman on leaving Yes (again):

"Alan broke his leg skating and we all went home and never reconvened. It was not a happy time. The record company wasn't happy and we, as a band, weren't happy. Nobody seemed to want to play on anybody else's songs at the time and in the end Jon had enough. He said he was leaving and so I joined him! I always felt though that my leaving was always in the best interest of the band. I cried on two of the occasions. The first time I quit and in 1979 in Paris. All water under the bridge now. The past only shapes the present. The present shapes the future and that's what counts."

3

1980s

•••

Theoretically, Yes should have been killed off so that rock in the 1980s could operate unhindered by 18-minute-long multi-disciplinary spiritual quests set to music only deciphered with calculator and slide rule. Punk, long dead, became post-punk in the UK, and in the US, a cheerier, more palatable and amorphous non-category known as new wave. We also saw a healthy industry in music made primarily by synthesizers and other adjunct technology, to the point where a debate was being had for real whether rock was dead, and indeed, whether computers could completely replace people in the creation of music.

As well, there was a New Wave Of British Heavy Metal, which sparked a massive interest in heavy metal in Los Angeles in the low 1980s, with the music evolving into thrash and hair metal. Filling the gap between those two, most hard rock dinosaurs of the 1970s were now doing even better business than they did back then, codified in the arid heat of California on Heavy Metal Day at the US Festival circa 1983.

And where did Yes fit into all this? Well, practical business men that they are, they bellied back to the bar with an album called *Drama* in 1980, which found Rick Wakeman replaced by Geoff Downes, but infinitely more of a travesty, Jon Anderson replaced on vocals by Trevor Horn. Fan acceptance of the album was stronger than fan acceptance of the band live, but even so, the meticulously crafted, audiophile-quality record was pretty much ignored. Over time, it's gotten its just due, and *Drama* is considered by most Yes fans as a very fine Yes album indeed.

Then, practical business men that they are (again), Yes call it a day and the members fuss about trying to slot themselves into various supergroups, given the currency they had built up as rock royalty in the previous decade. Chris Squire and Alan White try to get something going with Jimmy Page, which fizzles out. Steve Howe and Geoff Downes, on the other hand, find themselves with a surprise hit band called Asia, joined by John Wetton and Carl Palmer. *Asia* goes quadruple platinum, and wobbly follow-up *Alpha* does platinum. It's debatable what value there is to derive from the band's weirdly noisy, fence-sitting music—sort of pop with prog poked into all the wrong places—but the phenomenon does indicate that there is some love for these old rockers who, on paper, should have been consigned to obsolescence.

Into this era, which significantly is also when MTV is beginning to go gangbusters, an alternate nascent Asia called Cinema becomes Yes, with the re-attachment of Jon Anderson, and soon this Trevor Rabin-infused collective have a surprise hit on their hands with a tight, urgent, technology-laden album called *90125*, flagshipped by a jarringly incongruent smash single called "Owner Of A Lonely Heart," which sounds like a Police song, despite opening with the heaviest power chords ever pasted onto a Yes track this side of "Machine Messiah."

The success of *90125*, at triple platinum, along with Asia and a similar surprise second wind success for Genesis, puts these venerable progressive rockers at the head of a feisty, short-lived resurgence for the genre—but necessarily updated—that also brought along a few newer bands in the wake. The phenomenon was dubbed neo-prog, and its proponents at the time included the likes of Pallas, IQ, Magnum, Pendragon, Twelfth Night and, most successfully, Marillion, each hailing from the UK, which echoes the geographical reality of prog rock in the 1970s, save for outliers Rush and Kansas and maybe Italy's PFM.

Similarly, underscoring the currency of these 1970s manor-dwellers is the gold-selling success of something called GTR, with their lone self-titled record. This was, of course, Steve Howe together with ex-Genesis guitarist Steve Hackett, the former now further quelling his misfortune at not being part of *90125* with his second successful offshoot band of the 1980s.

Back in the Yes camp, just like Asia, initial massive success could not be followed up, with Yes turning in a difficult, belaboured son-of-*90125* record called *Big Generator*. Like Asia's *Alpha*, the unwieldy Yes album would nonetheless go platinum and, all told, Yes spend much of the 1980s as big an arena-rocking success as they were all through the 1970s.

As the decade comes to a close, we get a hint of the legal and paperwork weirdness that is always bubbling under in the Yes organization, when a self-titled album emerges by a band called Anderson Bruford Wakeman Howe. Again, proving currency, the complicated record sells three-quarters-of-a-million copies worldwide, and an expanding family of Yes members escapes the 1980s still rock stars by pretty much any measure, save for the good looks of youth.

1980

1980. Rick Wakeman marries for the second time. The marriage to Danielle lasts but a year, producing one child. Jon and Vangelis issue *Short Stories*, their debut album together, on Polydor.

January 10, 1980. The Buggles issue their debut album, on Island, called *The Age Of Plastic*. The band is a duo, consisting of future Yes members, Trevor Horn and Geoff Downes. The album hatches a smash single called "Video Killed The Radio Star," which hits #1 in the UK and #40 in the US.

Trevor Horn reveals why he called the band The Buggles:

"We were getting the third degree from other labels that wanted to know if we were going to tour, if The Buggles was a band. In fact, when we took the demo around, we weren't a band at all. It was a studio concept. You see, as producers, we had become very cynical about names, about categorization. We decided to find a name that was a horror and The Buggles fitted the tag perfectly. If anything, the name is a play on an electronic bug. But then again, The Buggles means absolutely nothing."

April – June 1980: Yes work on what will be their first album without Jon Anderson as lead vocalist, and without long time keyboardist Rick Wakeman. A Buggles song is offered by Trevor for possible inclusion on the new Yes record. With Trevor and Geoff Downes in the studio with Yes to help them get the song straight, the absence of Rick and Jon is immediately noted and soon the duo are asked to join the band. The suggestion comes from Chris, who had struck up a friendship with the guys through their mutually shared management.

Alan White on getting Buggled:

"That lineup was really started by Steve, Chris, and myself. Jon wasn't involved at that time, and we just went into rehearsals in Munich with the idea to do a new album. In the next studio was Trevor Horn and Geoff Downes, and they were fans of the band, and they kept coming in and listening to us, and finally one day Trevor said, 'I've written a song that you guys can do really well,' and then all of a sudden we were playing the song and they're both kind of in Yes. We had a meeting, and then we went in the studio and recorded. That was another album [*Drama*] where a lot of people brought a lot of music from a lot of different areas; it was compiled really by all of us, and we had a great time. I think it's an underrated album, one of the band's better albums."

Geoff Downes on *Drama*:

"A lot of people like *Drama*. It showed that Yes were prepared to access and push new boundaries. From my standpoint, a piece like 'Machine Messiah' is a worthy contender to sit along with some of the best Yes stuff. It has the hallmarks of a Yes piece, as does the whole album, which doesn't really sound like anybody else. It sounds very disciplined as a record but actually we were all over the place in terms of recording. I mean, that's why the album name *Drama* came up, because the amalgamation of the other three guys and me and Trevor was not holding great reverence in some corners, certainly with the diehard Yes fans.

"But I think once they got to hear the album, and over time, people have warmed to it. It was put together with a lot of rehearsing and care. Eddie Offord came for some of it, and then he left, and we had to finish it off on our own. It ended up as a kind of group-produced album. Eddie Offord did the backing tracks, but everything else was done as a group production. That's where it usually can sound absolutely awful, where the band are all hanging over the faders. But it actually does stand up and sounds pretty powerful and punchy still. So it had a lot of ups and downs, but if you look at it in the cold light of day, it's a solid album."

Steve Howe on *Drama*:

"I think at times *Drama* is underrated because Jon and Rick aren't on it. But there is a segment of our audience that believes Drama is a great album. And if you take the record at face value and don't overly read who's on it, and say this is a record from the '70s or 1980 by Yes... I mean, it fooled us. Chris, Alan, and I weren't really aware that we made anything different than what we used to make with Rick and Jon, because, strangely enough, Trevor was so much, in his writing capacity, not much different from Jon. And I think the lyrics on *Drama* are pretty true Yes lyrics in most respects.

"And Geoff had his own kind of subtlety to bring to Yes, which was a great thing. Because you can't have a guy just twiddling. Yes never wanted to be a band where people just twiddle away. And I think Geoff brought a new level to it, a new kind of keyboard player that had a Fairlight and a Synclavier. He was a guy who was going somewhere with his keyboards and not just carrying around a Hammond and a piano, which, you know, is a great tribute to somebody's simplicity but at the time we wanted so much more. We'd got Rick in to replace Tony who really didn't want to be a multi-keyboard player. And Rick was a multi-keyboard player, who would sometimes eat curry while we were playing on stage. He did things that left us kind of a bit cold as far as what kind of commitment he really had. So when Geoff came along, we wrote *Drama* which is the main one, I would say, that's underrated... if you could say that, because we rate it anyway. But by some, it's totally missed, because they won't go there because Jon and Rick aren't on it."

How Trevor Horn became a Yesman:

"The [Buggles] honeymoon was over with the record company, and we realized that we would need a manager to keep things rolling for us. We couldn't continue to hide

The first Yes lineup looking sartorial in 1969.
L–R: Peter Banks, Chris Squire, Jon Anderson, Tony Kaye and Bill Bruford.
(The Estate Of David Gahr/Getty Images)

Top left: Alan White arriving at Morgan Studios, in style, in 1973. *(Laurens van Houten/Frank White Photo Agency)*

Top right: Rick Wakeman wasn't happy with *Tales From Topographic Oceans* and checked out of the band for the first time six months after its release. *(Laurens van Houten/Frank White Photo Agency)*

Above: Jon Anderson wanted to record *Tales From Topographic Oceans* in the country, but it wasn't feasible. So manager Brian Lane brought the country to Morgan Studios, hence the cut-out of a cow behind Chris Squire, apparently the band's new drummer. *(Laurens van Houten/Frank White Photo Agency)*

Top: Eddie Offord doing his best to record what Yes had in mind for *Tales From Topographic Oceans* while Jon Anderson (barely) looks on. *(Laurens van Houten/Frank White Photo Agency)*

Above: Jon looking distinctly fed up at Morgan Studios. *(Laurens van Houten/Frank White Photo Agency)*

Chris Squire and Alan White on the Tales From Topographic Oceans Tour at Carolina Coliseum, Columbia, SC, February 10, 1974. *(Hunter Desportes)*

Top: Steve Howe and Jon Anderson at the Carolina Coliseum.
(Hunter Desportes)

Above: Rick Wakeman at London's Rainbow Theatre, October 21, 1973.
(Laurens van Houten/Frank White Photo Agency)

Above: The Yes lineup for 1980's *Drama*, an album that history has judged more kindly than reviews would suggest at the time.
L–R: Alan White, Geoff Downes, Chris Squire, Trevor Horn and Steve Howe.
(Michael Putland/Getty Images)

Opposite top: Talented multi-instrumentalist Trevor Rabin plays guitar hero at the Knickerbocker Arena, Albany, NY, April 25, 1991.
(Frank White/Frank White Photo Agency)

Opposite bottom: Bill Bruford at the same upstate New York gig; Bill re-joined Yes from 1990 through 1992.
(Frank White/Frank White Photo Agency)

Above left: Jon Anderson at the Spectrum, Philadelphia, PA, Aug 26, 1994. *(Steve Trager/Frank White Photo Agency)*

Above: Dr. Chris Squire, with intern Billy Sherwood looking on, at the Upper Darby Theater, PA, December 12, 1999. *(Steve Trager/Frank White Photo Agency)*

Left: Billy Sherwood, although his tenure was brief, brought a tougher, more modern sound to Yes. *(Steve Trager/Frank White Photo Agency)*

Left: Steve Hackett has worked with both Steve Howe and Chris Squire. Noted Hackett, of Chris, for this book: "I loved working with him. We had great times, both in the studio and recording in my home." *(Neil Thompson)*

Below: Alan White circa 2011: over 40 years with the same band, which is quite an achievement given the physicality of drumming, especially for a band like Yes. *(Greg Olma)*

Bottom: Asia have always had close links to Yes. Here's Steve Howe and Carl Palmer in 2006. *(Jomelia)*

Above: Benoit David, from Yes tribute band to the real deal. *(Greg Olma)*

Left: Jon Davison, in possession of more of a Jon Anderson vibe than Benoit, is the band's current vocalist. *(SolarScott)*

Top: Oliver Wakeman believes his value to Yes was playing the songs live as they were recorded, whereas father Rick championed improvisation. *(Greg Olma)*

Above: And it's goodnight from the boys in the band. *(Greg Olma)*

Chris Squire, 1948–2015.
Thank you for the music. *(Greg Olma)*

in the studio. Anyway, Brian Lane, who manages Yes, had heard the cut of 'Video' and he liked it. We sat down and decided he was the man to handle our affairs. Through meetings with him at the office, we started to meet Steve Howe and Chris Squire and friendships started to develop. And Chris invited us down to his house one evening—the two of us—and we ended up talking right through the night. It was at that meeting that the first discussion came up of us joining the band. Now I knew every Yes song already; I owned every single one of their albums and so it wasn't a matter of having to learn everything from scratch. We went into the studio and did a few rehearsals and from there we became co-members of the band."

August 18, 1980. Yes issue *Drama*, which features Steve Howe, Chris Squire, Geoff Downes, Alan White, and controversial new vocalist Trevor Horn. The album is recorded at Town House, London and mixed at SARM. The production credit goes to the whole band, but in the main, Trevor Horn produced, with "backing tracks" produced by Eddie Offord. Engineering is Hugh Padgham, who's signature gated drum effect can be heard on "Run Through The Light."

Steve Howe muses on this period:
"It was a telling time, when Yes tried to continue—or did continue—without Rick and Jon. Obviously a lot of people held their breath and thought, 'I don't

know what this band...' and we didn't really know. But when Geoff and Trevor came along, their skills, their talents, were so obvious to us. We'd met a keyboard player who was going to write with us more, in a way, than Rick did. He wasn't so flamboyant a technician as Rick, but he had a great feel and he had a great British approach to being a keyboard player. With Trevor, it was like having a genius in the group. Trevor's skills were going to come through in his production, very much, but his writing and his singing also. Because after all, he started as a bass player; obviously he wasn't going to play bass in Yes, because Chris was playing.

"But I guess the emotions that were around there were the challenging emotions of perpetuating the group. The manager used to say, 'We surely don't change the singer! Can we really get away with it?!' And for a few people, we didn't. For Jon Anderson, for instance. But that's a bit like asking me what I think of *90125* and expecting me to have a lot to say. So I don't expect Jon or Rick to have any views on *Drama*. Putting the touring aside, the recording was done with full Yes determination, and I think 'Tempus Fugit' shows that.

"One of the things I like about Yes that doesn't always come through very seriously, is that this band started as a rock band. We might have orchestral influences and we have classical this and that or we can play these funny guitars and keyboards which have got nothing to do with rock. But the return point, the mid-ground, is rock. And when you listen to 'Khatru,' you know that's true. When you listen to 'Tempus Fugit,' you know that we were still rocking at that point. That is not a piece of dirge. You can't write a song like that unless you're going somewhere with it. 'Tempus Fugit' flies, it rocks, like anything. I compare it to 'Sound Chaser.' I put it next to 'Siberian Khatru,' this sort of league. It's a fast song, it's tricky, it's dynamic."

Chris Squire on *Drama*:
"*Drama* was a good album. In the last couple of years we've been playing tracks from that album. I think *Drama* has some of Steve Howe's best guitar playing on it, so it's a pleasure to play that material with him now on stage because he still plays really, really well—probably, better. It was an interesting time for us and the first time that Geoff Downes and Trevor Horn were performing with us. Good memories from that time."

Geoff Downes on *Drama* (again):
The Yes thing had been enormous for quite some time and when I joined it had really gone full circle. They had come off the album *Tormato* which I think for them was the very least successful album for quite some time. So it was very much me stepping into someone else's shoes. And the band was obviously at a low ebb because both Anderson and Wakeman had moved off to other things. I wouldn't say that it wasn't a great experience, but when you are sort of learning other people's parts, it's OK for a bit, but there's also your own stuff you want to get on with. And that's why the album itself was really good fun because I think

we brought quite a lot of interesting approaches to Yes's music. And I think even after that, Trevor's influence on the *90125* album really gave Yes a new lease of life, which they continued through the Trevor Rabin period. They'd shown that they were still a force to be reckoned with, even as a live band."

August 29 – December 18, 1980. Yes execute their Drama Tour, another strictly European and North American affair. There are tensions all around as the band (and their wives and kids) spend way beyond their means, and as the revolt from the fans against Trevor as the singer grows.

Geoff Downes on Trevor Horn sounding like Jon Anderson:

"He [Trevor] got a lot of support from Chris Squire because Chris was very in tune with the way Yes sounded vocally. He sort of helped steer Trevor in that direction, and I think that's why, despite the fact that you did have two of the key members missing, I think it still had a Yes flavour to it."

Trevor Horn on joining Yes:

"I've always been a Yes fan and the chance to work with this band is a really exciting opportunity, if not something of a bizarre situation. There was a need to change in the band; both Steve and Chris wanted to play again and that change was needed to make it work."

October 1980. Yes issues as a single "Into The Lens" backed with "Does It Really Happen?"

Journalist Rick Johnson on *Drama*:

For a group that eats personnel changes for breakfast, they sure have come up with a consistent style. Closely clipped, weightless vocals splatter on the paralyzing underdrone of slightly dimwitted vocoders mulling over 101 ways to cook mud puppies (on a long stick is best). Even with the last-minute grafting on of the Buggles (?!), this is fairly solid stuff.

Geoff Downes's keyboard inspirations:

"The early rock keyboard players like Emerson and Wakeman influenced me a great deal, as did orchestral music. I tended to move more into an orchestral sound with a lot of layers, as a sort of one-man ensemble, if you like. I did that even more so than say Emerson or Wakeman, who are very much lead instrumentalists. That wasn't my thing, particularly. I was more of a textures merchant."

November 1980. Jon Anderson issues his second album, *Song Of Seven*. The album includes four tracks that were demoed during the sessions for *Tormato*. Two singles are generated: "Some Are Born"/"Days" and "Heart Of The Matter"/"Hear It." *Song Of Seven* reaches #38 in the UK and fails to chart in the US.

Author review of *Song Of Seven*:
Years since his last solo flight, Jon Anderson is in a very difficult frame of mind. No longer defined by Yes, Jon spices this truly solo, truly on-yer-own record with oscillations between fresh optimism, soul-searching panic, and stale regression. The overall vibe however, leans towards hope, if tinged with escapism, Jon assembling a hybrid of shameless, mystical hippie musings, bouncy R&B rhythms, and occasional new-ish electronic technologies (see the anthemic "For You For Me"). But even that catch-all refuses to catch all, "Hear It" and "Days" harkening back to the fireside madrigal feel of *Olias*, "Don't Forget (Nostalgia)" half-heartedly courting the blues, and "Heart Of The Matter" sounding like something off of *Sesame Street*.

The biggest advance however, is the fact that *Song Of Seven* is a full-band record, most noticeable performances being the electric jazz/Jeff Berlin stylings of John Giblin (he is one of four bassists on the project), and the sax work of Dick Morrissey, who adds a *Young Americans* dimension to the lighter, bouncier side one.

But come side two, Jon tends to slip back into his acoustic prog cocoon, blowing the record out with the 11 minute title track, a sort of delicate Yes pageant with too much emotion and therefore a belittling of emotion through over-beratement: Jon and his band of strangers functioning as Starcastle. Sum total of the *Song Of Seven* experience? One of fragmentation (think Peter Gabriel's first two records, or the Ian Gillan Band), too many disparate pop rock styles, long tracks next to short, the only constant being Anderson's unflagging spiritualism, a bright light that illuminates every track with hope, despite often maudlin musical beds on which that hope bounces like a toddler.

November 12 – December 16, 1980. Jon Anderson plays one date in Germany and five in the UK in support of *Song Of Seven*. The band is billed as Jon Anderson with the New Life Band.

November 24, 1980. Yes issue their second live album, a two LP set called *Yesshows*. Although released after *Drama*, the album features Jon Anderson on vocals, given that it is composed of tracks from 1976 through 1978. Indeed the band had scheduled the recording and issuing of a double live album back on the Going For The One Tour, planning to use shows from the tour leg in Australia and Japan. Many shows in fact were recorded, with plans also set at that time for a feature documentary on the band.

December 1980. Yes has, to all intents and purposes, broken up. Meanwhile, Geffen A&R wizard John Kalodner envisions a new prog supergroup, now that both U.K. and Yes are no more. Brian Lane, first

fired by The Buggles and then Yes, within a few weeks is on board as the manager of Steve and Geoff's bright new idea, which at that point had included a bass player as well, namely John Wetton. Eventually joining would be Carl Palmer, but not before Simon Phillips (a baby Bill Bruford in both looks and sound) had been suggested for the drum stool.

Geoff Downes recounts how Yes disintegrated after *Drama*:

"It happened largely because I don't think Trevor was that comfortable being the lead vocalist. We finished in the UK, and he wasn't really enjoying it that much. He felt that it wasn't really for him. He wanted to be more of a record producer, which, I think he made the right choice, because he's an incredible record producer. Time and time again, he's done some ground breaking albums over the years with a variety of artists. But it had been difficult because Trevor himself was not actually a singer's singer. He was a bass player really, and singing was something else that he did. It wasn't really his instrument. Under the circumstances, he carried himself particularly well, especially on the record.

"But by the time we came to do the dates, it was much more difficult. Because someone like Anderson sings for two, two-and-a-half hours every night and doesn't miss a note. It's also very high register. For someone to come in and carry that off, I'm surprised that Trevor actually did it as well as he did. It's a formidable prospect. I think the UK tour particularly, Trevor got a lot of stick from the Yes fans here. People were more understanding and prepared to listen in America, but I think here there was a lot of prejudice that me and him had come into this situation and were not suitable replacements for Anderson and Wakeman. So after that UK tour, Trevor felt, 'Look, I can't carry on with this', and I was pretty much of the same opinion. So that's when we went back and started to do another Buggles album."

1981

1981. The big news this year is that Steve Howe lends his talents to the new supergroup Asia. Alan White ties the knot with Gigi. They are still married, and have two children, son Jesse and daughter Casse. The Whites live near Lake Washington, Seattle area. Jesse has worked as a ProTools engineer for Trevor Rabin. In this year, Alan and Chris Squire attempt to fashion a band to be called XYZ, with Jimmy Page.

Chris Squire on why XYZ never got past its ABC:

"That was fun, naturally. That came about because, unfortunately, it wasn't long after John Bonham had passed away, and Jimmy wanted to get back into playing, but he wanted to sort of ease into it. I can't remember exactly the first time I met Jimmy but in the '70s we were always at the same *Melody Maker* and *New Musical Express* awards lunches, so probably it was one of those. Plus, Yes and Zeppelin were both Atlantic Records bands, so maybe I met him in the office. Anyway, because we lived relatively close to each other, in the Windsor area of England, we just ended up getting together and jamming. And Alan came in, and we just played together and we were really just giving Jimmy some time to come back into enjoying playing again.

"Robert Plant was supposed to come and join us, but I think it was all a bit too early for him after John Bonham had passed away. So he never actually made it to the studio. We just ended up doing four demos. But because Robert didn't want to come and go back to work at that point—and I understand why—the XYZ project never really became XYZ. It just got to the stage of becoming four demos. I was the singer but we didn't want to do a three-piece band.

"Actually, parts of it have been used. We recorded the song 'Can You Imagine' on the *Magnification* album—that was one of the songs we had done with Jimmy. And there was another song that we did with him going on the Firm album, and I think they called it 'The Hunter' or something. Also, I'm not quite sure what album it was on—I'm going to say *The Ladder*— but there was a drum riff that Alan came up with. So bits of ideas from those sessions did end up getting recorded in various ways."

Alan White on XYZ:

"It was just a weird time when Chris and myself were floating free around London, and Steve was with Asia. We were released and people were doing different things. So Chris knew Jimmy Page pretty well, and he had a house on the river. Actually, a lot of the stuff that we did was written by Chris and myself. So we had ideas and we'd go down there and start work late in the afternoon and work into the early hours of the morning. It was quite an experimental period. It started to sound really good, and then management got involved and they had all these ideas which got in the way of the music, and that's kind of why it fell apart. I think Yes's manager wanted to be involved and then Peter Grant wanted to be involved, and they were at loggerheads on how to do this. They started to have a one-upmanship kind of thing.

"At one time Robert Plant came down and listened to the music, with a view to try to sing on some of it and see how he felt about it. But he just thought the music was too complicated, so it never panned out. But Jimmy was a lot of fun. On Led Zeppelin tracks, he used synthesizers with his guitar and things like that, so he's really into moving forward and being on the cutting edge of anything new. But he added the element of Zeppelin to it, so it was progressive rock meets Led Zeppelin."

January 1981. Yes issue "Run To The Light"/"White Car" as a US single.

February 12, 1981. While Yes encounter difficulties due to their fragmented lineup, fellow proggers Rush attain their career peak with their classic eighth album *Moving Pictures*, issued this day. In contrast, over the ensuing years, as Rush stumble with their attempts at modernization, Yes will find surprise success, as will both Asia and Genesis.

July 1981. Jon and Vangelis issue their second album, *The Friends Of Mr. Cairo* which scores a #1 hit in Canada with the title track. "State Of Independence" would be covered at least three times, with Donna Summer scoring a hit with it in 1982. The album reaches #64 on Billboard.

August 1, 1981. The Buggles' "Video Killed The Radio Star" is the first video aired as MTV opens for business.

September 22, 1981. Robert Fripp re-constitutes and reinvigorates King Crimson with the landmark *Discipline* album. Two more would follow in the ersatz trilogy, *Beat* and *Three Of A Perfect Pair*. Arguably, it is King Crimson—and at a similar heady creative level, Peter Gabriel— that brings excitement back to progressive rock, so that Genesis, Asia and Yes can clean up.

October 1981. With XYZ stalled, Chris Squire and Alan White issue a bright and cheery Christmas single on Atlantic called "Run With The Fox," orchestrated by Chris's long-time collaborator Andrew Jackman, with guest vocals by Chris's wife Nikki.

November 11, 1981. The Buggles issue their second and last album, *Adventures In Modern Recording*. The album includes a synth-pop version of Yes's "Into The Lens," re-titled "I Am A Camera." Two demo tracks from the album's sessions would be reworked for Yes's 2011 studio album, *Fly From Here*.

November 30, 1981. Yes issue a hits pack called *Classic Yes*, which eventually goes platinum. The original vinyl issue includes a 7" that plays at 33 1/3 rpm and features live renditions of "Roundabout" and "I've Seen All Good People." *Classic Yes* is in essence the most widely recognized Yes compilation.

1982

1982. In 1982, Trevor Rabin moves to Los Angeles. Just prior to rejoining Yes, Jon Anderson creates a project revolving around spoken word, some singing, and electronic music celebrating artist Marc Chagall.

Jon Anderson waxes lyrical about Marc Chagall:

"Aha! My favourite! I want to do it with projection and animation and talking about my life with Chagall, thoughts about what I did with him, and the songs that I wrote for him.

"I think I didn't know of his work until I met him. When I met him, I went into his house and he showed me his paintings, and I was stunned by his way of thinking. He was 90 years old but he was thinking like a 9-year-old boy! He was like a child! His paintings were very, very innocent. He had an amazing life; he travelled all over the world and created some beautiful art. I became friends with him in the south of France for five years; that's why I wrote this music. Initially, I wrote a dance piece with two songs and sang it to him, and then I wanted to make it into a big musical. Which I did."

January 1982. After XYZ fizzles out, Chris Squire and Alan White form Cinema, with South African multi-instrumentalist Trevor Rabin. Needing a keyboard player to fill out the sound, Chris suggests Tony Kaye.

Trevor Rabin muses about the record industry and Jon Anderson:

"I started sending things out to record companies. I got one reply back and it was from Clive Davis [a record company bigwig who founded Arista Records, amongst many other things] that said, 'While we feel your voice has pop appeal, we don't feel the songs. We feel it is way too left field and it will never happen.' I wonder what he thought when the Yes album went to #1. I sent out other tapes. Ron Fair was the guy who heard me first and he was amazing. He was the A&R guy at RCA. Had I done the RCA deal then I would still be wondering today how I was going to pay my bills.

"After Ron, I heard from Phil Carson from Atlantic who suggested I meet with Chris and Alan, who were in Yes at the time. We met up and we started playing my songs. Things were going really good and we decided to call the band Cinema, but some other band said their name was Cinema and that we would have to pay them a fee to use it. So, we dropped the name and that is when Jon heard the music and he got involved. People say that Jon and I had a lot of animosity between us but it couldn't be further from the truth. Jon stayed with me some months ago when I was doing orchestra for a Steven Spielberg thing I was doing. We get along to this day. In fact, Jon, Rick Wakeman and I have been talking about doing something for ages."

March 18, 1982. With their bold new name suggested by manager Brian Lane, Asia, featuring John Wetton, Carl Palmer, and two ex-Yes members in Steve Howe and Geoff Downes, issue their self-titled debut. The radio-friendly "arena rock" album is a massive hit, selling quadruple platinum, on the strength of singles, "Heat Of The Moment," "Only Time Will Tell," and "Sole Survivor."

Steve Howe on what's in a name:
"When people ask me, 'Why did you call Asia Asia?,' I can't remember the other nine group titles on the list that we cancelled. And really, we just looked at Asia—which nobody liked—and said, well, it's the only one we haven't blown out [*laughs*]."

Geoff Downes dismisses criticism that Asia were AOR:
"The *Drama* version of Yes had said, well, I don't know if we're going to carry on with this. It was shortly after that time that Steve had started working with John Wetton on another project, which turned out to be Asia. I went back and was working on that second Buggles album with Trevor, and they gave me a call and said, 'Look, we've got a lot of interest in the stuff that we're doing; do you want to come on over and get involved?' And by that time they had got Carl involved and it became Asia. And you know, a lot of people tend to pigeonhole that first Asia album and say, 'Well, that's AOR.' But we had a lot more going for us than that. It was performance music and that gave it that certain rawness. But there were also certain technological developments we used on it. There was a lot of overdubbing and production ideas that went into it that made it different than standard AOR, if you like that term. Certainly bands like Journey, who were around at the same time and doing albums that were similar, didn't have the same quirky aspect that we put on the music."

Carl Palmer's take on the Asia albums:
"I don't think they were raw sonically and from the point of arrangement, I think we were quite developed and mature, personally. The first album was the most successful. I think that album was balanced incredibly well, from the point of view of having a certain amount of protest music like 'Time Again,' pieces

like that, which were obviously longer than the two or four minutes. 'Wildest Dreams' was another piece which featured me a little bit.

"I think that the production at the time was suited to the music. I think the actual boomy sort of sounds would come from more of the commercial songs like 'Only Time Will Tell' and especially, 'Heat Of The Moment.' The first Asia album was obviously, I think, a real musical statement, an unbelievably well-balanced album, from the point of view of having prog rock musicians trying to develop 20 minutes into a seven-minute version, which, again, we did with 'Wildest Dreams' and 'Time Again,' and a few pieces on there that definitely lock into that area. And we had obviously pop tunes on there.

"I think the balance, coupled with MTV, was absolutely superb. It wasn't too over-the-top; it was still advanced enough for people who were into the prog movement, who followed bands like Yes, ELP, Jethro Tull and whatever, who could still listen to that, and they would find something they could really enjoy, apart from the obviously radio plays. To be honest with you, the hits that we had, 'Heat Of The Moment,' which was #1 for nine weeks, was actually a country and western song that John Wetton had written. It was written in 3/4. So it was a nice piece of music, but it didn't really suit what we were doing. But we rehearsed for six months, so we could really remodel and define and restructure and rebuild everything, every idea that every one of us had gotten. So we had plenty of time to put an album together, without really having to copy or steal from anyone."

John Wetton on how Asia got their unique sound:

"I can tell you this—Mike Stone, our producer, had a lot to do with it. Mike had been involved with lots and lots of projects that involved our kind of rock at the time, leading up to that, everything from 'Bohemian Rhapsody' to Journey. He was just about perfect for us, because he knew how to record the band. He was one of those guys, back in the days of analog, whatever you need in the track, he could find it. The big difficulty in those days was working in the 24-track format because it meant constantly multi-tracking and bouncing down, and he was good with us with that. Nowadays it's not so difficult because you've got Pro Tools. But he was great; he had an idea how he could translate what we wanted to do.

"I suppose I had the strongest idea of what I wanted the band to sound like. Because if you listen to the precursor of *Asia*, which was the solo album I did called *Caught In The Crossfire*—it was two years before and one year before we started rehearsing—you can actually see the way I was heading. And that kind of translates into the first Asia album—it's a bridge rather neatly to that. And Mike was just the perfect person to do that. He was also keeping everybody's personality in check. I mean, we got accused of pandering to the radio airways, but in fact, if you listen to what was going on at the time, in 1981, early 1982, it was all keyboard synth bands who were more concerned with image than with musical image or sonic image. And Asia was very much equally guitar- and keyboard-driven, but more importantly, I think, vocally-driven and song-oriented. We had it all kind of wrapped-up. I think it was a very good package at the time.

"And it was just progressive enough that people wouldn't say, 'Oh, it's just pop.' It was rock enough in its sound and it hit quite hard, so it couldn't be dismissed as another one of those synth bands. And it had real songs which were about real things and real emotions, and yet, something happened that was magic. There's always an endpoint in a recording where you realize that the sum is greater than the four individual parts. I think The Police described it as the ghost in the machine. Something is being added that you're not putting in. There's something coming out that's not physically being put in. The easiest thing to do is to put your feet up and get dragged along with it."

Author review of *Asia*:

Looking back, one can see that it made a sort of miserable sense that Asia went on to become the biggest selling album of 1982. Product-engorged music fans were tiring of progressive rock, but not heroes or legends, and Asia rescued a few of these and thrust them into the world of stadium AOR, a radio-friendly realm that rarely saw a squinty-eyed and artsy music school guy from England.

Time And A Word

So raise the odds with Roger Dean painting modern and manly, one godly and divine logo, a name the size of the world's biggest land mass, and you pretty much can't lose. No question Asia was a supergroup, which guaranteed them press, but the pieces were definitely less than the whole (not much less: this was barely humming synergy). We had John Wetton, a love-it-hate-it voice that always sounds a chore (rejuvenated after his *Caught In The Crossfire* solo record in 1980), Carl Palmer, the thunking, thudly Cozy Powell of prog, from one of the world's most ridiculed rock contraptions, Geoff Downes, a new boy with questionable buggy pedigree, and Steve Howe... well hey, no diminished chord there.

And what the band came up with was a surprisingly brash, punchy boisterous AOR display, loaded with sappy songs that romped, hooks to the fore, with lots of room to throw in prog flourishes (see "Soul Survivor" and the positively Drama-tic surreptitious metal of "Time Again"). But Asia was a smash, popping out hits like "Heat Of The Moment" and "Only Time Will Tell" that drove everybody nuts for better or way worse, those choruses the snicker subject of many a prog flameout on behalf of weary rock fans.

But probably the most overt characteristic of this record was its tone-deaf mid-range intrusion, a sound built perfectly for the limitations of car radio but horrid at hi-fi. Vocals way up, keyboards constantly washing ashore like scuttled shrieking seagulls, Palmer's stiff beats all ham-fisted drums and destroyed cymbals, Howe sounding thin and out of place amongst such projected and crowing corporate bombast. It all coagulated to define Asia's perplexed sugary mayhem, and like I say, it drove old school proggers around the bend worse than Wakeman's wardrobe. But hey, the cash rolled in, much to the amazement of the art crowd, placing Asia in the rarified company of Dire Straits as funniest-looking surprised stadium draw pushing wheelbarrows to the bank.

Why Trevor Rabin missed the boat to Asia:
"I was producing Manfred Mann at the time and that is how I met Kalodner. He had never heard of me as a guitar player, so I sent him some stuff. I actually met David Geffen, who I met first as we went out to lunch. A few weeks later, Kalodner had me getting my stuff together to move. I was given a development deal in order to write music for an album that I thought was going to be a solo album. Kalodner told me in order to go the fast route I should join some other known musicians and write some music with them. He told me doing a solo album would be much harder. I met with Carl Palmer and we got on quite well. John Wetton then came in to try out as a bass player.

"Time went by and I didn't hear anything for a few months. Kalodner phoned me one day and said, 'Look, I've got this thing with Steve Howe, Carl Palmer and Geoff Downes. We would very much like you to go and check it out.' I said, 'I don't want to have some big name supergroup-type of vibe that eclipses anything musical.' I was very cynical about it and I didn't want to do it. Kalodner told me, 'You've got to do this or we will be dropping you.' I said, 'Fine.' I went and I just hated it. From their point of view, they really didn't need me, as they were great. I think we had two days of rehearsal and I went back to John and I stuck to my guns and said I was not doing that. It was quite amazing, two days later I got a call that I was dropped. I should have done it [*laughs*]."

June 1982. Jon Anderson issues his third solo album, *Animation*, which finds Anderson moving from the traditional progressive rock of his first two records into more of a modern electronic sound. Aiding and producing with Jon are Neil Kernon and Tony Visconti. The album generates two picture sleeve singles, "Surrender"/ "Spider" and "All In A Matter Of Time"/ "Spider." Jon tours the record through August 26, closing in New Orleans.

Author review of *Animation*:
Now fully and freshly charged with the electric flow of new technologies (work with Vangelis couldn't have hurt), Anderson creates his most layered and belaboured collection of songs yet. Adding to the maelstrom of synth dynamics is the collective fussing of players like guitarist Clem Clempson and genius session drummer Simon Phillips. So call *Animation* a record of excesses, prog's most piercing and projecting vocalist fighting it out with poly-complex rhythms ("Pressure Point," "Animation," and "Much Better Reason"), while everybody else attacks his own particular sound stratum.

Less snobby experiments include the anthemic nouveau-Genesis clomp of "Olympia" and "Unlearning," the sunny feel-good Caribbean rhythms of "Surrender" and "All Gods Children," [*sic*] and the Christmas chime of "All In A Matter Of Time," all combining to demonstrate that Jon remains an all-pop kind of guy, celebrating with modern buoyancy many genres, perhaps becoming master of few. But there's way more happening here always, making every wayward directive that much more forceful and deliberate, *Animation* sounding like *Song Of Seven* with loads more confidence, arrangement and production, even if said production remains mid-to-trebly claustrophobic.

September 17, 1982. Thin Lizzy's Phil Lynott issues his second and last solo album *The Philip Lynott Album*, which contains a track called "Don't Talk About Me Baby," originally worked on by Phil along with... Chris Squire and Alan White.

Alan White talks about the track renamed "Don't Talk About Me Baby":
"Chris Squire and myself did a track with him, with some ridiculous name that just came out of the blue, dreamed up by, I think, originally Phil, but then we spent about seven hours in the studio. It was something like 'Silly Willy' [*laughs*]; it was a really, really silly song. I wish I could find a copy of it. It came out of

Chris's friendship with Phil Lynott. Chris knew Phil better than I did, because he lived in the same area as Phil—Virginia Water—in England. But I was around, and we just went into the studio and just worked it—a bit of lunacy, actually. I think Phil played guitar and Chris played bass, and Phil sung it."

Chris Squire remembering Phil Lynott:
"Phil used to come visit with his family, and when I had a studio in my house, we put down a couple of tracks. One was called 'Little Silly Willy,' It was a tongue-in-cheek kind of song. And there was another song that might have been called 'Hurricane'–some weather condition [*laughs*]. Phil was a great guy. Of course, as we all know, he was a dyed-in-the-wool drug addict, but he was a lot of fun as well. We had some good times and we had some creative times together. I'll always remember him fondly."

November 1982. Cinema work in earnest on what was to become their debut album, with recent Yes vocalist Trevor Horn suggested as lead singer for the band. Horn indeed sings on some of the early demos, but quickly moves over to a producer role. The material is a mixture of unused XYZ ideas and songs Trevor had from a shelved solo album. Into the new year, Tony Kaye is elbowed out of the band due to his lack of skills on the new hi-tech keyboards such as Synclaviers and Fairlights. Eddie Jobson is soon enlisted, being around long enough to appear in the "Owner Of A Lonely Heart" video. Tony is enticed back, and for a spell, the band has two keyboardists, until Eddie leaves, unsatisfied with sharing those duties.

1983

1983. Genesis-soundalikes Marillion issue their debut album, *Script For A Jester's Tear*, which goes platinum in the UK, creating a sort of "new wave" of British progressive rock. As it turns out, the main outcome of the emergence of new bands such as Marillion, IQ and Pallas is that the old guard, reconstituted, enjoy a second life.

April 1983. With neither Chris Squire or Trevor Rabin being strong enough vocalists for their new project, Atlantic's Phil Carson suggests Chris meet with Jon Anderson to see if his involvement could be secured. Much animosity had passed between the two, but on the strength, mainly, of "Leave It," and "Owner Of A Lonely Heart," Jon agrees to join the project. At both Phil Carson's and Jon Anderson's behest, and with considerable trepidation from Rabin, the band adopt the name Yes. Phil Carson, having spent all the label's money already, plus $150,000 of his own dosh, now finds himself in the position of having to re-record all

the vocals, which had been handled by Trevor Rabin as the band neared completion on the project. Carson plays the tape for Ahmet Ertegun at an impromptu meeting in Paris, upon the sorriest little portable cassette player. Fortunately (but not surprisingly), Ertegun could see the gold cracking out of the speakers, and the finances are quickly put in place to finish what had been originally been titled *The New Yes Album*.

July 1983. Jon and Vangelis issue their third and final album (while still operating as a group) called *Private Collection*.

July 26, 1983. Asia issue their second album, *Alpha*, which is considered a let-down at only achieving platinum status. The album reaches #6 on Billboard, buoyed by the hit single "Don't Cry."

Steve Howe reflecting on *Alpha*:
"Asia 2, *Alpha*, was a record that I'm not saying is actually bad, but it was just terribly finished off. Mixed in completely ass-about-face values. *Alpha* had all the merits of a reasonably good record. But there is *Alpha* material that has never been heard, which of course is some of mine, which offered more of a progressive sort of balance. So *Alpha* was a complete disaster. There is one person in Asia still going around loathing and hating and moaning and complaining when, hang on, we had a good time in those days.

"You don't have to spoil it all just over a bit of spilled milk. I know it sounds like I've got a few hatchets to fly, but they're really just actually things I've come to terms with. I've said look, this was a disaster but it doesn't mean to say I hate the guys, you know what I mean? I don't blame John Wetton for Alpha, not wholly. I think

John and Geoff did take the lead there; they took a few leaves too many out of the 'Let's lead the group' book. But there were people who allowed that to happen. It's a combined effect, not one person at all. So if people could lay down the hatchet, maybe one day there will be a reunited or original Asia. But it won't happen now, because there are too many people that have too many axes to grind."

Geoff Downes on why Asia was such a success from the outset:
"I'd say it was because it had the integrity of the players that were involved. The bands that we were involved in, it had that integrity. But also, when we started working on the material, we consciously, or subconsciously, directed it in a much more, not middle-of-the-road, but much more mainstream direction, I suppose. I think we all wanted to do that, and certainly John and Carl and Steve had done a lot of big progressive rock pieces in the '70s, and it was a fresh start for all of us. From my own standpoint, having that stint with Yes, I really enjoyed going out there and playing live to big audiences. So it was a good opportunity for me to continue with that. Mike Stone was very integral in helping us achieve what we wanted to achieve on that first album, in terms of production. Mike let us be ourselves, and he recorded it really well. And I think the eccentricity in the production is more from the eccentricity of the arrangements. No one else was doing anything like it, so it was a fresh sound for people—it sounded like it was recorded in a stadium."

Carl Palmer on *Alpha*:
"The second album was a complete mistake, and was put together, possibly, through greed, the 'chasing the single' syndrome. It was just full of pop tunes, and that just died miserably. I'm saying that, but it nearly sold a million copies, I believe. There was always egos; I think there's always arguing. I don't think anyone can sit on the fence. If you're in a band and you sit on the fence and like and agree to everything, then you don't want that guy in the band.

"You want a guy who's got an opinion. You want someone who can voice something in an intelligent way and be constructive. You don't want it being awkward for the sake of being awkward. Asia was pretty much a targeted band. We knew what we had to do. We wanted to use the media, we wanted to get involved with things like MTV. We were looking at our previous bands and seeing that radio play had practically ceased on anything recorded in the past, so we knew we had to change. How radical the change was going to be—who knows? Fortunately enough, the balance on the first album was quite an organic affair and we didn't have lots of discussion or arguing or anything like that. It just happened fairly naturally."

John Wetton's take on *Alpha*:
"If *Alpha* had been the first album and *Asia* would've been the second album, everybody would have been as happy as Larry. Because the progression would have been, in people's minds, more organic. What we did was, we were forced

back into the studio by the machine that is the business. Geoff and I had to come up with material on the spot. And there are really good songs on *Alpha*, and the third album as well. But because of the monumental success of the first one... I mean, I don't regret anything that I've done, but, to look back on it, I can pick out the good bits. And I look at the album as an important step, but it came out too soon. We could have toured on those sales for about four years. Instead we came out with an album exactly 12 months later.

"As the old saying goes in the business, it takes you 20 years to write your first album and 20 minutes to write your second one. That was the position I was in [*laughs*]. And I even remember, after we recorded *Alpha*, in the control room, in the studio, we played the album and I was just about on my last legs. And I heard this voice behind me that said, 'Mmm, I don't hear a single.' So, that evening, Geoff and I sat down at the piano and wrote 'Don't Cry.' It was tough. So obviously, the writers get bashed. They get no credit if everything goes well, but they're the first ones to get bashed if something goes wrong.

"And me being the singer as well, I got a fair amount of stick, when it didn't perform as well as the one that sold 10,000,000 12 months previously. It's a pretty tough act to follow. The record company and the industry assumed that everyone who bought the first one would go out and buy the second one. But it doesn't work like that. I don't think we made any train crashes or big mistakes on the second album, but it didn't sell as well as the first one. And that, after a monumental success, is considered a catastrophe."

Author review of *Alpha*:
Uh, ladies and gents, "Don't Cry," Asia are back and sounding like the Bay City Rollers rocking the bus with Abba. *Alpha* is just *Asia* all over again, except it's all the bad bits, the cute but blaring ballads wiggling like fishies. And I've never heard a drummer with so little swing or rhythm, Palmer just slamming those toneless round things of his like every tender moment is a hockey barn sound check.

Pretty well every song included for your listening displeasure is an uptempo, uptown romantic ballad at full blast at the mall, each rendered in turn as a sort of march to robotic backbeats, written with dull uniformity exclusively by Wetton and Downes, neither of whom is a progger at heart, despite some of Wetton's high-falutin' credentials (Roxy, Crimson, U.K., Heep).

Sum total: even less Howe, less hard rock, louder keyboards, and soapy sappy tones galore. It's also pretty well void of chartables save for that abomination 'Don't Cry.' A round of yucks is in order. *90125* showed the world how to make smart, current and commercial progressive rock. Alpha methodically blows it in all departments in which that record got it right, and as a result, Asia became a laughing stock. Note: Wetton soon left the band (replaced by Greg Lake), but was back in time for the next record.

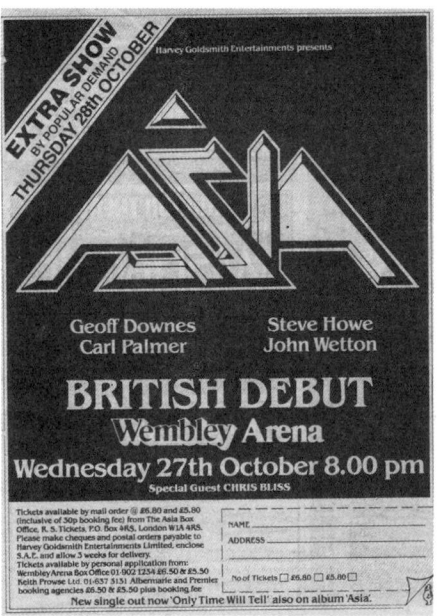

October 3, 1983. A month before Yes drop their new record, Genesis builds upon the double platinum success of *Duke* with their 12th album *Genesis*, which is eventually certified quadruple platinum.

November 7, 1983. Yes, issue their *90125* album, which scores a huge hit single for the band with "Owner Of A Lonely Heart," which goes to #1 in the US, drawing the album to a #5 placement on the *Billboard 200* chart. "Owner Of A Lonely Heart" is also issued in the UK, rising only to #28, despite hitting the shelves as regular 7" and 12" single, picture disc and shaped picture disc.

Trevor Rabin on Yes vs. Cinema names:

"I was never happy that the band was called Yes. I thought it really didn't represent the band. I knew if anything positive ever happened then there would always be the question of whether the songs were really that good or was it just the name of the band. My wife says to me, 'If you'd called it Cinema, then maybe it would have been easier for you to get into movies' [*laughs*]. We were all amazed at the success of the album. I remember being in Los Angeles and a song came on the radio; it was on this big, cheap stereo system that sounded like shit. I heard us on that radio and it sounded to me that it just didn't have it and it sounded terrible. My manager called a few days later and told me that the album was starting to take off and I breathed a sigh of relief."

1980s

Jon Anderson discusses Yes's two biggest songs:
"It became a #1 pop song. Yes had two big hits, 'Roundabout,' and 'Owner Of A Lonely Heart,' and that's what the majority of people know you for. But your fans, they understand who you are, they know what you've been doing, they know the creative process, so I'm pretty happy about that. I enjoy doing both of them very much. You always want to sing it good, you always want to do a good version."

Alan White on the band's drastic new direction:
"We were all into it. We spent quite a while rehearsing. We rehearsed the material for *90125* over a period of about nine months, and we were redirecting the course of Yes. Initially the band was supposed to be called Cinema. But then Jon Anderson got interested because he liked the songs so much, that he sang on it and we couldn't call it anything else but Yes."

Author review of *90125*:
If, in some squinty-eyed way, *Tormato* was a reaction to punk, and *Drama* was a reaction to the reaction, *90125* would convolutedly prove another reaction again, a sort of curt, sassy, commercial nu wave, reaffirming (by way of a new leader, of course) that this new version of an old brand name can be vital and vigorous and bouncy and, most pertinently, relevant. With Jon Anderson saucily and belatedly back in the fold, things surprisingly spring ahead, the man's hippie-regressing flightiness no match for the jaunty pop juggernautiness of South African jack-of-all-trades Trevor Rabin, who single-handedly transforms Yes in his image, basically writing and commandeering the whole thing.

And so, after Jon's return, the band's cleanest, most transparent graphics yet wrap a record that would become Yes's most successful and sociable album ever. Its flagship track, opener "Owner Of A Lonely Heart" served as metaphor for the *90125* vibe, with its hi-tech electro-drum intro collapsing quickly into clear, stinging heavy metal chords from a heavier-than-Howe Trevor Rabin. What ensued would be perhaps Yes's most recognizable song, even though it possessed few Yes characteristics, sounding more like a *Zenyatta*-era hit from The Police. Yea and verily, this was Yes chucking conventions, marrying prog rock callisthenic thinking to a half-dozen or so new wave ideas; not punk, but the second wave after punk, the skinny tie set, the romantics, the dance and synth crowd.

There's the story of Ahmet Ertegun telling Chris that a hit single must happen this time... or else, and indeed this was to be the case, all members of the band past and present getting quite a kick out of this fresh success with a crazy, left field sound. Once the shock settled, this newly configured machine made sure that other twisty tricks popped out all over the record like magician's flowers, and *90125* blossomed into a rich album experience with legs and, more pertinently, additional smash singles.

1984

January 17, 1984. *90125* is certified platinum, two months after release. The album reaches reach triple platinum, with over eight million copies sold worldwide. Canadian sales clock in at double platinum, with the album going platinum in Germany and gold in the UK.

Rick Wakeman is generous about *90125*:

"I'm a great *90125* fan. I think *90125* is one of the most important albums Yes has ever created, because I think without *90125*, there wouldn't be a Yes now. Because it was that period in the '80s, the mid '80s, where prog rock was dead, really dead. And bands like Yes were in a death throe. A lot of bands were. So the album... I know it was originally a different name, and then Jon came in and sang on it and various things, and then it became a Yes album. But because it was so, shall we say un-Yes in various respects, but with Jon's classic voice stuck over the top, it just about fit into a genre that was acceptable without it being prog rock, if you know what I mean. Very song-oriented, great Trevor Horn production. I mean, I'm a great Trevor Horn fan and, of course, not so much in the UK and in Europe, but certainly in America, it was a monster album, and I'm convinced that saved the life of the band. I'm convinced if the band did another album like *Drama* or something like that, the band wouldn't be here now. It wouldn't have survived. So it was a crucially important album."

February 1984. Yes score another hit from *90125* with "Leave It," which originally had appeared as the b-side of debut single "Owner of A Lonely Heart." "Leave It" is sent to market in various formats, accompanied variously by *a capella* and remix versions of the song, reaching #24 on Billboard. Reflective of the song's hi-tech sonics, the music video for the track made pioneering use of CGI graphics.

February 28 – October 1, 1984. Yes conduct their *9012Live* Tour, blanketing the US, then Europe, then returning to North America for a second leg.

Chris Squire, in 1984, comparing Yes with Asia:

"I can see certain similarities in the bands, but not that much. Perhaps the major reason for even a superficial similarity is that Trevor Rabin has a very good pop feel to his writing. Asia has that same feel in some of their material. The way we approach music shares a common root—after all, Steve and Geoff went through a lot with Alan and I. But Yes is still a very distinctive band. We don't have to take a backseat to anybody. We are proud of the music we're making now."

May 22, 1984. Yes sign a legal agreement stipulating which members can use the Yes name. It would cause a ruckus over Anderson Bruford

JULY ■ 11th & 12th Wembley Arena, England ■ 14th Birmingham NEC, England ■

CAT NO. 89723

JON ANDERSON • CHRIS SQUIRE • TREVOR RABIN • ALAN WHITE • TONY KAYE

A · *IT CAN HAPPEN*   B · *IT CAN HAPPEN (LIVE VERSION)*

PRODUCED BY TREVOR HORN

Wakeman Howe five years later, although the document isn't clear enough to settle all discrepancies between the mildly warring parties.

June 1984. Yes issue a third single, "It Can Happen," from *90125*, backed with a live version of the same song. The track reaches #51 on Billboard, but fails to chart in the UK.

June 24, 1984. Yes play Dortmund, Germany; five of seven tracks from the forthcoming *90125Live: The Solos* will be sourced from this show, with the balance being lifted from a concert on September 28, 1984, at Edmonton's Northlands Coliseum.

November 10, 1984. Rick Wakeman marries for a third time; his 20 year union with actress, singer and former *Sun* Page 3 girl Penny "Nina Carter" Mallett produces two children, son Oscar and daughter Jemma, who has sung on Rick's records. Men of a certain age will remember Nina as one half of pop duo Blonde On Blonde with fellow model Jilly Johnson.

1985

January 17 – February 9, 1985. Yes play South America for the first time, beginning with a stand at *Rock In Rio* and closing off with single dates in Uruguay and Argentina.

November 1985. The final single from *90125* is "Hold On," the song coming into being from two separate Trevor Rabin compositions called "Hold On" and "Moving In," before additional contributions from Jon and Chris.

Alan White on getting the right drum sound:
"'Hold On,' where we reverse the rhythm around, turn it around a bit, that's a creative highlight up there with *Relayer*. There are spasmodic parts that I pick out of every album that have a lot of creative direction coming from the drums, but in the end, create an entire picture. But, oh boy, you can't get away from the fact that the drum sound on 90125 is one of our best; we spent a long time on those drum sounds."

November 1985. Asia issue their third album, *Astra*; significantly, guitarist Steve Howe is replaced by Mandy Meyer.

Geoff Downes lauds Asia for not standing still:
"Certainly the big change we made initially was when we got Mandy Meyer in for the third album, because that offered a completely different guitar perspective to Steve Howe. Although commercially it wasn't a particularly successful album, it shows that we were prepared to not just regurgitate what we had done before and take it in new directions. Over time, we definitely went through some periods. The range of the music has been quite wide, from a pop influence to a jazz influence to heavy rock to progressive music. As I see it, rightly or wrongly, we managed to explore quite a few musical avenues."

November 7, 1985. Yes issue a 33-minute short live album/long EP called *9012Live: The Solos*, which rises to #81 on the Billboard charts, during a stay of 11 weeks.

Trevor Rabin reflects on finding his own style:
"One thing, from a technical and maturity standpoint, I'm a lot better player than I was in those days. Going back to age 16, I have always been able to play whatever I wanted to play. Yes is very complex music but when I had to go back and learn all of the albums, I realized it is really not very difficult to play. I realized that was Steve Howe and that made me question who I was. I needed to find out what my style was and who I was as a musician."

Late 1985 – Early 1987. Yes work at studios in Italy, then London and Los Angeles, on material that will comprise their all-important follow-up to *90125*. Italy was chosen for tax purposes. In London, the sessions were tough, with songwriting battles erupting between Trevor and Jon that were not present on *90125* (due mostly to the finished nature of the music when Jon arrived), with producer Trevor Horn stuck in the

middle to sort them out. Trevor Horn would soon bow out, with the guys finishing the record in LA with the production job now on the shoulders of Trevor Rabin and Paul DeVilliers.

Trevor Rabin on the dangers of self-importance:

"Chris Squire is like a brother to me. When we used to play together, we would do a gig and then go to a pub until like three in the morning. He once said to me, 'You need to focus on being a guitarist. If you keep going like you are, which is a keyboard playing, producing, guitar player, then you're not going to get the focus that you deserve, which is for being a great guitar player.' I said, 'Yeah, but I love playing piano.' Chris said, 'You're a way better guitar player than you are a pianist.' I said, 'That is a real insult.' I get that, but at the same time I don't want to get that big head. I saw it in Yes and I saw it in Rabbitt. You get successful and you think that you're the only one who is successful and you live in this bubble and you are the world's axis and the whole world revolves around you. I never thought like that, but I've seen that. I have seen it happen in bands that I have produced. I have seen bands that were not even that big but they create a self-importance which diminishes being open to stuff."

December 1985. Jon Anderson issues *3 Ships*, which includes a number of Christmas-themed selections. Producer for the project is Roy Thomas Baker. "Easier Said Than Done" is issued as a single, backed with "Day Of Days" in most territories.

1986

March 1986. *9012Live: The Solos* sees UK release, reaching #44 in the charts.

May 2, 1986. Mike Oldfield issues a single with early CGI video called "Shine," on which Jon Anderson is guest vocalist.

June 9, 1986. Yes rivals Genesis enter an entirely different league with *Invisible Touch*, which goes 6x platinum.

May 1986. GTR, featuring Steve Howe and Steve Hackett, issue their self-titled debut album on Arista. The Asia-like album peaks on Billboard at #11 and is certified gold, on the strength of singles, "When the Heart Rules The Mind" and "The Hunter." On tour, the band include a rendition of "Roundabout."

GTR producer Geoff Downes on working with two guitar virtuosos:
"It's a difficult situation to feature two guitarists equally. You've only got so much space for a guitar solo and which guy plays the solo? [*laughs*]—that's what it comes down to. So they kind of moved further and further and afield as the album went on. So instead of actually working on things together, it was very much, 'Right, that's my bit, that's your bit.' In the end, that spoiled any real fusion between the two, which, as the producer of the album, was what I was looking for. In the end, I just ended up being a referee. If I had been able to step away from it and not have the two guys breathing down my neck, and been able to mix it the way I wanted to... but the trouble is they were both so keen on how they wanted it to sound, and it ended up being a compromise. The rough mixes I did on my own were considerably better than the final mixes that ended up on the master."

Steve Hackett on GTR:
"With GTR, we had the unenviable position of having a hit album in the States and a bankrupt company in England. And so the price of success came very, very high indeed, to support that level of activity, meaning a very expensive album etc. I also feel that the best of GTR was perhaps left behind in the rehearsal room, with long solos and lots of blasting away that never made it onto record. Because it was not just Steve Howe and myself that were making the decisions there, although we were the prime creative team. At the end of the day, there may have been 20 people involved with the decision-making process with that outfit. So it became unwieldy, hard to steer.

"It's a funny period, really. There were a lot of things pulling in different directions. With Steve, I think we were aware from the word go, that it was a band that would have to do well instantly, or it was going to be 'call it a day.' So the pressure was on us in a way that neither of us had felt before. But I decided to embrace it, and at that

time I felt I was proving my bankability again, and so it really was a case of doing it by the book and following the rules. I think that, if anything, it was the closest to a formula-made album than anything I had done before, and will ever undertake in the future. I'm not really a great believer in formulas. I'm a bit of a formula-buster."

Steve Hackett on Steve Howe:

"The similarities between us are that we are interested equally in acoustic stuff as well as electric stuff. So we used to kick off the GTR show with acoustic guitars; we did 20 minutes of that. Sometimes Steve would do something like 'The Clap;' sometimes he would do a set of country music things; nobody really knew he was capable of doing that, with Yes. I would do stuff that was perhaps a bit more Spanish-influenced. But those were the similarities. He tended live to use a cleaner sound than me. But I was very impressed with his work, not just with Yes and Asia, but stuff that he did with the earlier band called Tomorrow, with Keith West—that was an interesting band, obviously before Yes. And I think that is what sort of got him the job in that band. So everything that he did was very interesting. We shared a love of nylon guitar strings of course.

"I think there's a lot of the country player that is in his approach, and of course he does play pedal steel—that's part of his sound as well. I think the best of Steve Howe can be heard on *Relayer*, 'Gates Of Delirium'—lovely stuff there, and 'Yours Is No Disgrace.' Great iconic guitar work on both those tracks."

Author review of GTR:

As if realizing how crude and unkempt Asia really was, Howe assembles a similar if slicker vehicle, perhaps also challenged to succeed by Yes West's [Trevor Rabin, Chris Squire, Tony Kaye and Alan White's version of Yes, more of that anon] monetary windfall with a tighter prog-pop sound. And shaping another Asia-like supergroup, Howe yields half the limelight to a guitarist equal in stature, Steve Hackett from Genesis, whose string of solo records is one of the most impressive in prog. Vocals are handled by ex-Nightwing/Bronz belter and arena-ready sure-shot Max Bacon, who despite his ease of delivery, has pretty boy pipes like Styx 'n' Journey.

But the general vibe of the whole GTR spread remains one of a trickier, more musically articulate, forward-purposeful Asia, Geoff Downes's crackly cackly AM radio production sufficiently muddying all the detailed playing to the point of distraction. Hits were scored with Howe/Hackett's "When The Heart Rules The Mind' and to a lesser extent Downes's "The Hunter," and elsewhere many more could have been mined, most tracks riff-rocking quite heavily, sweetened by melodic, anthemic choruses and Bacon's teen dream vocals.

Two white-knuckle prog flip-outs close the show, "Hackett To Bits," which finds the band buzz-saw metallizing with stops and starts Rush would be proud of, and "Imagining," which jumps, twirls and hammers the record home with brisk electric verve. So come to think of it, the whole thing's pretty hard-hitting and aggressive, like ELP's professorial snobbery slumming it with Bon Jovi and Night Ranger at the mall, or more simply put, a raft of heavier Kansas tracks laid end to end. Kills Asia dead.

November 7, 1986. Jon performs a one-off show with Vangelis, at University College in LA. The duo try to record an album in 1986, but never release the material until a low-key issue of it as *Page Of Life* surfaces in 1991.

December 1986. *Fragile, Close To The Edge* and *Classic Yes* are issued on CD. However these are not the first Yes albums to emerge on the new compact disc technology, with *90125* being among the first wave of CDs to hit the market back in 1983. Five more albums would be issued on CD in 1987 and 1988.

1987

1987. Esquire issue their debut album, on Geffen. The Asia-lite-styled band features Chris Squire's wife Nikki on lead vocals. Both Chris and Alan White guest on it, Alan being one of three drummers credited. Chris also co-produces the album with the band. The album is recorded at Sun Park studio, at the Squire home New Pipers, plus Air London and Summa in LA. Trevor Horn gets a mixing credit on one track called "To The Rescue."

1987. GTR, struggling with financial issues and the inability of Steve Hackett and Steve Howe to get along, first lose Steve Hackett, who felt creatively stifled by the situation, then try to enlist Brian May, but ultimately settle on Robert Berry. The collaboration was short-lived, with Howe eventually winding up in Anderson Bruford Wakeman Howe.

Robert Berry talks about life in GTR:
"When I was in England I worked with GTR, Steve Howe's band, and that's how I hooked up with Rick Wakeman and I met Jon Anderson, although I didn't

do too much work with Jon Anderson. I also met up with Geoff Downes from Asia because I was working with Carl Palmer and Keith Emerson and we had the band 3. With GTR, I came on board for what was supposed to be the second album and I quit that band before the second album came out. The album hasn't really been released, although it's been released as a bootleg.

"I was brought in to replace Steve Hackett, and Steve Howe and I were writing all the songs and working pretty close together, and the band resented that. So whenever I wanted to sing a harmony part or do a little something that stuck out a bit, they tried to make sure it didn't happen. And I understood why, but it just got a little old after a while. So after I got all the songs written with Steve, they got their budget from the company, they OKed all the songs from Arista Records and they said, 'Yeah, go ahead and do the album.' And I said, you know, 'I've done what you need from me. I think I'm going to head home now. You don't really need me in this band.' And I wished it would have worked out because it was a great band. But I just wasn't really needed, you know [*laughs*]. Except for Steve—we had this great writing partnership down."

Steve Howe on the difficulties of GTR:
"Well, it's really unfinished, totally unfinished. What happened in that stage of recording was that we made quite a few backing tracks, bass, drums, rhythm guitar, and that's it, and guide vocals. So when I look back at those albums to see if there's potential, whether it's worth an arm-wrestle with this label to get these tapes released, to go back and revisit them, I said no all the time consistently. The tracks are nowhere near 'up' enough. They don't have enough on them. I would have to re-record all the guitars and all the voices. Because all we did really was put down the structures and that's a shame. I'm not pleased about that. I'm quite disappointed.

"It's mostly to do with the timing of Robert leaving. He had gotten another offer from 3, ELP if you like. And our management, stupidly, didn't realize how catastrophic it was going to be when we went back to Arista and said, 'We haven't got Robert now; he's gone.' So it was a very stupid thing to do, to go this far. But I've got to say I understand Robert's reasoning. I think it had a lot to do with the slightly aggressive British guys called Max and Phil. They were quite boisterous, pushy and boisterous, hard to deal with if you didn't know them. If you didn't know what they meant when they said, 'Fuck off!,' they would say that all the time. And in England, it's not really a big offensive thing to say that. It's just a mood swing. But yes, we lost a lot of momentum there and it's kind of why those tapes aren't presentable."

September 17, 1987. Yes issue their 12th album, *Big Generator*, which receives a Grammy nomination and is certified gold within three months of release. The album reaches #15, on the strength of *90125*, and three singles launched from the record, "Love Will Find A Way," "Rhythm Of Love," and "Final Eyes," the latter into the new year.

Trevor Rabin on *Big Generator*:

"I enjoyed every album we did together. *Big Generator* was emotionally a very difficult album. *90125* was a very weird album but it all worked with the guitars and the keyboards. By *Big Generator*, we had to make things work and we learned that Trevor Horn, who produced the other album, was going to be involved and I wondered how it was going to work. The songs were not as good but I still enjoyed making those songs and I loved playing them live."

Rick Wakeman begs to differ:

"Not that keen on *Big Generator*. To me, *Big Generator* sounds as if it's been produced 500 times and remixed 500 times. Even though there's some good stuff, it sounds tired to me. And it's interesting, in talking to the guys, that's exactly what it was. It just got done over and over and over."

Alan White on *Big Generator*:

"*90125* had more of a rock approach even though we had Yes elements in amongst it. It was one of our most successful albums of all because we just happened to hit on the right button with 'Owner Of A Lonely Heart,' which gave that album a lot of sales and a lot of play. *Big Generator* had some material that was as good as some of the material on *90125*, and it did pretty good. It was just a different album as we'd moved on down the line a couple years. But I wouldn't say it was that hard to follow up *90125*, no. The Trevor Rabin sound is running through both of those albums. *90125*, we spent a long time on the rehearsing and the material for that, and then also recording it. *Big Generator* would be a more, dare I say it, heavy metal-ish, but still with a lot of great song value on it. It was a little bit heavier, although *90125* had its moments of that."

November 14, 1987 – April 13, 1988. Yes tour in support of *Big Generator*, closing off with six dates in Japan. In Trevor's opinion, the new songs didn't translate as well live as did the *90125* tracks.

Jon Anderson on the music business as machine:

"When you start a band, it's amazing. The first five years are amazing, but then it becomes accountants and managers and money and problems. And then you get a hit record in the '80s and you're famous for ten minutes and then your managers and accountants are screwing you. There are always gonna be people around you just trying to make money; they don't really care about the music or the quality of creation. They don't care about what you're doing up on stage or what you're doing to people's thoughts by doing some wonderful, different music. They're always saying, 'Man, you gotta get a hit record.' And I

always say, 'Well, fuck you. Go on and get another job.' I don't play that game; I never did and I never will. I don't want to. I believe in great music."

December 1987. "Rhythm Of Love" is issued in the US as a dance mix single, backed with *90125*'s "City Of Love" in live version. The track charts at #40. Trevor Rabin's suggestion to employ real brass on the track as well as his rude guitar work rankled the band's more traditional fans.

Trevor Rabin on *Big Generator*:

"It obviously wasn't *Dark Side Of The Moon*, and on 'Rhythm Of Love,' I just went for shock value. But I was quite happy with some of *Big Generator*. And even though it was a traumatic experience making it, I thought it was the best album I did with Yes."

1988

April 29, 1988. *Big Generator* is certified platinum.

Alan White on Trevor Rabin, the mastermind of the band during this era:

"Trevor was a very, very talented musician, an all-round musician. He writes great music, plays incredible guitar, and he's an incredible piano and keyboard player as well. If he can think it, he can play it, one of those kind of things. And he's also educated in reading music, so he can write the whole thing out. He's one of those guys that's Beethoven-ish. Beethoven wrote his symphonies when he was deaf. He just wrote the notes down, but he knew what it was. Trevor could also do that, without picking up an instrument, and he had perfect pitch as well. He could write a whole orchestra section running through a melody."

Trevor Rabin on why he didn't ruin Yes:
"I think I have an understanding of what it was that maybe is different from the outside. I knew who I was and what I did, but I'd have a little chuckle reading articles where it said, 'He's ruined Yes. He's brought this silly pop, plastic element to the band.' When we finished *90125*, we were so excited. Chris Squire was really holding the flag, saying, 'This is the new sound. This is what we're about now.' I was really proud and happy, however we got there, with both *90125*, and 'Owner of A Lonely Heart.' We all were."

May 17, 1988. Jon Anderson, departs once again from Yes after the Big Generator Tour obligations and issues his fifth solo album, the commercial and accessible *In The City Of Angels*, which was recorded in Hollywood, with Stewart Levine producing. Two singles are generated: "Hold On To Love"/"Sun Dancing (for the Hopi-Navajo Energy)," and "Is It Me"/"Top Of The World (Glass Bead Game)."

Late 1988. Jon Anderson collaborates with Steve Harley and Mike Batt on "Whatever You Believe," a charity single in 7" and 12" format for the ITV telethon.

1989

June 20, 1989. Anderson Bruford Wakeman Howe issue their one and only studio album, a self-titled effort. The band was positioned as an alternate version of Yes, with Jon Anderson not happy with the commercial stadium rock version of the band as commandeered by Trevor Rabin and Geoff Downes. The Yes West version of Yes was so incensed by the existence of ABWH that they served an injunction that no mention of Yes be associated with the band. "Brother Of Mine" is issued as a single in various formats and track listings. Bassist on the album is Tony Levin, with additional keyboards from Matt Clifford. The album was recorded at both Air Studios locations, Montserrat in the Caribbean and London, after pre-production work in Paris.

Rick Wakeman on balancing virtuosity with emotion:
"Both have equal importance. I am so pleased I had a long and thorough musical training. It means that almost nothing is impossible. A musician is like a writer in as much as a writer can only write according to the knowledge of his vocabulary. His imagination will also be limited by this knowledge. Musicians are limited by

their knowledge as well, so the greater a vocabulary of technique and musical knowledge a musician can have, then the more possibilities can become reality. Having said that, too much knowledge can be a dangerous thing and a lack of it can make composers do some weird and wonderful things. A good balance within a band is crucial if you really want to create something special and different."

Bill Bruford, contrasting Tony Levin with Robert Fripp:
"Tony is probably the most secure. He's played with so many people that pretty much anything is all right with him. You can give him the phone book and say, 'Play that' and he could turn it into music. Robert is a brilliant mind. He finds it much harder to make music. If you gave him the phone book, he wouldn't know what to do with it at all, apart from look up phone numbers. But nevertheless a fine thinker and of course he was the guiding light of King Crimson."

Future Yes singer Billy Sherwood on the *Big Generator* lineup without a lead singer:
"In 1987, '88, around there, I was doing demos for the first World Trade album, which was signed on Polydor. And Derek Shulman, lead singer for Gentle Giant, and record executive, signed us to Polydor. And shortly after our record came out, he moved over to Atco, to become the president, where Yes was without a lead singer. So it was Chris, Tony, Trevor and Alan. And Derek is the guy who said, 'Jon's not here; you need a lead singer. I know this guy, Billy Sherwood from World Trade—he would be perfect.' So he made the introduction. And the rest is kind of history. But the initial spark was right around the World Trade time. So yeah, everybody around me was telling me I was gonna do it, and I was the only one who was saying, 'No, I'm not going to do it' [*laughs*]. Because that's not my role, and job, in Yes. I don't want to replace Jon Anderson. He's a one-of-a-kind character and lead singer. I felt at the time if I did it, I would be short-changing my own path and my own career, which is what I was focusing on, doing other things."

July 10, 1989. Trevor Rabin issues, through Elektra, his first solo album in nine years, and his first after becoming a star with Yes. *Can't Look Away* features Alan White drumming on two tracks. The record reaches #111 on Billboard, and generates a Grammy nomination for best video. It is essentially Rabin's first and last high profile solo record.

July 29, 1989 – March 23, 1990. Anderson Bruford Wakeman Howe tour in support of their lone album, hitting Europe, North America and Japan.

August 1989. "Let's Pretend" backed with "Quartet (I'm Alive)" is issued as a US single.

November 1989. "Order Of The Universe"/"Fist Of Fire" is issued as the final single from *Anderson Bruford Wakeman Howe*.

4

1990s

•••

It's been quite a run for Yes as we enter what is considered a sort of weird decade for rock music, a side-drift, as it were. Shorthand for the 1990s bespeaks of the grunge explosion out of Seattle, plus hard alternative, industrial rock and rap. Most old warhorses are put out to grass, and, in particular, all forms of heavy metal are considered an embarrassment best left to the 1980s.

As it turns out, Yes can't find a place in the rock culture of this decade. Rock 'n' roll is a young man's game—surely that must be part of it, as Yes take their place as a heritage act, although one that admirably keeps generating new music, despite the film and fog of nostalgia creating proportionally outsized demand for their old hits.

The decade, however, opens with Yes continuing to find ways to push boundaries, emerging with a record called *Union*, which finds, what is essentially, the two amicably competing versions of the band coming together as one eight-headed monster of throwback progression. *Union* manages to go gold, but creatively speaking, the exercise proves that eight cooks in the kitchen results in indigestion for the patrons beyond the swinging door.

The band would return for *Talk* in 1994, which would become the first record of many to come that would not achieve RIAA (Recording Industry Association Of America) designation. At this point, it's almost as if a switch is flipped, and Yes become the underground band they were in 1969 and 1970, content to serve their large cult fan base with unabashedly complicated progressive rock releases like the two *Keys To Ascension* albums, which are half live hits and half new studio material, and *The Ladder*, the tragic last production for famed Vancouver knob-twiddler Bruce Fairbairn, who dies during the making of the record.

Just before *The Ladder*, however, the band turn in a controversial album called *Open Your Eyes*, which points to a tougher, more immediate, guitar-charged sound for the band, fuelled very much by the creative input of youngster Billy Sherwood. As you will read as the story unfolds, the album causes much consternation for Steve Howe but then, as Sherwood intimates, it seems Steve has had somewhat of a change of heart concerning this interesting and vital outlier in the Yes catalogue.

As subplot, the members and ex-members of Yes, through the 1990s, prove the sincerity of their engagement with music by continuing to release solo albums and collaborate with each other and myriad other performers, mostly unknown and semi-famous. The effect is a heartening one, where the fan comes to realize that once the fame and fortune wanes, what matters to these guys most is the creation of more and more music, even if no label of note will sign it, because, in reality, not quite enough people want to hear it.

1990

1990. Rick Wakeman issues two albums this year. *Night Airs* is the follow-up to *Country Airs* and *Sea Airs*, with Wakeman completing his trilogy of piano albums, while *Phantom Power* is a re-imagined soundtrack to the 1925 version of *The Phantom Of The Opera*.

Summer 1990. Anderson Bruford Wakeman Howe work at a studio called Miraval in the south of France on tracks intended for a second studio album. Work is halted as a novel merger with the rest of Yes is strongly suggested by the label and management, who figured, according to Bill, that this was the only way to best the 750,000 sales of *Anderson Bruford Wakeman Howe*. i.e. duct-tape both bands together and call it Yes.

Steve Howe discusses the nature of the music business:
"ABWH was short lived. When it became Yes it came out as it was before as if nothing had happened. It was very disappointing. The basic headings, the main thing that artists love to blame are management. They usually are somewhat to blame but I wouldn't say that they can take all the blame. I think that personalities create tremendous problems in bands. The personality clash or the musical interference clash can be bad. When someone is bugging someone because they keep doing stuff that should not be there or they are doing stuff that was not there yesterday... there are so many levels. You can get stuck in ruts. You can think, 'He's really getting a bit out of it.' You get the imbalance in the group from working because that is really wearing.

"You can also let things come up more like a bad luck story. One thing keeps going bad and then another thing goes bad. That is not what you thought was going to happen and then someone is not even around anymore. People can sometimes walk out on the spur of the moment. Then they want to come back. You get all this paradoxical farting around.

"Another problem is the high-level business stuff. Somebody gets the needle about something or there is something that they don't agree on. Maybe they think they were not paid their share. People can make life pretty difficult for themselves. I think Asia may have suffered from that. Yes was, for a long time, an ocean-liner ship. It was always being boasted up and put back into operation. These other groups didn't get that chance. The original members went adrift. They were each problematic. Yes has a course of action that somehow keeps it alive.

"It is quite a management cliché to say that the band is falling apart but musical argument is good. It is sometimes good to stand back from the situation. People can push themselves down a ramp by what they say. Some of it they have to eat. There is a book in there somewhere and I have written it already [*laughs*]. There are a lot of inherent problems. Another thing that can affect a band is bad financial planning. One of the bands that we mentioned was like that. We got to a point where we overspent and over-expected and we were eventually in trouble. One of the first bands I was in had a van taken back; 30, 40 years later things haven't really changed. We might be talking about a Hummer now instead of a van [*laughs*]!"

August 14, 1990. Asia issue *Then & Now*, which marries six earlier hits with four new compositions, with "Days Like These" being issued as a single. The Geffen-issued album reaches #114 on the Billboard charts and goes gold on the strength of it, serving as the band's first greatest hits package.

1991

April 9 – August 8, 1991. The eight-man version of Yes tour in support of their forthcoming *Union* album. Rick Wakeman and Tony Kaye meet for the first time ever during rehearsals for the tour, even though Tony thinks the two met in the men's room once. Opening music for the shows is Stravinsky's "Firebird."

Alan White on the technology he has on stage:
"I use the MalletKAT for triggering an assortment of percussion samples and sound effects, like gongs and droning sounds. When I play my acoustic drums, I trigger a mixture of my own drum samples and live drum sounds. For instance, during the intro of 'Owner Of A Lonely Heart,' I'm triggering samples from the record."

Bill Bruford on the *Union* gig:

"With this band, all we have to do is turn up on stage—and not fight—and the people are thrilled. We don't even have to play a single note and they go absolutely wild. I'd say that's a way to make a living, eh?"

April 30, 1991. Yes issue their 13th studio album, *Union*, leaving their longstanding relationship with Atco for Arista. The ground breaking record is so deemed because it represented a coming together, essentially, of Yes West with Anderson Bruford Wakeman Howe. Essentially, however, four tracks are crafted by the Rabin wing of the band, and ten by the ABWH configuration, plus a Steve Howe guitar solo. Arista's ploy to blow up ABWH for a more successful band, results in a record that doesn't do much better sales-wise than *Anderson Bruford Wakeman Howe*, although gold certification is achieved in the US.

Steve Howe on *Union*:

"*Union* was a total disaster. The way that was mixed left everybody going, 'What?! This wasn't a record we made.' And it certainly isn't the record we made. It's got other people playing keyboards and guitars on it. And really, I don't care what Jonathan Elias [*Union* co-producer] ever says, but that was the most insulting thing he could have possibly done. To have no skill to procure from a musician what he had hoped to happen, shows that he was no kind of producer. Because when you work with a producer, all he is really doing is getting the best out of you. A producer doesn't play for you, he doesn't tune for you, he doesn't think for you, he merely manages to get the best. So, that didn't happen in *Union*. *Union* was probably the most dissatisfying record, I'll tell you, equal to Asia *Alpha*. The whole group was resonating with dissatisfaction. The drums didn't sound right, the arrangements weren't quite the same, the guitars weren't always audible or dynamic or exciting. And we ended up with... some say it is more what Jon would've wanted. That's what Jonathan Elias kept saying: 'You haven't got your voices in because Jon didn't want them in. The guitars aren't in because Jon didn't want them.' So, I mean, you hear the stories. It's too late now, I don't care."

Rick Wakeman on *Union*:

"We were doing the second ABWH album in France and the management of Yes and our management got together to discuss a merger, which seemed very logical. Sadly it destroyed the making of the second ABWH album. But we had a Wally of a producer thrust upon us anyway so who knows how it would have turned out?! We couldn't use the name Yes because we weren't Yes. It's quite simple really. If people leave a band, then they leave the name behind. It just so happened that four people who were quite important to Yes all happened to have left and joined forces. Whilst to a lot of people this was four-fifths of a Yes, the fact is that we weren't, and Chris was perfectly correct in keeping the name for the Yes that was then in existence. There was no fighting at all. The press enjoyed it and made up stories as they do, and we just got on with sorting the problem out in as best a way as possible. Hence the Union Tour, which for my money was the best tour Yes ever did, and the *Union* album, which is a piece of brown smelly excretion."

Billy Sherwood's take on *Union*:

"I wasn't really privy to the politics in the band at the time because I was a new entity working with basically what they call Yes West. I had 'The More We Live,' that I had written with Chris, which ended up on the *Union* album. And I worked with Tony Kaye, who I had met and we've been friends ever since. And I got to know Trevor through that process as well. In that period, I wrote the song 'Love Conquers All,' with Chris, which we tracked at the same studio that 'The More We Live' was done at, and a couple of other tunes that didn't make it to the record. So we were making music and I wasn't really paying attention to the politics that I knew were going on. Obviously it was crazy, bringing all eight of those people together. But from my perspective, I was just happy to be there working on my music with the guys. And at the end of the day, Jon came in and sang on 'The More We Live,' and it remained intact, which I was very, very happy about—the way it came out is pretty true to form."

Tony Kaye speaking in 1991:

"It's a combination of two things that were recorded separately and then put together. The fact that it worked out, and everybody is happy playing together, probably indicates that this was really a ground breaking kind of album. But, of course, six months ago that wasn't so obvious. Anderson Bruford Wakeman Howe were recording their own album in Paris, and we were working on material in Los Angeles, not really knowing what was going on, because we didn't have Jon at that point. The complicated thing was to join with a record company that really wanted to put out the album."

May 1991. The spirited and poppy "Lift Me Up" is issued as the only US single from *Union*, backed with the non-LP "Give & Take." All other territories (Europe and Japan) use "Take The Water To The Mountain" as the b-side. "I Would Have Waited Forever" was issued in promo-only CD format, including edit and album version.

June 1991. "Saving My Heart" is issued as the UK single from *Union*, backed with "Lift Me Up" in edit form. A US CD single was issued as well, but promo-only.

July 1, 1991. Steve Howe issues his third solo album, on Relativity, called *Turbulence*. Bill Bruford drums on all but two tracks. Steve has called this album his favourite from his solo catalogue due to its strong rock element.

Author review of *Turbluence*:

Steve's first solo record as an industry fringe-dweller shows all the signs of a diminution of attention: small label, weak graphics and hobby-level songs. Or at least one thinks demo first, because many of these tracks sound like vocal constructs with no vocals. Yep, *Turbulence* is all instrumental, but frustratingly so, sounding like a scrap yard of Yes bits. Indeed, Steve drew from Turbulence for pieces of Union. *Turbulence* had been written long before the release of *Union*, but *Union* seemed to shelve the solo effort. So Steve saw no reason not to borrow liberally from it for the Yes project (most notable lift: "Sensitive Chaos" metamorphosing into "I Would Have Waited Forever"). As it turned out, *Union* revived *Turbulence*, which was released shortly after the somewhat reviled Yes record.

But the present disc sounds even less realized than *Union*, Steve constructing a sort of unaggressive guitar wank record, a shred-fest with new age noodling replacing the shred. And neither Bruford nor other drummer Nigel Glockler help matters, both sounding stiff and secondary, unintegrated into the songs ("While Rome's Burning:" yuk). "Running The Human Race" is probably the most pleasant groove, Steve soloing electric slide and acoustic blues in convincing fashion, while "Corkscrew" is a lush Spanish recline worthy of inclusion in any Yes set. But much of the rest is rough-shod and unwritten, Steve visiting too many places, the mean average being a type of choppy electric jazz.

July 2, 1991. *Union* is certified gold.

August 6, 1991. Yes issue a four CD box set called *Yesyears*. Previously unreleased 1981 track "Make It Easy" is issued as a cassette single from the box, backed with "Long Distance Runaround." Roger Dean's cover art references bits of past covers, but the biggest innovation is the creation of a new Yes logo. A sister piece is the *Yesyears* VHS video documentary package, itself a nice companion item to the 12-song *Greatest Video Hits*, which comprises most of the band's MTV video clips plus some live material.

November 1991. "Owner Of A Lonely Heart" gets a reissue as a 7" and 12" single in the UK and mainland Europe in various formats, the largest of which includes the original version plus three remixes.

1992

February 29 – March 5, 1992. Yes take their *Union* show to Japan for five dates. All told, the tour does great business, the band is well paid,

but creatively feel stifled, confused, and bogged down in too many parts. This results in animosities, particularly between Steve and Trevor (they played, essentially, separately), and Bill and Chris, with Trevor bonding best with Rick. Wakeman, in fact, says that one of his biggest regrets is that there's never been a Yes studio album made with Trevor and himself in the lineup together.

Rick Wakeman recalls his funniest tour anecdotes with Yes:

"A giant fish appearing up from the middle of the stage during the Union Tour. Some strippers appearing courtesy of the crew on a last night somewhere. I can't remember the tour or the venue, but I can remember the strippers, although their faces are a bit of a blur."

June 8, 1992. Asia issue their fourth album, *Aqua*, which features the return of Steve Howe to the fold, with Steve still smarting at having ABWH hijacked by Yes, and then not being part of the regular-sized Yes that was to continue after the eight-man *Union* configuration. John Wetton is gone from the lineup, replaced with John Payne. Geoff Downes is still part of the band, with Steve considering himself a "special guest," sharing guitar duties with Al Pitrelli.

Author review of *Aqua*:

Major personnel shuffle here, and surprise, Asia are a classy and worthy commercial prog band–an entity they never were before. Steve Howe seems like a bit of window-dressing, with most of the large performances coming from leader Downes and powerful new vocalist John Payne, who puts on a dramatic and thespian performance over a batch of thoughtful compositions, a few of which would have stood their ground on *90125* or *Big Generator*, like good Foreigner singles should.

Harmonies in particular are vastly improved, the rough edge and tension provided by Wetton gone the way of steely perfection. Gun-for-hire Al Pitrelli also burns a few metal fills here and there, texturing the show just right. Heck, even the lyrics are greatly improved, those short stumbling love tunes intellectualized and stretched a bit up to 1990s standards. Ultimately, *Aqua* sports an ambitious slickness missing from past Asia cheez-fests, a mature reconciliation with the damnations of AOR, and a recognition that this band can only be what it can be, a fully committed soft rock treasure for but a few. Soapy and slurpy as they get, but ever so perfectly rendered.

September 15, 1992. A version of the *Yesyears* box distilled down to two discs is issued, as *Yesstory*.

November 1992 – July 1993. Yes work at The Jacaranda Room and A&M Recording Studios in Los Angeles on material that will become their *Talk* album.

1993

May 8, 1993. Having divorced Nikki in 1987 after 15 years of marriage, Chris Squire marries for a second time when he weds actress Melissa Morgan.

August 24, 1993. Steve Howe issues *The Grand Scheme Of Things*, his second release for Relativity records and his fourth in total.

September 21, 1993. Yes issue a hits compilation called *Highlights: The Very Best Of Yes*.

Jon Anderson on the quest for meaning through his lyrics:

"I've always been very interested in the search for the truth of why we live, and what the point of living is. I think that's in everybody's mind all the time, so I'm not the only person thinking that [*laughs*]. So lyrically, I tend to jump into that ocean of possibilities, as to why we live, and then come up with some form of understanding on my side, which I put it into a lyric. And that's how it stems forth."

October 12, 1993. Anderson Bruford Wakeman Howe issue their second and last album, a two CD live album (and DVD) called *An Evening Of Yes Music Plus*, which documents a show from Mountain View, California, on September 9, 1989. Issued with "Starship Trooper" and without. The phrase "an evening of Yes music plus," as applied to the original ABWH touring run, was one of the main irritants in the legal battle over the Yes name four years earlier.

Author review of *An Evening Of Yes Music Plus*:

Also immortalized in an excellent video (that is longer than the album, including Jon Anderson's hilarious intro segment, plus "I've Seen All Good People" and "The Meeting"), this disc is the product of a blessed outdoor amphitheatre gig, the last of ABWH's US tour. And the performance is wonderful, the band full-on creative (note: this review wantonly mixes video and audio). After a taped classical intro, Jon Anderson begins the show by ambling into the crowd singing "Time And A Word," resplendent in one of his (ahem) curious white jumpsuits, simple electro-acoustic accompaniment from Milton McDonald. Then Jon segues into a campfire version of "Owner Of A Lonely Heart," arriving back at "Time And A Word" after a slightly outclassed "Teakbois."

All told, this warm opening segment from Anderson is one of the most inspiring pieces of the whole show, "Time And A Word" really hitting home, warming the fires of a crowd ready, willing and ecstatic. A Steve Howe medley follows, Steve as expressive and energetic as usual, followed by a trim-looking Rick Wakeman who uses some of his solo material to burn up the keys in awe-inspiring fashion. The show enters full spread with "Long Distance Runaround," on which Bruford gets to go nuts, hitting all sorts of his patented Simmons tom-toms, uniquely arranged for the walkabout approach, then chomping down on a full set solo. Bruford's playing as usual is effortless in the conservation of energy, the man resembling a mad but reserved scientist, neutral poker face, focus personified.

ABWH track "Birthright," like "Teakbois," seems vaguely outclassed, but that just may be curmudgeonly snobbishness speaking. It is of note that the band's funky and fun "I've Seen All Good People," enjoyed early in the video, is omitted from the CD set, although "Starship Trooper" is attached to the end of disc one as a bonus track. "And You And I" is of course, gorgeous, again a high point, really driving home how well-recorded this set was, and how spirited the band was.

Disc two begins with a flawless "Close To The Edge," again Bruford and his electronic drums punching through, his attack reminiscent of his work on Crimson's *Discipline* opus. After this, things bog down a bit with the newer, mechanical and stiff proto-prog of ABWH tracks "Themes," "Brother Of Mine" and "Order Of The Universe." But Jon does a crafty request-taking, resulting in an extra large but comfortable oldie, "Heart Of The Sunrise," and eventually a fairly relaxed, loose and funky "Roundabout." All in all, a fantastic show, no doubt buoyed by the fact that it was a tour closer.

Bill Bruford debates youth versus experience:
"The young guys I work with are very distinguished players in one way or another. They can play anything. There's no time lag at all between them hearing something in their ears and their ability to produce it from an instrument, which is the mark of a very good improviser of course. As soon as I think of something to say, I can say it to you verbally. The mark of the good improviser is that the minute he hears something to play, he can play it to you down an instrument; that's a very fast reaction. And they're very good players. And yes, like tennis and so forth, it's just getting faster and bigger and more and more amazing.

"But no, they don't intimidate me because there's something experienced musicians have that the inexperienced don't. And I think we have a good balance in a sense, that I can offer them an international platform in that my band travels globally and has a high degree of respect and is a working band that gets them out there and allows them to do their thing in front of audiences. And in return for that, I get lovely compositions and red-hot playing.

"I practice the drums a lot. It takes a lot for me to stay in shape, and indeed I do. And I think at this level, most of the drummers practice quite a bit to keep fluid and to keep the fresh ideas coming. Every year people want new approaches, new ideas on the drums, and that's partly what I do. I started before punk rock, I started before prog rock, I started before jazz rock and all these things I hope to have contributed to. You know, I hope to find drumming in a different place when I leave drumming than when I started it. And indeed, it already is."

October 26, 1993. The London Philharmonic Orchestra issue the 55-minute *Symphonic Music Of Yes*. Guesting are Steve Howe, Bill Bruford and Jon Anderson. Arranging and conducting is David Palmer. The orchestral recording is produced and engineered by Alan Parsons, with the "album production" credit going to Steve Howe and David Palmer.

1994

March 21, 1994. Yes, once again essentially purged of its British membership, issue the Trevor Rabin-produced *Talk* album, on Phil Carson's new label Victory. "Walls" is issued as a single from the album, reaching #24. The album reaches #33 on the charts, and hangs around for eight weeks, but ultimately stalls at a disappointing 300,000 copies worldwide. Trevor has said that the long hours spent assembling the album on computer, without traditional audio tape, prepared him for his successful career doing movie soundtracks.

Jon Anderson on *Talk*:

"In those days, it was a question of making good music, as much as making a hit record again after *90125*. *Big Generator* just didn't happen. It was overblown and overdone. I really had no part in that project; I just went in and sang. They wanted to keep me out of the way, so I went and did an album with Vangelis. I kept myself busy. But then after that, I did Anderson Bruford Wakeman Howe— and then got a really good energy with the record company at that time. They just wanted me to do what I wanted to do. With Steve and Bill and Rick, it was so easy, because they just wanted to make music. So, the album worked. Then the next step was, we all got together, of course, and did *Union*—and then me and Trevor started to really bond at that time. We hadn't really bonded before, so it was a real interesting time. Trevor asked if I would come stay at the house, and work on some music, and that became *Talk*. The album ended up having so much of the classic style of Yes, and that's something very unique about it. But the record company went bankrupt, and the album never got any promotion— so, it was onto the next project."

Trevor Rabin on *Talk*:

"I enjoyed the *Talk* album; Jon feels that album is the best piece of work that he and I did together."

Alan White on *Talk*:

"One of the main proudest moments is when you finish an album that you're really proud of, for instance *Talk*, which I thought was great, but didn't get the attention that some of the old albums did. I mean, 'Endless Dreams' is an amazing song, one of my favourite of all Yes songs. And it's not easy to play; it's a very difficult piece of music."

Author review of *Talk*:

After two laborious attempts at recreating the prog octopus that was Yes in the 1970s, key parties felt it was time to make another purely "Yes West" record, i.e. a Trevor Rabin album with a bunch of Yes guys helping out. *Talk* would be the third of these, after one wildly successful debut (*90125*) and one under-rated sophomore (*Big Generator*). Significantly, Rabin worked quite closely with Jon Anderson, resulting in lyrics that are a hybrid between the pedestrian sentiments of Rabin and the flights of fancy Jon takes with such enthusiasm.

Lead tune "The Calling" rewarded the band with a minor hit, the track swaggering like a bloated arena rocker that actually grows in stature come chorus time, a few fleeting moments that are in my opinion, an early climactic point never reached again throughout the rest of the album. "I Am Waiting" follows with similar chart-slobbering aspirations, leading into an elephant of a song called "Real Love," which is a bothersome elbow in the ribs similar to *Union*'s "Shock To The System." Not a bad chorus once more, but overall, heavy-handed and overproduced.

"State Of Play" continues with the record's blast of computer pops and kicks, Rabin making sure that the performances of Alan White are indistinguishable from his own. And surprise, once more an obnoxious and ostentatious verse opens up for a softened, melodic chorus. Miserable patterns are afoot. "Walls" lightens things up a bit, the track actually being an older one that Rabin had kicking around, one that he had worked up with Roger Hodgson of Supertramp. And, yes, it could be a gormless Supertramp thingie from the anonymous 1980s, or a Traveling Wilburys or Tom Petty or ELO hit, what with all those glossy acoustic guitars. The track's only redeeming factor are the vocal harmonies and Rabin's various guitar tones, but otherwise, a smarmy attempt at a hit, nothing more—it's the last tune worked on for the record.

"Where Will You Be" is a second success for the album, with Rabin's musical track (originally written as a soundtrack piece for an Australian movie), perfectly in sync with Jon's thought-provoking lyric. Interestingly, both the lyric and the music contain the essence of Australian aborigine dreamtime, the contemplation of a long, outback walk, the connectivity of soul and earth.

Closing the record is "Endless Dream," a three-part loud, rocking prog freak-out which collapses into an odd bit of piano-driven Beatles-like psychedelia before finding a more comfortable verse structure. Then it's once more sent into a sort of futurist prog rock heaven, Rabin splicing together a couple of dozen tracks in demonstration of his latent Yes-ness. Even though most of the tomfoolery is computer-driven, it's successful given its uniqueness. Although things droop a bit, the manic, rapid-fire hysteria of things returns in widening arcs, until another series of good to great melodic choruses and chorus-like structures leave us with that giddy feeling that only Yes can find and deliver. After a slow, dramatic fade, the record ends, and months later, Rabin would leave the band.

May 1994. Asia issue their fifth album, *Aria*; the only Yes alumnus at this point is Geoff Downes.

May 4, 1994. Yes issue "The Calling" as a single from *Talk*; the anthemic, hi-gloss track makes #3 on the *Billboard* sub-chart, Hot Mainstream Rock Tracks. "Walls," also from *Talk*, would make this chart as well (at #24), as would the title track from *Open Your Eyes*, three years later, at #33.

July 18 – October 11, 1994. Yes tour in support of *Talk*, omitting Europe (due to poor sales projections) but playing both South America and Japan. Trevor Rabin leaves the band after his tour obligations, to become a composer for film.

July 19, 1994. Jon Anderson issues his sixth solo album, *Deseo*, more of a world music affair, issued on Windham Hill Records.

Jon Anderson on *Deseo*:

"I had actually been recording it over the last three years. It's a Latin-American album where I sing in both Portuguese and Spanish, and it has numerous guest artists from all over South America. It was a really exciting project to work on, and they're actually doing a dance mix for the clubs in South America."

Late 1994. Yes issue a CD-Rom called *Yes Active*, mixing album tracks with instrumentals, demos, videos and multimedia content.

October 17, 1994. Jon Anderson issues his seventh solo album, *Change We Must*, which is orchestral, classical music-based.

Jon Anderson on *Change We Must*:

"This is me singing with the London Chamber Orchestra. This is very different from anything I've ever done before. It sounds just fantastic and features some of my piano works as well."

1995

1995. In 1988, Steve Howe collaborates with composer Paul Sutin on a joint album called *Seraphim*. The duo follow this up with a second record entitled *Voyagers*. The release of *Voyagers* was in conjunction with a reissue of *Seraphim*, both through SPV in Europe and CMC in the US. Steve looks upon the past few post-Yes years fondly as a productive time for his solo career, and also one in which he gained much satisfaction from touring all around the world.

Author review of *Voyagers*:

Falling somewhere between synthetic, clinical, electronic-steeped prog, light jazz and new age, *Voyagers* is a slight, unobtrusive listen, much more Sutin than Howe. Too much slick synthesizer dimensions cloud the innocent playing of Howe and indeed Sutin himself, who is clear, concise and cleansing when playing what is, or what is close to, acoustic piano. Indeed, with all its layers and compositional heft, this is great movie music, peaceful (of course, all instrumental), and eventful enough. But too many sounds are faked and approximated by computers, *Voyagers* becoming something with many melodic Yes (and Jon Anderson!) characteristics, even if it's ultimately an exercise dehumanized by bits and bytes.

Early 1995. Jon initiates a reunion with Rick and Steve, ringing up Steve, who is immediately enthusiastic. The three follow up with a meeting in LA in the summer.

September 27, 1995. Jon Anderson issues his new age-y eighth solo album, *Angels Embrace*.

Fall 1995. What is arguably the classic Yes lineup reunites—Anderson, Howe, Wakeman, Squire and White—conducting the first set of sessions that will result in their *Keys To Ascension* album, working at Yesworld Studios.

Jon Anderson on writing with Yes:

"When I would go to the band, I would say, 'Don't play my chords. You should play other stuff. Play different stuff.' And I'd help them come up with ideas and I was very interested in classical music and how the structure worked. I would invest that energy into the band and suggest that rather than just ramble. Because we never did solos; we'd create solo structures. Every solo was sort of written down so that each night, the performance would be exactly the same so that you could make it better and better, rather than have the kind of situation bands have where the guitarist just wants to solo for five minutes and he just rambles on and he might do a couple of bad nights. That might be boring. So Steve Howe knew what he was going to play every night; he performed the music like it was written."

Alan White defines the Yes sound:

"That could be an all-day answer [*laughs*]. It's individualistic people involved that have a particular style of playing that seems to work. With Chris and myself, we've been playing together for almost 40 years, so there's a chemistry going on there, where we almost know what each other are going to play before we play it. Chris has a very percussive sound, because it's the sound of the Rickenbacker, which is edgy and toppy, which makes the bass sound almost like a lead bass guitar. But that works for me and we work very tight together—I work with that to try to get it as tight as possible. But yes, we can read into each other's playing a lot. And similar with Steve and whichever keyboard player we have at the time [*laughs*]. When we create it, it's a movement toward seeing something, always looking over the horizon, into the future, and trying to find something that nobody else has really done."

1996

January 30, 1996. Jon Anderson issues another new age album, a Native American concept album for High Street/Windham Hill, called *Toltec*. The material was originally recorded in 1992 for release as *The*

Power Of Silence, which was shelved by Geffen. *The Power Of Silence* is a spiritual quest book by Carlos Castaneda.

Jon Anderson on his evergreen vocal prowess:

"I like singing. I sing almost every day. In some ways, I was never a screamer. I was really not methodical about singing a certain way, even though I did sing in the high register. I'm not quite as high register anymore. But I sing in a certain style that I can feel comfortable about. Now and again I go wild and I go crazy on stage a little bit, but I don't overdo it. I just keep myself within myself when I sing, and make sure I don't strain. Because there have been times on tour, where you're on tour for two or three weeks, and you start feeling like you need to get some more medication for your throat because it's getting sore. You've got to be very gentle with your throat and your larynx. Like anything, it's my instrument, so I've got to take care, and I do."

February 1996. Asia issue their sixth album, *Arena*, Downes further shuffling his pack in order to perpetuate his cult rock franchise.

March 4 – 6, 1996. The reunited Yes record three San Luis Obispo, California shows that will yield the live material for their *Keys To Ascension* and *Keys To Ascension 2* albums. The shows mark the return of Steve Howe and Rick Wakeman, the latter quitting the band again directly after, before rejoining in 2002.

Spring 1996. Yes conduct additional studio sessions toward the completing of *Keys To Ascension*, working at The Office in Van Nuys, California.

Billy Sherwood on *Keys*:

"On *Keys* I was just a producer and engineer. I mixed the first *Keys* record. They worked at my studio and we mixed, and they enjoyed the hang, and they appreciated and liked the work and the way it sounded. And I got along with them all great. And so shortly after that I got a call from Chris saying, 'Hey, that was fun; do you want to produce the next album? We'll just come to your studio and make it right there.' And I said, 'Yeah, let's go.' So we did that, but that was my role as an engineer/producer, just trying to get sounds, and having opinions about things along the way [*laughs*]. *Open Your Eyes* was done there as well. Those two records, *Open Your Eyes* and *Keys To Ascension 2* were made in my studio from tip to tail. But in terms of input, you know, just try that solo again, or what if this vocal harmony was like this? All things that the band appreciated and accepted, and for the most part took in. Drum fills and parts and talking with Chris about moving things around. And they obviously had a very clear vision of where they were heading on the *Keys 2* material; it came in pretty well intact, knowing what they wanted to do. But along the way I just would push and pull here and there, where I felt it was warranted to pipe up."

August 28, 1996. Yes issue *Keys To Ascension*, a double album that is roughly a third studio and two-thirds live material. Packaging includes a large booklet, card outer sleeve and poster. The studio tracks are "Be The One" and "That, That Is".

Steve Howe on capturing emotion on stage versus the studio:

"I always believe that recording and, dare I say, overdubbing, isn't an unnatural process for modern musicians to create in. When I heard Les Paul's stuff from the '40s and '50s, I noticed that his overdubbing sounded just great. I wanted to be able to do that but also be able to keep the type of spirits, whether it was psychedelic in '67 or progressive in the '70s. I still wanted my playing to have a bite. I guess that is what I am doing. It is mainly because I am more of an emotional player. I respond to the things around me. I think people see this clearly when I am working on stage. The air of spontaneity is obviously great there. It is demanding. On records, I think that being able to overdub and get a good feel is very important. It is important to not just get the parts right, but to make sure they actually have the right spirited ingredient."

Alan White on Steve Howe:

"Attention to detail on everything he does, and he makes sure it's kind of meticulous before he even records anything. I mean, he doesn't just go on the fly for certain things. He works on his parts intensely so that when the time comes to record he executes it. Steve lives in a total guitar world and totally thinks guitar. But most of the things that he plays, he works out ahead of time, basically. There's not that much spontaneous playing once he gets into it. But it's great; it all fits in."

October 4, 1996. Steven Seagal action flick, *The Glimmer Man*, opens in theatres. The movie marks Trevor Rabin's entry to the film business, Seagal offering him the job of putting together the soundtrack, after Trevor taught Seagal how to play Jimi Hendrix's "Red House" on the guitar.

November 1996. Over an intense and compact five-week period, Yes record the studio material that would emerge on *Keys To Ascension 2*.

1997

1997. Jon Anderson issues an album of Celtic music called *The Promise Ring*.

Spring 1997. Jon Anderson marries for the second time, having divorced Jennifer in 1995. Jon and Jane Luttenberger Anderson remain married to this day, living in California. Best man at the wedding was Alan White.

June 12 – June 27, 1997. Yes cancel all dates of a slated US tour, when Rick exits Yes... once again.

Time And A Word

Summer 1997. Yes work on the material that will comprise their *Open Your Eyes* album.

Steve Howe on the title, *Open Your Eyes*, and the making of the record:
"Titles are fun. *The Ladder* was spun from a song title, but *Open Your Eyes*, even more. There's a song there called 'Open Your Eyes.' But we didn't know we were going to focus on the track, and when they said, 'How about calling the album *Open Your Eyes?*' I went nuts, because Asia had a song on the second album called 'Open Your Eyes' [*sings it*]. But nobody cared, gave a toss. And then the next thing you know, we have an album called *Open Your Eyes*. *Open Your Eyes* was a most disagreeable time when stupidly—and I'll say it today: stupidly— Chris involved Billy to such an extent in his music that Billy had to join the band to sort of exercise this operation. And I've not met anybody who liked that time at all, really.

"*The Ladder* is quite good, but *Open Your Eyes* was a hodgepodge of unrelated— to Yes anyway—musical ideas. I had nothing to do with hardly any of that album—and I objected to it. And there's a point I'd like to clarify: Jon and I agreed to get on with those tracks on the condition that there were going to be new tracks written by Jon and I, which were going to sort of rebalance the whole direction of the album, which heavily leans towards Billy and Chris. So that never happened, due to time. And all we did was 'From The Balcony,' which only happened because all Jon and I had to do was walk into the studio and we had a track. It's a bit like 'Nine Voices.' So it's really that Jon and I didn't get the time or the control over that album. Pretty frightening. I never play it, I don't want to see it, I don't want to hear about it, I don't want to talk about it. It's just something that I've buried—and I've buried a few albums in my life."

Billy Sherwood on *Open Your Eyes*:
"Steve came in very late on *Open Your Eyes*. Even though he was invited in early, he decided, 'No, I'm gonna stay here in England for a while.' And things were moving quickly, so when he came in at the end, a lot had been done, which I think is probably the major contributing factor to why he wasn't too happy. But, you know, there was nothing I could do. The pace was being set by more than just me. Otherwise, we all contributed. He was never comfortable with two guitar players being in the band at the same time. But I've read recent interviews, where he reflects back on it, and he has a bit of a different perspective now when he refers to it, which is quite nice to see.

"And, obviously, I've worked with him quite a bit since and I continue to. He's the guy that called me. I picked up the phone one day and he says, 'Hey, can you mix *Heaven & Earth* for us?' [*laughs*]. We're both very headstrong and opinionated in our ways, but I think that created a certain amount of respect between the two of us as well. So, we became friends and continue to be."

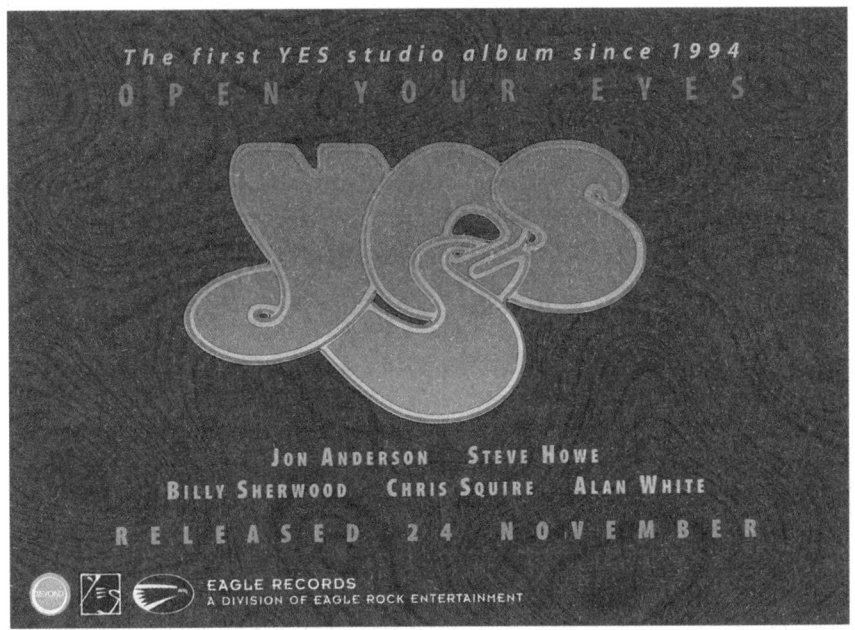

September 9, 1997. Jon Anderson issues *Earth Mother Earth*, an album of conventional acoustic songs, recorded at his home in Maui.

October 14, 1997. New Millennium Communications issue, in the UK, an archival live Yes CD called *Something's Coming: The BBC Recordings 1969–1970*. US release date is April 28, 1998, issued on Purple Pyramid/Cleopatra with a poster a different cover and title as *Beyond And Before: The BBC Recordings 1969–1970* and then later as simply *The BBC Recordings 1969–1970*.

October 17, 1997 – October 14, 1998. Yes hit the road for a year, in support of their 30th anniversary as well as *Open Your Eyes*. The extensive tour covers much of Europe and the US, and also includes trips to Mexico, South America and Japan.

Billy Sherwood on *Open Your Eyes*:

"Well, it's not composed in those massive, lengthy pieces that Yes is known for. I felt at the time that that would be a shift the band could benefit from, where they could do something different. Because they'd just come off of *Keys To Ascension* and all those other records that were long pieces of music, I just thought some real straight-ahead, concise music would get them back on the radio and back out there on the road doing big things. And to a certain degree it worked. *Open Your Eyes* had a ton of radio play, and wherever we saw that radio play, ticket sales spiked. So everything kind of worked out— one hand washed the other there. But my goal was that I really wanted to get back into a mode where Yes was being heard by the masses, and by masses I mean radio. Radio isn't about to play a 12-minute song—it just won't. So it was targeted and designed in a way to hit those targets, and to a degree it worked."

November 3, 1997. Castle Communications issue *Keys To Ascension 2*, which consists of one live CD and one studio CD, comprising five new songs that clock in at about 44 minutes. The label had demurred on issuing a second *Keys* album, but is persuaded by the fact that the band was going to crank up the touring machine again. So the album emerges in elegant digipak packaging with poster. Rick Wakeman, having quit the band again just after the release of the first *Keys* album (quashing the band's many touring ideas), complains now that the band erased most of his work on the second one, pretty much out of spite. Still upset, Rick later turns down Alan's request to return for UK tour dates. Two weeks after that, Rick finds himself at dinner with EMI's Richard Lyttelton discussing his massive multi-million dollar plans for *Return To The Centre Of The Earth.*

Billy Sherwood praises Steve Howe's sound:

"Steve carved his own unique path by taking that Chet Atkins sort of country thing and a bit of a jazz thing, and merging it into rock 'n' roll, and along the way, created some amazing compositions. On his own, and in Yes, in the chordal progressions, the voicings, they're very unique to him. And there's really no other guitar player like Steve. Whereas, maybe now, the world we live in with Guitar Institute Of Technology, and how to play fast on YouTube, there's a lot of guitar players that tend to sound like the other guy. But no one really sounds like Steve. And I think that's a testament to his craft and his creativity, and the kind of playing that he's carved out. It's one-of-a-kind.

"As for tones, we never really got into tones. We just kind of looked at each other, 'That sounds cool; let's record' [*laughs*]. I suppose that's just taste at that point. Some guitar players lean towards that bright and edgy thing, and other ones lean towards that lower, mid, woofy thing. I know just how he mixed Yes albums, and also on a basic instrumentation level, to be in a band where the bass is rumbling around like that into all these octaves and moving around, a more brighter guitar sound is gonna be heard. That might have a little to do with it [*laughs*]."

Steve Howe reveals the vagaries of writing credits:

"You have to give respect to everybody but you have to give credit. Sometimes we give credit primarily to the writers, but more generally we give block credit to everybody in the band because most of our music is pooled. But sometimes people lose a lot by that. You might say that for instance 'Bring Me To The Power' on *Keys To Ascension 2* was all my music, but Jon wrote all the words. But then again, he had melodies from me on which to construct those lyrics. He could change them, but that is just an example out of the blue, an example where we collaborated in a different way than it might look like.

"*Close To The Edge* has quite a lot of contribution from me, as does *Tales From Topographic Oceans*. But I didn't make many on *Relayer* or on *The Yes Album*, not much at all. But we've always been able to say, 'Jon, that line does sound a bit funny; how about saying it this way?' And even on *Tormato*, he would say to me, 'Oh, that's a really good statement you just made.' I said one day, 'Rock 'n' roll is the music of our generation' or something, something really simple [*laughs*], and he goes, 'That's great, I want to use that!' So there's contribution and there's collaboration. Like 'Onward' is Chris's song so it's credited to Chris.

"But there was a big band on TV the other day that still admits to arguing over songwriting splits and it is one of those areas that is close to home. So you have to get it right. It's either a group split or it's a songwriter credit, where who writes song gets the credit—that's a pretty fair idea. But that can create imbalances where the work that other people do in the songs has to get credited. That's where you get contradictions.

"We always thought *Topographic Oceans* would say Anderson/Howe, but it doesn't. But it should do. Those are the incredibly accurate titles. But then there are arrangements. The band would share in the song credits due to the fact that they wouldn't have sounded that good if Yes weren't playing it. I don't care. It's all history; it's all water under the bridge. But what you've always got to do is get it right, get it right straight away. Because if you don't, you'll never get it right. So we've always argued about that. But we find solutions to those arguments, rectification."

November 24, 1997. Yes rush-release their 17th studio album, *Open Your Eyes*, reacting to the news that Castle have decided to put out *Keys To Ascension 2*. New keyboardist and full writing member is Billy Sherwood. The album reaches #151 on Billboard and sells about 200,000 copies worldwide.

Steve Howe on playing to your strengths:

"Sometimes these guys come into Yes, and some of their strengths... like Billy Sherwood, when he came in for *Open Your Eyes*, some of his strengths weren't there. It was almost like Billy became so preoccupied with playing the guitar, what about all the other things he did great? We wanted him to be a more general, rounded musician, as opposed to just another guitarist, which was obviously getting on my nerves. But that said, *Open Your Eyes* probably shows the sharpest contrast in the sense of direction we were taking. I guess in the story of Yes it's pretty compatible, but then again it's the first in a long time, since *Time And A Word*, where there hasn't been anything like it since that album. So I guess you can say it's a first, but I guess it's a bit precarious saying that, because it's actually a second [*laughs*]. The last one was in 1969 when most of your readers weren't even alive, I suppose. So this is different for us.

"This was a step that a group takes when it feels it's ready. And we felt we were ready and we felt that we wanted something to happen around us that would take away from the emphasis we've had for quite a few years around, you know, where is Rick Wakeman? Why don't you get Patrick Moraz back? What happened to Geoff Downes? What happened to Igor Khoroshev [keyboard player on *Open Your Eyes* and *The Ladder*]? All these people asking about the keyboardists just needed to lie down and shut up. We were fed up with talking about it."

Chris Squire on *Open Your Eyes*:
"That was the album where Billy Sherwood became a member of the band, and he and I had been writing together for a while previous to that, and had our own side-project called The Conspiracy. The fact that Billy and I had been writing, that sort of formulated the basis for the music on *Open Your Eyes*. Yeah, there's some really good stuff on there. That was a good period, I thought, for Yes's creativity, when Billy was involved. And then of course down the line, it didn't really work out with Steve Howe to have another guitar player. He's not really that kind of guitar player [*laughs*]."

Alan White on *Open Your Eyes*:
"Much of *Open Your Eyes* had been something that had been worked on by Chris and Billy Sherwood, and I was involved in that for a bit, because we had a band around the same time as that was being conceived called Conspiracy, a band that was the three of us. And that turned into Circa because Chris was doing other things. But I guess there was a whole period of time when we were just writing and working and there was lots of material coming out, and some of it ended up on *Open Your Eyes*."

Billy Sherwood's lyrical contributions to *Open Your Eyes*:
"'New State Of Mind,' the whole message was about getting back on track with a new state of mind and bringing Yes back into a higher plane than it had been at the time, getting the band back on the map in a bigger way than we had been at the time, with the spirit of positivity and forward motion and the idea that nothing can stop you if you focus on your desired target. Eventually you're

going to hit it. But it does take a new state of mind from the band, and from the business and all those things.

"'Universal Garden' was just thinking about the cosmos and the wonders of space and time, and how it all relates to us here, and how vast it is out there. Things that we'll never even understand because we can't physically reach them in our lifetimes. And how strange it is to live in a universe like that. We just don't know—we think we know, but we don't know at all.

"'Fortune Teller,' at the time we were making that record, every ten seconds on TV were these fortune teller ads, where you can call in and they would tell you your fortune over the phone. And I found that to be pretty intriguing that anyone would bother [*laughs*]. These people are just selling their fortune-telling over the phone. That's where that lyric stemmed from—the idea of how crazy that is."

Author review of *Open Your Eyes*:
After many fits and starts, delays and promises, the first *bona fide* new studio album from Yes in three years emerges, almost stealth-like, with little fanfare, except for an immensely successful and vigorous concert tour. And *Open Your Eyes* is quite the surprise, brimming with youthful energy, in essence, presenting the thick, well-tanned hide of a Yes West record, without Trevor Rabin, but with Billy Sherwood assuming the position of detail man, commercial sounding-board and fresh legs.

And it rocks, oddly enough. "New State Of Mind" announcing this newly hefty entity with a big, infectious Zep lumber, upon which heavenly multi-tracked vocals deliver a standard Yes-affirming tale of optimism, enthusiasm and ethereal headspace-ism. Overall, the record oscillates between this glossy pound and softer imprints from Steve and Jon, although at either extreme, one still remains distracted by a sense of over-production, a clinical embracing of too many new sounds, guitar effects, keyboard effects, snappy, impertinent drums, layers of uber-pop overwhelming the humanity of the thing.

But great successes abound, the runaway best seller being the title track and lead single, which combines a tough, forward drive with a quixotic, melancholic and tense, thoroughly addictive melody, a bridge upon which to build, steady but progressive advances, a chorus of fresh vitality, and a lustful solo from Steve. But the sequencing of the record, with this masterpiece at track two, ultimately undermines *Open Your Eyes*, all the best music crammed into the first three compositions, the record wearing a bit like *Talk* or the ABWH slab by the back end, the jarring of the band's elephantine hard stuff chafing against Jon's attempts at connectivity on "The Solution" and "Man In The Moon," while "Love Shine" rings just a bit trite for this usually dangerous band.

But all told, *Open Your Eyes* is a bold return to participation in reality, an affirmation of commercial viability, song sense, and bravado, while repeated listens reveal that the prog is just broken up into micro-bites, tasty fills, exotic flourishes and background skronks. And don't worry, Jon is still all about love, hope, faith, perhaps more so than usual, with *Open Your Eyes* reading like a flood of inspirationals, Anderson perhaps renewed by the obvious continued interest in the band.

1998

1998. The RPM label issue a Tomorrow compilation/rarities album called *50 Minute Technicolor Dream.*

April 10, 1998. *Highlights: The Very Best Of Yes* is certified gold. *The Yes Album, Close To The Edge, Classic Yes* and *Yessongs* are all certified platinum. *Fragile* is certified double platinum and *90125* is certified triple platinum. The band are presented this spate of awards amidst a festive atmosphere at the Hard Rock Cafe in New York City.

April 14, 1998. Jon Anderson issues the poppy, urban R&B and near adult contemporary *The More We Know*, most compared by fans to *In The City Of Angels.*

April 21, 1998. Steve issues his *Quantum Guitar* album, on Voiceprint; drummer on the very guitary instrumental album is Steve's son Dylan.

Summer 1998. Rick Wakeman's health deteriorates due to overwork and too much fast food during the hectic making of his forthcoming classical opus, *Return To The Centre Of The Earth.* Hobbling back to London from LA after having ballooned to 231 pounds from his fighting weight of 210, he collapses on the golf course and is diagnosed with a collapsed right lung, a partially collapsed left, double pneumonia and pleurisy.

June 27, 28, 1998. A first official Yes fan gathering called *Yestival* is held, in Cherry Hill, New Jersey.

August 25, 1998. Eagle Records issues a two CD compilation of Yes solo and collaborate work called *Yes, Friends And Relatives*, the highlight of which is the opening track, a 1998 remake of "Owner Of A Lonely Heart."

September 22, 1998. Kiss issue their reunion album, *Psycho Circus*, Bruce Fairbairn's last major production before working with Yes on *The Ladder*, his final one before his death.

November 1998. Yes conduct writing sessions for their next album; moving up from guest to member is keyboardist Igor Khoroshev, suggested for the band by Steve and Jon, after almost hiring back Geoff Downes, and mulling over the likes of Eddie Jobson and Patrick Moraz.

Billy Sherwood on Igor Khoroshev:

"Amazing keyboard player. I kind of kept to myself on the road, so I didn't really know him personally. I never really got to know him that well. He was very tight with Jon at the time, so those guys would hang out quite a bit. The guy's just a killer player. As far as the politics of Yes go, and knowing how to play inside the lines, I don't know if he was as skilled at that [*laughs*]!"

Alan White on Khoroshev:

"He's still a sideman, but he's contributed a lot like in the writing on *The Ladder*, and changing chords and stuff like that. So, he's on a good salary, let's put it that way!"

1999

1999. Eddie Offord, associated with Yes as much as artist Roger Dean, retires from the music business. His last major productions take place in the mid-'90s for alternative rockers 311.

February – May 1999. Yes work at studios in Vancouver, BC, on material for their 18th album, *The Ladder*.

Alan White enjoys recording *The Ladder* in Vancouver:

"*The Ladder* was more driven by Jon Anderson, who had some very creative ideas. We rehearsed for about three months in Vancouver, Canada, and we would all go to the small room every day. So Jon had a lot of great ideas that we took inspiration from, but then took it in a different direction. We'd spent like six weeks writing prior to Christmas of '98, and then we had Christmas off, and then went back into the studio in February and did a couple of more weeks of rehearsal, and just slammed into the album. There was a great vibe between everybody. We were all living up in Vancouver, and we'd all get up and go to work every day, and that's a very good positive way to make an album, as opposed to some albums where everybody lived around the area and you lived in your home and then had to go into the studio every day. When you're living away from home it tends to go faster.

"It was very uplifting. Bruce took the helm, and he was very good sitting behind the board, making decisions. We might have been scratching our heads for a while, but Bruce would say, 'No, no, that definitely doesn't work; you should do this.' He had good control over what was going on in the studio. It led to us being more positive while we were in there because we thought that an outside idea—we should take that advice and go down that path."

Steve Howe talks about coming up with titles:

"Some of it is very straight ahead but the way it convinces us, is in the way it comes about. What I'm really trying to say is that when it comes about in a certain way, people say, 'Oh yeah!' When we fall into liking it, that's the title [*laughs*]. It doesn't matter how it got there or what the reason is. Each one is different, but it usually relates to a particular song.

"'The Ladder' was really the title, to be honest, of 'Homeworld.' 'The Ladder,' the song, was slightly rewritten as a song that would include the song 'Homeworld.' It was kind of coloured to meet the criteria of what it was going to be, which was part of a video game [Homeworld, by Sierra Entertainment], which some people were excited about. People get excited about it, but I don't get excited about it. It doesn't warm my heart much. People were going, 'Yeah! It's going to be a huge game!' People were walking around keying themselves up all the time. 'It's going to be huge, monumental!' I've heard it all before! All this stuff is going to happen, and it didn't.

"So the video game wasn't a big deal. 'Homeworld' was really a nonsensical title. 'The Ladder' certainly wasn't, and that's why the album got called *The Ladder*, and the track is even called 'Homeworld (The Ladder),' which is kind of juggling about. Jon sometimes does this on most of the albums. Sometimes Jon will juggle with a title, almost to the point of, not to everybody's frustration and annoyance, but you know, haven't we changed this one enough?! And suddenly it's changed again [*laughs*]."

February 1, 1999. EMI issue on CD, with bonus tracks, the self-titled Tomorrow album from 1968.

April 20, 1999. Rick Wakeman issues a high profile new solo album called *Return To The Centre Of The Earth*, the sequel to his gold-selling *Journey To The Centre Of The Earth* from 1974. The album was financed by EMI Classics to the tune of $3 million. With a company goal of 300,000 units globally, the album stalls two years later at 195,000 worldwide, meeting targets everywhere except the US, where it only moves a disastrous 25,000 copies.

Rick Wakeman muses on *Return To...* and playing live:

"It was something I had wanted to do for years. Technology meant that I could really fuse all the musical ideas I had live within a symphony orchestra and choir. I knew that I could put Ozzy Osbourne in the orchestra and make it work for example. Ozzy was brilliant! I had many friends on board, such as Trevor Rabin and Bonnie Tyler, and I was really knocked out with the end result. The album was given target figures to sell around the world and it reached these figures everywhere except for America where it became more difficult to find in the shops than finding a condom machine in the Vatican! I was really disappointed about this but life goes on. Luckily it sold well elsewhere in the world.

"I have worked with the London Symphony Orchestra before. The time was in 1974 when I did the original *Journey To The Centre Of The Earth*. I love writing for orchestras and orchestrating in general. My heroes in this field are Rimsky-Korsakov and Prokofiev. I don't think I was difficult, but being the only one who knew what it would sound like completed... this was difficult for all concerned, to see the pieces of the jigsaw coming together and then being put to one side for the final piecing together. What also didn't help was the fact that I contracted pleurisy and chronic double pneumonia during the latter stages of the recording. It wasn't helped by the 22-hour days for three months. I was given less than 48 hours to live.

"But, yes, I have invested much of what I have earned in the live extravaganzas and why not? I like to do things properly wherever possible and if people have bought an album with an orchestra on it then I try to give them that orchestra in a live setting. I don't do that so much these days, sadly, as most of what I earn and have earned is eaten up through my very poor record of having been married and divorced three times."

May 17, 1999. Legendary Canadian producer Bruce Fairbairn dies during the mixing sessions for what would be his last production, Yes's The Ladder. He is discovered dead by Jon Anderson and studio manager Sheryl Preston at Fairbairn's Vancouver home.

Billy Sherwood on *The Ladder* and Bruce Fairbairn's death:
"It's a shame that Bruce died during that process; it was shocking and really sad. I don't really know what the cause was. I never really investigated it. I just kind of moved on in life. I regret that he wasn't there, hands on, to see the whole thing through. Because he had a certain vision that he was going for, I don't know if we really achieved it at the end of the day. That said, I think it's still a really cool record and holds up. It seems to be a lot of people's choice—Yes fans seem to like it. And the tour was a lot of fun, that's for sure, playing all that stuff live very much like the record. So I think it was a good period of time spent, and good things came from it. But as for what Bruce would have done, it's hard to say. I just felt that he had an edge to how he was doing rough mixes that didn't quite translate to the end product when I listen to it. You know, all the parts are there that we recorded, everything was there, but whenever Bruce would play a rough mix for me, it always had some edge to it. It's hard to explain, but that was his ear and how he heard blends. It was very good."

July 13, 1999. Steve Howe issues *Portraits Of Bob Dylan*, including, as guests, Jon Anderson and Geoff Downes.

September 6, 1999 – March 25, 2000. Yes tour in support of *The Ladder*, beginning this time in South America.

Alan White on augmenting *The Ladder* with additional percussion:
"We actually had a percussioner come in, and played a vast array of world

instruments that we wanted to use, but we only used about as half as many as anticipated. We had that kind of 'world feel' to some of the drumming. We wanted to get across Caribbean/Afro-American rhythms, but in a progressive kind of way, a progressive style; and that was the idea behind all of that. Different people like different things. At the moment they're playing 'Homeworld' a lot, but I like the Caribbean tracks. For me, it's hard to say because, to me they're all so different because you kind of live every track. I have a kind of feeling for all the tracks myself. 'Homeworld' to me is a stand-out track, it's a combination of the '70s and what the band used to be and the very modern way that we played in the '90s."

September 20, 1999. Yes issue *The Ladder*. It is the only album featuring the band as a six-piece, the only album with keyboardist Igor Khoroshev as a member of the band, and the second (and last) with Billy Sherwood in the band. The rest of the band consists of Anderson, Howe, Squire and White.

Steve Howe remembers *The Ladder* and Bruce Fairbairn:

"Well, to us, *The Ladder* was a big re-learning process. And we had a master teacher, if you like, in Bruce Fairbairn, and he did things for us that nobody seems to care about doing for us anymore. People were tentative and cautious about coming in and taking over. You know, for somebody to come in and say 'I'm going to take over Yes.' Nobody had done that for a long time. And basically Bruce was quite clear about it, that he was going to take over, that he was in charge, that he did make the decisions. And we would do, much like an airline hostess would tell you, you know, 'While you're on this plane, you'll do what I tell you.' And Bruce kind of said the same thing.

"And the reason we wanted that, and the reason I talk about it so positively, is because we were kind of desperate for something that was better than what we had. Obviously, *Open Your Eyes* was a very argumentative period. We couldn't even play it on stage. It wasn't just that we had trouble making the record, we couldn't play it on stage either. So we didn't want to make any more records like that that undermined our fans' enthusiasm and didn't become great live music.

"But Bruce really did offer all the answers, all the solutions. He really was a top producer who had his own location. When we really didn't have to work, it was a great location, we could go off anywhere we wanted. And the other thing was, we needed some consistency which was lacking in the work we would do ourselves. And Bruce came in and he was authoritarian, disciplinarian, all these things, but we liked the guy [*laughs*] and we had some great moments in the studio, where he would whisper down the talkback to every member and say something to every member. Like he would say to Alan, 'Leave this first drum break out and put the bass drum on the downbeat when you come back into the middle eight.' 'Jon, do this.' He would tell everybody things. And sometimes he would call me Swami, which was a nickname he never really described. He would say, 'Swami, just keep doing what you are doing there.' That was the kind of confidence he instilled in me. Sometimes he would give me directions but he would often generalize and be very easygoing with me. Because he found that I was flexible. I would do a rhythm part, anything that was needed. And I usually found out what was needed without asking.

"So I admired him for the respect he showed the band and the way we worked together. So the whole record was about Bruce. We were back to being children in kindergarten and we thought of him as the teacher—seriously, we really did. So it wasn't like somebody forced a producer on us. We wanted him to take control because we were lacking agreement in how to do that. We can do a Steve Howe Yes record, we could do a Jon Anderson Yes record, we could do a Chris Squire Yes record, but to do a Yes record that fairly represented all of us, we didn't know how to do that."

Alan White on *The Ladder*:
"It's coming across to the people as having elements of the '70s, the '80s and the '90s all rolled into one package there, kind of a modern version of all that material. So there's elements and sounds from the '70s and '80s, but played much more in a '90s style. Bruce Fairbairn was a big fan of the band; he also understood the band's music, and he always wanted to get his teeth into something that was challenging, like this, a more progressive type band. It was a perfect relationship we had, and unfortunately, as you know, it never worked out in the end for him. They were about three tracks into mixing when he had his heart attack. But the engineer, who we had been working with, Mike Plotnikoff, he actually had been working with Bruce for about ten years, and kind of knew how he wanted the album to sound. So, basically, he wanted to carry on and finish the project. As for the writing, we all throw things into the pot, as it were. I usually come up with some keyboard chords and rhythms, and Jon comes up with melodies and lyrics. People have different kind of things they bring to the table. It's very amicable."

Billy Sherwood on not producing the album:
"After *Open Your Eyes*, the band kind of thought, now that you're a full member and you're playing on stage and you're doing guitar and this, that and the other, you really shouldn't be producing anymore because you're too close to it now, and we need another objective viewpoint coming in. And so the idea of Bruce Fairbairn was brought up. I thought that was a great idea, because obviously Bruce, his track record speaks for itself and he was an amazing musician in his own right. And so he knew music. We went up to Canada and

wrote all the music together in one room. Literally, everything was contributed by everybody. You'd come in with this part, play it, and it would expand, and Steve would throw in a thing, Jon would come up with something, and we would get in on that. Or I would start something with Chris and Alan and we'd work that. But it was all very much a collective process, which, at the end of the day, it comes out with very much of a band feel on that record because we tracked it all live."

5

2000s

•••

If the 1990s for Yes was an era of commercial decline, but otherwise, one of writing and recording and touring as much as any vital band, the 2000s found Yes on a decade-long form of victory lap, not much new music to speak of, but lots of live work and some of it innovative. Furthermore, there was lots of celebration of the band's career through product, during a transition in the business when it was considered that elaborate packaging and value for money in terms of quantity of music, along with DVD augmentation, might counter the growing popularity of downloading, free or paid.

The new century starts out with the Masterworks Tour, on which the band amusingly and obstinately plays mostly long songs. There's also the first of many live albums to come in *House Of Yes*. In 2001, the band indeed hatch a new record, *Magnification*, which finds the guys considerably progressive and playing with an orchestra, which carries over for the album tour, the first live milestone for the band as we start the decade.

An additional theme through the decade is more solo work from members and ex-members, particularly Steve Howe, who proves prolific. Then there's Conspiracy, pairing Billy Sherwood with Chris Squire, and Circa, featuring Billy with Tony Kaye. There's Jon Anderson releasing solo albums, Rick mounting a monumental live stand plus solo work, and Asia continuing to record and tour in various configurations, very much a cult band with small label deals at this point, although a late career highlight for the band arrives in 2008, with a reunion of the original lineup.

Speaking of Rick, he rejoins Yes in 2002, an event that is captured in the spirit of the Full Circle Tour, Yes now fully settling into their identity as a band that is always on the road despite not always having new songs to display.

In 2003 and 2004, there are further permutations of product, with the *35th Anniversary* two CD and three CD set, an odd *Yes Remixes* album, Trevor Rabin's *90124*, the *Yesspeak* documentary, accompanied by a 35th Anniversary Tour and an acoustic DVD. As we spill over into 2005 and 2006, there is the inevitable live album and DVD, a live box set, more work for Conspiracy and also a revitalized Syn reform.

The bold headline for the Yes camp comes in 2008, when Jon is sidelined with a serious respiratory illness. Here we get an additional peek into the concept of Yes as a business: no hard feelings, as the rest of the band decides, well, we need a new vocalist. Enter Montrealer Benoit David from Mystery and Yes tribute band Close To The Edge, who hits the road with the band, and not a beat is missed.

It's a strange concept, this idea of no hard feelings, because Jon, ever the wheeler dealer, ever the practical one in the band, exhibits a degree of pragmatic understanding, but also grumbles that the guys could've waited. But you get the sense that communication and friendship isn't completely severed, that everybody understands that the guys have to put food on the table, that the show must go on, that if Yes doesn't tour, catalogue sales will drop off.

Eventually the idea settles in that it is all for the best, because the creative life that Jon had been subtly choosing all along, and is now forced to adhere to and feed even more, seems to suit him well and make him happy, pushing 70. In essence, his creativity is unbridled, his enthusiasm to work with others is easily fulfilled, and his wish to not be part of a touring machine that is both large and always running... well, it seems that the fate and the karma that he heeds and respects so reverently has dealt him the hand that his soul desires.

2000

March 21, 2000. Billy Sherwood and Chris Squire issue a self-titled album under the band name Conspiracy.

June 20 – August 4, 2000. Yes execute the short *Masterworks* US Tour, with a set list consisting of a few long epics. Support comes from Kansas, the closest thing to Yes to come out of the US.

Steve Howe discusses long songs and way-out clothes:
"When I said to Jon, 'Let's do a tour where we only play 20 minute pieces because that will really show them!,' what I was saying was that Yes had done

many things that were verging on things that other groups could do, but we were the only group that did that. *Masterworks* came out of that discussion. It was a slightly watered down discussion of that idea. Some days we might get closer to the ultimate *Masterworks* and only play the 20 minute pieces that we kind of created our major mystique about us.

"I always wanted to close with 'Gates Of Delirium.' We are not doing so but I would like to. The responses we have been getting with 'Gates' have just blown us away. We just take it musically with however well-tuned our egos are! Jon says, 'It is the way you listen that helps us play better.' It is a nice touch. We are an interactive group. We use a lot of mental telepathy with each other and the audience. One member of the group does go over the top to make it a show. I have never felt that is totally in line with Yes but it is certainly in line with what Chris does. He likes to perform a lot.

"I think all of Yes is into the music much more than anything else. Sure, we look weird! I will openly admit that in 1973 I went onstage in a complete Afghani outfit. I had boots that tied up my legs. Everything I had was from Afghanistan. It was the right thing for *Topographic* because I was this kind of folk guy. We all took on certain personas. Chris had very outrageous clothes. Over the years we have kind of played that down and got more stereotypical rock 'n' roll look.

"Of course, Trevor Rabin wore his famous leather trousers for a while. The group changed image and look in the '80s. I think we were left with that in the '90s. Yes was a mixture. Jon was still looking a little bit hippie. I have gone more lethargic. Chris definitely wanted to be outrageous but he played it down. It used to shout but it just kind of barks now! You never see Alan because he is behind the drum kit. People find out what he has on at the end of the show. We never ever talk about what we are going to wear. We used to laugh at each other the first night of every tour. We would go, 'You are really wearing that?' After that you were not allowed to say anything more about it. You just got one shot at it!"

September 25, 2000. Yes issue *House Of Yes: Live From The House Of Blues*, capturing a show from Halloween 1999. The album includes Billy Sherwood and Igor Khoroshev, both out of the band by the time the album was released.

Billy Sherwood talks about playing long sets in legendary venues:
"That was a very special event, to be able to play with Yes in my hometown [Las Vegas]. That was my favourite band growing up—everyone I knew, knew it. So to have me kind of seeing my old friends there, and being on stage with these guys was just really special. And I'm glad we got a chance to make that video, especially making it there. It's there forever, a particularly cool moment. It's really just great memories for me playing places that I never thought I would

be playing—Madison Square Garden, the Royal Albert Hall, all the touring that we did in Brazil at all these different venues. People were freaking out.

"And being able to play a set that is three hours long, and really have time to enjoy what you're doing. I mean, most bands play for an hour and you get up and you get off. But there were some times we were playing for three hours and 20 minutes. You would really feel immersed in the whole experience. You had a chance to soak in it, so to speak. And we were all cracking our own individual whips to keep the level of integrity up, especially during the tours I was doing with them. We always wanted to maintain a certain standard of excellence. There was a lot of rehearsing and talking about stuff and getting things together. And it was always snapped to the grid. By the time we got on stage, everything was pretty much on autopilot. Now you could just perform it and enjoy it all."

Alan White on the rare two-guitar lineup of Yes:

"Steve Howe is going to be Steve Howe, and he has a very definite style. And some of the material we do from the '80s, Billy kind of latched onto that a lot more, some of the stuff that Trevor Rabin did. Billy comes to the table with his own material too. He comes from more of an '80s standpoint, whereas Steve is probably more '70s. Billy and Trevor are very good friends, actually. Billy feels he's good at emulating what Trevor did in some of that music, but there's no comparison to draw between them."

2001

In the spring and summer Yes work with Tim Weidner at Sound Design Studios in Santa Barbara, California, on material that will comprise their *Magnification* album.

Steve Howe on working with an orchestra:

"There was certainly a challenge. Tim Weidner worked with Seal and Trevor Horn, and also on my album *Turbulence* a few years ago. I recommended Tim, and Tim came in basically to engineer, and he took on the production decisions. So we joint-produced the record. And once the tracks were recorded, there was a sort of nightmare period where they needed careful mixing and careful control and a little bit of an ingenious stitching here and there to make it actually as good as it is.

"And it is pretty damn good. To us, it didn't start out quite so good, but with careful molding and direction and perspective, I mean, you can't just put a group with an orchestra and kiss it goodnight and walk out of the studio. There's a lot to do with dynamics and perspective and particular positioning of things. So it was much harder than doing a Yes record without an orchestra, that's for sure.

But you can't really define what was difficult. It was just the putting together of these two ideas that took some molding and consideration and patience. It was a difficult time, but out of it came what might be one of our best recordings in a long time."

May 25, 2001. Yes issue *Keystudio*, a compilation of the studio material from the two *Keys To Ascension* albums.

June 5, 2001. After what is more of a duo instrumental album in 2000 called *Rare*, Asia issue *Aura*, which features Geoff Downes and John Payne working with a number of session musicians; Steve Howe guests on one track.

June 30, 2001. Rick Wakeman performs *Return To The Centre Of The Earth* in its entirety in Trois Rivières, Quebec. The album has only been played completely twice, the second time also in Quebec, on the Plains Of Abraham on July 15, 2006, where the piece was performed with full orchestra, full choir, rock band and special guests including Jon Anderson. The event was augmented by a fireworks display.

July 22 – December 13, 2001. Yes embark on the Magnification Tour, which finds them playing with an orchestra, reflective of the experience of working with an orchestra on the album. The Amsterdam show is recorded for DVD release.

Further thoughts from Steve Howe on working with an orchestra:
"This is new to us. We haven't been particularly tainted by it. We've only started it two months ago. It's a natural progression of East meets West sort of thing that you would expect with this. Due to our conductor Wilhem [Keitel], and initially Larry Groupé, who was the arranger as well, but the conductor works his backside off. He's rehearsing in the afternoon. He's there for show time. He has a long day. And basically it's that expertise that makes it easy for us. The reason I say easy, is that we have views, opinions and for the most part, we get on stage and play, and the orchestra is our ship. We're the captain, but that's the ship. That's what comes along with us and doubles our sound value or reinvents our orchestrational ideas which were originally synthesizers and samples and all that.

"So what we're excited about is the lack of things we have to do [*laughs*]. We don't have to do very much to make the show sound pretty amazing. We have to do our end. And Wilhelm, in his day, and maybe Larry, is going to return and do a couple more shows in America before it's out. But I mean, these guys basically hold it together. The orchestra is like the biggest add-on you can imagine. We've always had our difficulties, rather than playing with an orchestra and worrying about them. So we don't worry about them. They take care of themselves and they are well-controlled by Wilhelm.

"In a way, it's been more pleasurable than I imagined. I thought there might be more times when there was frustration or annoyance, but those things just don't come into it. This is a pleasurable opportunity, and many nights these people get a real kick out of doing this. There might be some people [in the orchestra] that can't wait for it to end and go home. That's OK also. They don't have to love Yes to play this music. They have to be able to read music very well and have a very high standard. But what aids it and improves it is the fact that there are a lot of people who do the show that really do get a kick out of it from the orchestra. I think that makes the point that this isn't a one-way street, that we're not just hooking up with these guys. Some of the people are very pleased to do something with a band that is more original or less predictable than a lot of other bands who've done this kind of work.

"And Wilhelm rehearses with them very thoroughly. Quite often he'll go through the set twice. They'll start with the introduction and look at 'Close To The Edge' and they'll look at particular bits that he knows are quite tricky, like 'Gates Of Delirium,' where he spends a bit of time and makes sure they understand it. First time around it's only three beats, then it's four beats. There are complexities that we are used to. The orchestra has it written down for them, so that makes it easy, but it's also quite confusing.

"We're not able to be compared to bands like The Moody Blues, because our music is more restless, more key change, more tempo change, more twists in it. And they're not playing to anything like tapes or what have you; it's quite amazing. The conductor has such a vision and he actually knows what's supposed to happen. It's actually one of the nicest times to hear the music. I'm actually there towards the end of rehearsal because I still do favour a sound check. And I arrive and sometimes I hear the most beautiful thing. I hear a segment from any of our current songs, particularly things I wrote, or things I helped to write a lot of, like 'Ritual' or 'Close To The Edge.' And I hear those tunes, things I contributed to, being played just by an orchestra in the open air and it's really quite rewarding. It's not a big like stroke on the shoulder but it's a subtle awareness that your music has reached the point where it can be reinterpreted now by an orchestra.

"It's great to hear them on their own; it helps their clarity not to have a band thundering along. If they play their parts and they understand what it has to sound like it's really going to help when we are thundering along and the room is full of people and it's all intense. And suddenly they will just vaguely remember that the music stands alone. It comes together at night, but in the afternoon it's a bit misleading—it's a very gentle and airy creature. But when it gets on stage, it pushes it, it rocks it, it forges ahead."

September 11, 2001. Yes issue *Magnification* in the UK—on 9/11. The American release date is set as December 4. The tour with orchestra rolls along without pause. The 2004 reissue from Eagle Records will include a bonus live CD.

Steve Howe on *Magnification*'s lyrics:

"I don't think it differs a lot. I don't think Jon is suddenly going to write a book about gardening. Our songs have a certain style and there's a certain anticipation in them. And there's always room for improvement. I'm not saying that they're so good that we don't need to improve them. I'm just saying that they are so 'us' that we don't need to worry too much.

"Obviously Jon has had a leading hand in lyrics, but I need to clarify that sometimes and explain that at various stages of our work, for instance, I've written a considerable amount of lyrics as well for Yes that Jon gets most of the credit for. But I'm not really bothered. I mean, Jon is seen, rightly so, as the lyrical magician if you like in Yes. So he pulls together my lyrics when it's appropriate or when it has been appropriate. On *Magnification*, a song like 'Soft As A Dove,' that has some lyrical ideas from me. Jon, if he likes them, he'll sing them; if he wants to change them he can.

"But *Magnification* was quite different from *The Ladder*, where he and Bruce Fairbairn kind of took it under their patch to get the lyrics up. This album was a little different where there was much more cross-involvement. When Jon came to do final vocals, I'd come up with what I thought were improvements here or there or developments: 'Jon try this' or 'I don't like that word.' So the input level was quite different from *The Ladder*.

"Each album is different. We never do things stereotyped, [or] the same. But there were times, like when we were doing *Keys To Ascension*, Jon wanted to steer the lyrics much more himself and I wasn't really pushing—or Chris for that matter—any lyrical ideas forward, knowing that Jon wanted to have that freedom. It kind of curves, like in the '70s when it was a bit more like it is on *Magnification*. There's input from Chris and me, there are some changes, songs that had lyrics that would then go through Jon's mill. But sometimes they'd go there and they'd just stay. And, of course, Chris and I are pleased with that. And then other times Jon will expand them or steer them more toward something he was thinking of. All that is fine, and in a way it doesn't really matter. As long as we get there."

Journalist Pete Pardo:

The big issue over the last few months was who would be the band's new keyboard player. Well, the answer is basically no one. Instead Yes chose to hire composer Larry Groupé to add layers of orchestration in place of where a keyboard player would normally fit in.

The results, while different and immediately shocking, really work after repeated listens.

October 2001. Steve Howe issues, on Spitfire, an all-acoustic album called *Natural Timbre*.

Steve Howe "unplugged":

"I've had it in the pipeline and been wanting to do one for a long time, but I had other opportunities. Last year the record company asked me, 'What about an all-acoustic album?' I was thrilled that they wanted it. I knew there was a time where I could come through with something strong that had a lot of guitar solos. The idea of it being completely acoustic as well really appealed to me. It was part of my fantasy that one day I would do it and *Natural Timbre* is the first of it.

"When you take away all the devices and mucking around that you can do with the electric guitar, it becomes intimate. There was a time of reckoning where it was really down to the music, performance and the construction and arrangements. It was demanding in its own way, but it was also refreshing because I had left out a part of my world of electric guitars. It really made me hone down with some personal endeavour work. Solo guitar playing isn't something anyone told me to do; I just wanted to do it. I am influenced from Chet Atkins. I wanted it to be quite obvious that I come from a learning curve that includes people like Chet."

2002

2002. Steve Howe issues *Skyline* with long term collaborator Paul Sutin on the InsideOut Music label

Steve Howe on *Skyline*:
"Because of my work with Paul Sutin, it may have a hint of *Voyager*. I wanted to make an album that was more laid-back than before, a little improvisation, a little more, not flimsy, but an invisible sort of structure, where the vitality of it wasn't so much about arranging it to pieces. Sort of try to build it up, but actually kind of stretch it out and make it... I guess what it is, is what I wanted it to be [*laughs*]. It's more melodic and ambient than anything I've done, but that doesn't mean to say I'm going to make ten albums now like *Skyline*. But it does mean I wanted to make this kind of album.

"I don't want to get on a treadmill about any of my styles. I just made an acoustic album, and I'm not going to make a load of those either. But these adventures are good for me, especially after *Magnification*. I mean, I did *Natural Timbre* just before *Magnification*, and I didn't expect *Magnification* to be quite as difficult as it was, but we got there in the end. It just took a lot of reminding people that we did set about making an album that would please the whole band [*laughs*]. And we got there with that one pretty well.

"So with *Skyline*, the texture of the album suited me within the things that I'd just gone through. In fact, I take the piss a bit out of Yes by calling one track 'Simplification,' for the very reason of what it is, which is synth guitar. It's basically one guitar. You can't get much simpler than a guitar. It doesn't sound like that terribly, but that's what it is. So I had a bit of a laugh, just because I like playing with titles. But simplification is what this album is about, more than elaboration, magnification, and the other sorts of things I've been doing."

April 16, 2002. Yes management announce that Rick Wakeman has rejoined the band, yet again.

Steve Howe remembers the return of the prodigal keyboard player:
"Well, I'm hardly going to say anything negative, because there isn't anything negative to say. I mean, Rick coming back is of major importance. Rick's presence in Yes, by itself, is important. His interaction with me as a guitarist is incredibly important to me. Plus he tells jokes and he's really tall and he's got masses of keyboards, and the fans like him—that only compounds the fact that I'm excited Rick's back. It doesn't mean that it's the end of our problems. The group really doesn't exist without moving between states of happiness and achievement to states of unhappiness and lack of achievement. It depends on expectations. Some of the band do expect more as a result of our work than I do. They go with their heart sometimes, wanting, hoping, anticipating that all these remarkable things will happen. And sometimes they don't [*laughs*].

"And I'm the least unhappy about that, because I guess I'm more accepting in my life. I accept what happens. Like today, the weather is crap and I have to get to Ottawa, and I can either get a train or I can drive. It's a risk driving but sitting on a train is going to be a very uncontrolled environment. I can't control it. We're playing there tonight and the conditions are bad. So we have these choices to make along the way.

"And that's the same with everything about Yes—it's about making decisions. We're not very good at that. We're not very good at agreement on anything. But that doesn't mean to say that we don't get results that are fitting. And certainly this tour, and the previous tour we did in the summer, show that Rick coming back is more important than 'somebody' coming back—the sound of that is reasonably passé. His musicality is what I want in the group. His virtuosity is what I want, very much. Because I'm tired of either not having that kind of a guy to work with, somebody to understand the intricacies and back me up when I say, 'Chris, you can't play E flat in that scale. You can't play F sharp in this scale.' I have problems where people don't really listen, always, to my musicality."

Rick Wakeman, on what he brings to Yes in 2002:
"For me it is the natural affinity I have for both the music and the other guys. I can read them both as musicians and as individuals and I suspect they have the same abilities. This particular lineup also has the uniqueness of having five highly individual musicians and five individual personalities. Put this particular combination together, and for some inexplicable reason the sum of the individuals as a whole, becomes immensely greater than the value of each individual. A genuine case of $1+1+1+1+1=25$! Will it still be there? Of course, and I think that this time it could be even stronger. Everything has met at the right time to make this happen and it is happening for the right reasons too: the music and the desire to make it together."

July 17, 2002 – October 4, 2003. Yes embark on the Full Circle Tour, a world tour, featuring the return of Rick Wakeman. In October and November of 2002, support on select US dates comes from Porcupine Tree, who will soon become the UK's biggest and best new progressive rock act.

Further thoughts from Steve Howe on Rick Wakeman's return:
"Rick's come back with a full commitment to stay with us and record. But that doesn't mean he's going to be a puppet. Nobody's going to control him, any more than anybody controls me. Rick has good, sensible opinions that can translate to us very, very well. Rick is not complacent or silent or *blasé* about it. And I think that's going to wake up the rest of the band a lot, because I think there's a similarity between Rick and me, in that we tend to let things go a bit, when we see everybody's happy thinking they're making decisions for everybody. And then we get serious and say, 'Now, hang on.'

"So Rick draws the line and I draw the line, and maybe we draw the line together and say, musically, we'll just not go in this direction. Or business-wise—I mean, we've both existed, or parts of our career, we co-exist running our own affairs. I have a personal manager, but Rick and I pride ourselves on having a lot of control and direction. Otherwise we wouldn't be sitting talking about yet another studio album. So, we're kind of constructive in that way. And that makes for a powerful Yes. It's not a negative; it gets us to give our utmost to Yes. I think that what I would like to see is an album that does have very forceful guitar/keyboard parts, like Rick and I used to play. Because it hasn't happened with *Open Your Eyes*, *The Ladder* and *Magnification*. Purposely on *Magnification*, if you like, because there is no exact keyboard virtuoso present."

Rick Wakeman on being called a legend:
"It's better than 'dinosaur!' Recently I was down in Argentina and a journalist said to me, 'I'm going to call you Rick if you don't mind.' I said, 'Of course, but why did you say that?' He replied, 'By calling you Rick I am implying that you are still heavily involved in the industry of music. If I call you Mr. Wakeman, that implies that you are in semi-retirement and are much older than me. If I call you a legend then that probably means you are about to die.' I told him to call me Rick!"

July 30, 2002. Yes issue a 5CD box set called *In A Word: Yes (1969 -)*.

Steve Howe, speaking in 2002, on playing "Close To The Edge" live:
"We were doing 'Close To The Edge' last night in Toronto, and I was thinking, now, I wonder if those people can feel the conviction that we have about this song? You know, Jon and I wrote it together. We sat down, and I played him bits of it and Jon played me other bits of it. We were throwing these ideas around that were going to become 'Close To The Edge.'

"But we were doing it last night, and I was thinking, boy, you know, that's a lot of words, there's a lot of music, there's a lot of chords. In other words, in that 20 minutes, we put a lot of ideas together, but they were very deep ideas. You even have a white lace drifty song in the middle of it. 'I Get Up I Get Down' was just as important as 'Seasons Of Man' or the chorus, 'Close To The Edge.' So all those ingredients were just telling of Jon and me as writers.

"But also, eventually, Yes as an arrangement concept is what the key to it is. You've got to have songs that we believe in, not just songs that someone says, 'Oh, the radio will like that, so we'll record it.' That's the kiss of death for any band, let alone Yes. And Yes have been there—believe me—but not very much when I'm around, but unfortunately sometimes when I'm around. So I see that as a quintessential record, where everything about it was detailed to the nth degree. And there was nothing omitted; there was nothing... we didn't forget, you know, the beginning, the middle and ending [*laughs*]. Sometimes there's things you get right about records at the expense of other bits you don't. But that record has a true perfectionism.

2003

2003. Chris Squire marries a woman called Scotland, the marriage being his third. They have one child, Xilan, born 2008.

February 4, 2003. Trevor Rabin issues, through Voiceprint, *Live In LA*, recorded on the tour for his major label attempt at a solo career back in 1989. The album includes solo renditions of Yes songs, "Love Will Find A Way," "Changes," and "Owner Of A Lonely Heart."

March 2003. *Classic Rock* votes *Tales From Topographic Oceans* seventh greatest concept album of all time in their Top 30; Rick Wakeman's *Journey To The Centre Of The Earth* takes 25th. In case you're wondering (though you could probably guess it anyway), Floyd's *Dark Side Of The Moon* takes top spot.

July 2003. Conspiracy issue a second album called *The Unknown*.

July 8, 2003. Rhino issues *Yes Remixes*, featuring radical re-engineerings of Yes classics by Steve's son Virgil "The Verge" Howe.

July 22, 2003. Trevor Rabin issues, on Voiceprint, a solo album called *90124*, which offers material worked on during the lead-up to *90125*—solo and Cinema—highlight being an early version of "Owner Of A Lonely Heart." Additionally, 1994's *Talk* album track "Where Will You Be?" is offered here in instrumental form. Another *Talk* track "Walls" is presented with Supertramp's Roger Hodgson on vocals.

July 28, 2003. Yes issue *The Ultimate Yes: 35th Anniversary Collection*, in the UK as a two CD set, five months later as a three CD set, with the bonus disc being acoustic-themed; packaging for the three CD set is four-fold digipak with poster booklet.

Rick Wakeman on 35th *Anniversary* and other compilations:
"Funny enough, on *35th Anniversary*, I'm really, really so glad we did the acoustic stuff. Because that's made us all open our eyes because it was so popular with people. We all went, now, hold on a minute. Because if you revisit these pieces, and you don't try to play them acoustically as you play them electrically, but you go, 'Hey, how can we do this now?,' you can have a lot of fun with the music. That was a highlight for me. To be very honest with you, I'm fed up with compilations. Sick to death of them! There have now been so many, both Yes compilations and

compilations of my own stuff over the years, that I just throw my hands up in the air. You know, how many combinations of things can people put together? But unfortunately, the powers that be do deals that the band has very little influence over. And you know, the *35th Anniversary* is well put together. But apart from the acoustic set, it's like the other ones. Basically, there's been so many bloody combinations. There's been loads of my own. There's another one of mine that's just come out. And they're doing great promotion and things on it, but you go, 'Pffft!'"

Steve Howe on rocking again, now that Rick is back (and the band is all British):
"Having a rock element... our last three albums don't have that, seriously. I don't necessarily think that *Open Your Eyes* or *The Ladder* have that true rock element. It was more, I wouldn't say superficial, but I would say that the kind of rock that is on *Open Your Eyes* and *The Ladder* and *Magnification* is more drummed-up rock than felt rock, you know? And I like to feel the rock of 'South Side Of The Sky,' things like that. Last night, we tore the audience apart, on 'South Side,' particularly.

"Because I think the writing has just got to come from the internal British band. You know, as soon as we've got people who weren't from our country, we make a different kind of music. It gets watered down and it just doesn't wash. And I think that goes for the recording venues, the producer and the personnel. You know, I love the whole world, as a race, but I think when we work closely, we work best closely with our own people. Because a lot of other people have to either think they know what you're talking about, or say, 'Oh yeah,' when it should be like, 'What the hell do you mean?' So we've had that, we've been there, and it applies.

"So for me, the fact of changing members and getting back to an all-British lineup is more for the communication. You know, and telepathy. You don't talk about it because you don't need to. So there is that going on, and it don't count for much when you haven't got it. When you haven't got it, you might be playing together, you might come in on the same beat, but I think that there is some respect for communication that happens telepathically. And that happens best when you don't have to ask questions.

"It's like me when I'm playing with my son. Well, I have two sons that I work with, but particularly my eldest son [Dylan]—he plays drums. Somebody said to me the other day, do you have to tell him what to do? Exactly the opposite! He listens to my guide drums and he says, 'Do you want something vaguely like that?' And I'll say yea or nay. Or, 'Let's make it more off-beat or have fun.' Other than that I don't have to say very much. And that's what communication is about. Communication is so you don't have to talk for hours."

2004

January 26, 2004. Yes issue a documentary called *Yesspeak,* narrated by Roger Daltrey and directed by Robert Garofalo. It was launched into theatres with Yes following up with an acoustic set via closed-circuit transmission.

Steve Howe on interviews:
"There's not a lot you can say about music. I've managed to pad my career out a great deal talking about music. But honestly, there's not a lot you can really say that's particularly significant; even reading a book about a great musician. I just finished a book about Gil Evans, the jazz arranger. I think Gil would agree with me that, don't ask the musicians to talk. I mean, we're always asked, so we always will, but eventually, there's only so much we can say about what we do. But I can talk a lot about other people's music, and I like doing that a lot. I like talking about my favourite guitarists, like Chet Atkins or Wes Montgomery or Julian Bream. I adore them, and I adore the music they've made."

Early 2004. The Syn reunite, without Chris Squire, but with ex-Yes stalwart Peter Banks, who soon leaves the group. Later in the year, Chris returns to the fold.

February 24, 2004. Rhino reissues *90125* in expanded form, offering as bonus tracks three alternate versions of album tracks, plus the unreleased (but fully produced and album-ready) "Make It Easy," "It's Over," plus the Cinema version of future hit single "It Can Happen," before Jon Anderson changed the lyrics and made it his own.

April 15 – September 22, 2004. Yes embark on the 35th Anniversary Tour, supported by a 35th anniversary compilation. At the close, Yes wouldn't play live again for four years, with Jon suffering from acute respiratory failure, prompting his eventual replacement by Benoit David. Support in August and September comes from American progressive metal titans Dream Theater.

Rick Wakeman on the contours of the 2004 tour:
"Basically the last two years were, you know, the old lineup of the band is back together. It was very nice, and we were playing pretty much an old favourites type of set. And we decided at the end of last year, the end of the tour, that it was time to move on, that we didn't want to do that anymore. Not that we didn't want to do it anymore, but a lot of the hardcore fans said, 'OK, that's great. What are you going to do now, then?' So we wanted to put together a whole new set. This set is 85% different from the set from last year. Huge difference, doing stuff we've not done before ever, and it's really working. I think in all seriousness, it's the most enjoyable set I've ever done with Yes. Because it's really different.

"The main difference is that we've actually revisited some of the music, and rearranged it, re-done it. We've taken 'Mind Drive,' which we've never played live before, and split it into three parts. And that was a sort of catalyst to join a lot of the other music together. The first half is almost nonstop music, with a mixture of old stuff, stuff, as I say, that we haven't played for a long time. We've even gone back and revisited the very first album and taken stuff off that that even Jon struggled to remember. Trying to do things that people just really wouldn't expect us to do, but rearranged them, revisited them.

"We did some acoustic numbers last year and we did a couple of in-stores, and it was so popular that we thought we would throw it into the set, see how it went. And it's almost like the most popular thing we do. The website has been hounded with people saying how much they've enjoyed it. We all huddle together in the middle and do this 25-minute thing, and it really works fantastic; great fun.

"So, the whole thing is top to tail completely different. And the other thing we wanted was a Yes stage to look like a Yes stage again. Not just the band onstage playing. So we all decided during the last tour, to get Roger involved to build us a stage set, so we can almost like play in an album cover. And one of the things that Rog said was—which is very true—one of the main problems with bands onstage is it becomes very one-dimensional, very flat. It becomes like a wall and you're there. So we've had these incredible inflatables built which you can light from inside and outside, which give that 3-D effect with a cover. And it's a real buzz to play on it. It's very Yes in every respect. So it's like moving another stage on, which is great.

"And obviously to do that, you need to play in arenas where you can have a stage size big enough to fit in all on. It's full-up as it is, and it really does work and a lot of the scenery moves, and there's a lot of gear coming on and offstage throughout the set. It's actually a very clever stage because it's like a little maze. There must be about 12 permanent crew onstage at all times, bringing stuff off and on, doing bits and pieces. Quite a bit of choreography involved; it works really well."

Mid-2004. Yes issue *Yes Acoustic: Guaranteed No Hiss*, a DVD release of the closed-circuit concert that accompanied the release of their documentary.

Steve Howe on bringing a sense of mystery back into the band:
"On our own most loved records, I think we worked very hard, and we worked with a belief that we didn't really know what we were doing. I think this is what the '90s albums say of Yes, is that it sounds like we thought we knew what we were doing, which is very dangerous. And jaded—jaded in the respect of jaded to think we know what we're doing. Yeah, that's jaded. I try avoid that. And I think with

Rick coming back, hopefully, there will be a sense of realization that we are better not knowing what we're doing, because we make the best music when we don't know what we're doing. And just experiencing each other and sharing that honour, where we can work with each other. And Jon of course is a wonderful singer, and the way we work together is important to me—obviously we respect each other."

Rick Wakeman reveals which are the difficult bits to perform:
"For me personally, the areas that are hard are some of the pieces where we've changed keys; that are not in their original keys. There's a certain... it's different for guitarists. All they do, for that particular piece, is they de-tune the guitar. It's easy. De-tuned bass, de-tuned guitar, and they play exactly what they played in the first place. If you are using a single keyboard instrument, you could in fact, re-tune it, but I don't. They are, in fact, all midi'ed up together and all connected together and that just can't be done. So there are some pieces that I've had to re-learn in new keys. And you have to fight hard—there's always a certain in-built knowledge filed away. You can go up to a piece you haven't played in 20 years and the brain sort of clicks in and automatically goes where it needs to go. When you're in a different key, and you're at the keyboard, it's not as easy as people think. It becomes a completely different ballgame. So that's the hardest. For the first few shows, every now and then, I suddenly found myself wanting to go back to the original key.

"'Turn Of The Century' and 'Going For The One' are the two main ones. 'Ritual,' I have to keep my wits about me, because we've revisited that. I never liked it on the record, and I think we do it 100 times better now. To be honest, there aren't that many places where you can sit back and relax. It's not that sort of set. And Yes music was never intended like that. I think if it ever got like that for us onstage, we would be in all sorts of trouble. We all have to have our wits about us all the time."

August 31, 2004. Asia issue their tenth studio album, *Silent Nation*. Billy Sherwood guests on guitar and bass.

2005

2005. Chris Squire moves back to the UK from California.

August 9, 2005. Yes issue a DVD called *Songs From Tsongas: Yes 35th Anniversary Concert*, documenting a show from May 15, 2004. The set would be reissued in expanded edition on September 23, 2014 on DVD, Blu-ray and 3CD.

Rick Wakeman's tips for staying sane on the road:
"We've all got our own way of doing it, I suppose. I think one of the things is we all understand each other extremely well now. We realize that we are five

completely different personalities. So it's not always party time where we go, 'Hey, we're at the hotel; what are we going to do now?' Everyone manages to do their own thing. I suppose our days are pretty full as it is. I mean, I'm an early riser, so I always get up early, because I have stuff to run and look after back in the UK. I put on the computer and there will be 40 or 50 emails from England—because they are so many hours ahead—that have come in, and I try to answer them before having my shower and whatever it is and then you're normally traveling off to the next place.

"And you arrive, and your day tends to be, throw your bags in, do some interviews, down to the gig, sound check, and then back to the hotel. I suppose, when you get back to the hotel, that's the only time when you get to relax. And the problem is, you're tired, but you can't sleep, because you've got the adrenaline rush. So, I'm at my happiest when I'm in a hotel that's got all the wonderful old channels like *Nick At Nite* and *TV Land*. It's great coming to Canada, because of course, you've got all the old British sitcoms that go on late at night. I mean, at 1 o'clock this morning, I was watching *Are You Being Served?*. I'm in my element then. And that really helps me to relax. And I make a cup of coffee or a cup of tea.

"I mean, times have changed. The days of going out all-night partying are, sadly, long since gone. And I know it sounds silly, but to some extent you have to pace yourself. We were saying today, we've had some pretty heavy schedules. I mean, today started at 6:30 this morning on the radio. So if you've been up for 13 or 14 hours and then go onstage to do a three-hour show... Sometimes the people that run us, and I don't mean this to sound unkind, because they all work very hard, but they forget sometimes that we're all closer to 60 than we are to 50. We're not the spring chickens we used to be. We like to think we are, but we're not really."

August 23, 2005. Yes issue, through Rhino, *The Word Is Live*, a 3CD box set, spanning the years 1970 to 1988. Highlights from an obscure perspective are the surprisingly fast and punky "Go Through This" and "We Can Fly From Here" from the Drama Tour. The latter is later reworked (a bit; mostly lengthened) into the centrepiece of the 2011 *Fly From Here* album. Also included is a cover of the Young Rascals' "It's Love."

November 8, 2005. The Syn (now Syn) issue, on Umbrello, *Syndestructible*, the band debuting live in London at the end of the year, playing into January 2006 with Chris on bass and Alan White on drums. Also this year comes another cringeworthy pun, *Original Syn*, a two CD set of original and reformation-era Syn material.

2006

May 16, 2006. Chris leaves The Syn, with acrimony amongst the members that descends into legal action.

June 27, 2006. Conspiracy issue A nine-track DVD called *Conspiracy Live,* which includes bonus interview and behind the scenes footage.

Billy Sherwood on Chris Squire:

"Chris and I have a unique relationship, and I love the guy like a brother. And while it may appear to somebody from the outside looking in... I know from the inside looking out, that his passion is Yes, his dedication is Yes—and that's his world. And he's been the only one who's been through it all and he continues to be. We have had a lot of laughs together. He's a funny guy, and I'm very much into having a better time than being grumpy [*laughs*]. I just saw him recently in Arizona. Every time I see him, even though a period of time has gone by between the two of us hanging out, it picks up right where it left off."

July 11, 2006. Laserlight Records issues an eight-track Yes package called *Greatest Hits Live.*

December 2006. Eagle Records issues a five CD Yes box set called *Essentially Yes.* The package includes the albums *Open Your Eyes, The Ladder, Magnification,* and *Talk,* plus an abbreviated version of the forthcoming *Live At Montreux 2003.*

2007

May 14, 2007. Jon Anderson issues *Watching The Flags That Fly,* a collection of demos that were the seeds for a second Anderson Bruford Wakeman Howe album.

July 30, 2007. Circa issue their debut album, *Circa 2007.* Three Yes members are part of the band; Billy Sherwood, Tony Kaye, and Alan White.

Billy Sherwood contrasting Conspiracy with Circa:

"Conspiracy is definitely songs that Chris and I wrote sitting there in a room together, sorting stuff out. And Chris's style is very unique; the textures, tempos, progressions and the bass lines and whatnot, the grooves, they have their own style. And to me, Circa, Tony Kaye, you know, amazing keyboard player. He comes from that gritty Hammond edge. He tends to rock in a way that pushes me in another direction, when it comes to the writing. They're different by edginess, I suppose. Proud of both of them."

2008

February 2008. Circa, with three of four members being ex-Yes old boys, issue a DVD commemorating their first live show from six month previous, at which a Yes medley was also performed.

Billy Sherwood gives Yes and Circa drummer Alan White the credit he's due:
"Alan's got a great feel unto his own, and one that I was always digging, and still do. When I was a kid starting to play drums, I played the Yes records all day long, and tried to emulate those feels, to get his kind of groove going. He's got a very cool, unique groove, his chops are amazing and his playing speaks for itself. He's a phenomenal musician and a super nice guy, really, really creative, and he's a cool writer. He'll come at you with certain things that are coming from a whole other place.

"There's a song on the Conspiracy record called 'Lonesome Trail.' Alan wrote the chorus to that thing, and the first time he played it for me, it's like, this is strange, how does it work? And then after a while, I went, wait a minute, that's the chorus! That's just too cool. It's cool to work with someone who presents you with stuff like that. I think he always respected the fact that I played drums on a level enough to be able to communicate with him and try to push him to even go farther than he might have wanted to or thought about going on some things.

"One of the more unique things that we came up with, with Circa, was 'Information Overload,' from the first record. He was out there in the room getting ready to record and I kind of gave him the signal that we were recording. And wherever I had started the tape, when he heard the click he assumed that was one, and it was actually... he started playing the song on the other side of the groove. And I looked at Tommy and I was going to stop and restart. Then all of a sudden I started listening to what was happening, and it made the whole song happen [*laughs*]. It was one of those moments with Alan—magical things just take place."

April 1, 2008. Asia's original and classic lineup—John Wetton, Steve Howe, Geoff Downes and Carl Palmer—reunite for *Phoenix*, issued on Frontiers in Europe and EMI America in the US. The album reaches #73 on the Billboard charts.

John Wetton explains how a lobby encounter kicked off a reunion:
"Historically, Carl and I worked together quite a bit after the demise of the original Asia. Steve and I hadn't seen each other for over 20 years. But, funnily enough, we bumped into each other in the lobby of the hotel where we were meeting that day, and it was all over in a hug, you know? I just knew that he was bringing nothing more to the party than hope, and me too. I didn't want to drag

anything from the past into that meeting we had that day in January. Steve, I was expecting to have a couple of skeletons in the cupboard, but he didn't, and I was really relieved about that. Because that would have made any progress very, very difficult. Whereas Carl, I've seen him on and off over the years and we worked together as recently as 1999. So there were no surprises there. We know what we bring to the party. But Steve was the unknown quantity—and it couldn't have been a better outcome."

May 13, 2008. Jon Anderson suffers an extreme asthma attack, requiring hospitalization. A smoker through the 1960s and 1970s, Jon had long cleaned up his act as well as become a noted and outspoken vegetarian. Nonetheless, he was diagnosed with acute respiratory failure and ordered by doctors to take six months off.

August 19, 2008. Steve Howe Trio issue their debut, *The Haunted Melody*, recorded October 7, 8, 2007. The band consists of Steve, Ross Stanley on Hammond organ and son Dylan on drums.

November 4 – December 17, 2008. Yes play their first dates in four years, bringing the In The Present Tour, featuring new vocalist Benoit David. An earlier planned Close To The Edge And Back Tour had been cancelled due to Jon Anderson's lung ailment. The new lineup also includes Rick Wakeman's son Oliver on keyboards, and the band was billed as Steve Howe, Chris Squire and Alan White of Yes. The 42-year-old Benoit David, from Montreal, had been with prog act Mystery but was discovered by Chris Squire through Youtube posts of his work with Yes tribute band Close To The Edge.

Alan White on the hiring of Benoit David:
"There wasn't a meeting, really. We just passed this video around to each other and said well, we should give this guy a try. Put his voice with us and see if he fits in with what Yes is. And we met and played for a while and just all talked, and basically said, 'Yeah, let's just do it; let's see how it develops.' Jon Anderson got really sick, and when he got better, he didn't really want to work. When he came back, he didn't want to do any of the arduous touring that we've been used to. We had these tours lined up, and then this situation turns up, and Jon needed a while to get himself well, and is now doing his solo show. I don't think he wants to do any kind of grinding, three shows in a row, flying every day, that kind of stuff which I just finished doing [*laughs*]."

Oliver Wakeman's preparation for the Yes job:
"When I started with Yes, I had a week's rehearsals on my own at home to learn the music, and then I had two weeks with them in a rehearsal room, for four or five hours a day, and that was it. And then we went out to the three-and-a-half-

hour show. That was a lot of music to learn! And what was difficult about that was, even though they hadn't played together for four years as a band, they had played that music before for 40 years, and I had never played any Yes music at home; I'd never sat down and worked out 'Roundabout' just for fun. So I had to learn everything from scratch, which was hard work. But you know, it's part of the job—you get there and do it. The same with The Strawbs: I knew some of the songs, but knowing the songs to listen to and enjoy is different to listening and trying to work out what part is there and helping make the sound. It's a different discipline."

December 13, 2008. Jon Anderson issues the 41-minute *From Me To You*, which consists of three long tracks, "Songbirding," "Birdsonging," and "Singsonging."

Jon Anderson's creative quest:

"I believe that some of the greatest music is still yet to come. Music comes from—well, we don't know where exactly—but music is so important to the human experience. I'm listening to a lot of Ethiopian music now; the old school stuff is so beautiful and the dance groups are so funky. I'm so tired of that disco 'boom, boom, boom' stuff; Ethiopian music is more upbeat and danceable and fun. It's ancient and we should protect our ancient musical knowledge because there's still so much great music to come.

"It's like when you watch a movie and you think, 'My God! What kind of visual is this?' Eventually, we're gonna get rid of the old stories, which are so brutal and silly at times, and we're gonna watch visual energy that's so powerful to our adrenaline factor. And the music is gonna be the same; whatever rush you get from listening to heavy metal or Yes or whatever it is that inspires you, you'll be watching these visual arc experiences in the next ten years that are all 3-D or animation. They'll really give you an adrenaline rush.

"We've freed ourselves from the gore, and video games will become more pure and enlightening. We have to go through this amazing change, and there are some incredible artists out there just waiting for the chance to create and develop their music and visual art. They'll be able to do it through the internet and through their home computer experience. You're gonna be able to work musician to musician, around the world, in time with each other."

2009

2009. In this year, serial marrier Rick Wakeman ties the knot for the fourth time. Rachel Kaufman, who is a quarter of a century younger than Rick, is the bride. Future Yes vocalist Jon Davison joins Chattanooga, Tennessee, prog rock collective Glass Hammer, established 1992. Jon also does double duty in Sky Cries Mary, in which he is bassist, along with roving his Yes chops through tribute band Roundabout.

January 14, 2009. Circa issue a second studio album called *Circa HQ*; the band is down to two ex-Yes members, with the departure of Alan White.

February 5 – 10, 2009. A second leg of the In The Present Tour, beginning in Mexico, is cut short due to a medical emergency concerning Chris Squire, who suffers an aneurysm in his leg.

July 26 – August 2, 2009. Yes continue on with their In The Present Tour, with Steve Howe pulling double duty, performing with Yes and opening act Asia.

Steve Howe's reaction to being called one of the greatest guitarists of all time:

"I am excited to be asked that in that way. I feel that I am quite a guitarist. You can say that I have my own sort of theme on the guitar and that my theme comes across in the way that I am playing. It has quite a lot to do with my personality. I think if you put a rainbow out there you could say that Steve Howe is all these different themes. The multi-guitarist role has given me a kind of smokescreen effect. I surprise myself playing something in one context of the guitar like a Spanish guitar solo and then five minutes later I have a fuzz box on! I like the way that I make the transition. As long as I am happy with the transitions as an artist then I'm OK. If they jar me, then I am doing something wrong. I like to be a chameleon. I like to change from electric to steel in a second. I like that side of me that I am still going there."

October 2009. Brought on as lead singer for live dates since the previous year, Benoit David is announced this month as an official member of Yes.

October 5, 2009. Rick Wakeman issues *The Six Wives Of Henry VIII: Live At Hampton Court Palace*. We've not cited all of Rick's solo albums in this book, reason being that the current record is, loosely speaking, Rick's 90th solo album!

Can Rick Wakeman remember all his albums?:

"Um, yes, I do, actually. I couldn't put them all in the right order, but certainly I do recall all of them—every single one that I did. To have a hundred of those, for you, I think you need to seek medical help, 'cause that's certainly strange to have so many [*laughs*]. Recently, *Vignettes* is one that I do enjoy and *Romance Of The Victorian Age* was good fun to do, but the thing is, I don't know what I'm going to write. I know that it sounds silly, but if you're sitting down to play and you start to write music, sometimes for whatever reason what comes out is suitable for a band or suitable for orchestra, and sometimes you just go, 'This is a piano piece!' So I never try and adapt a piece of music to make it fit a band or fit an orchestra. If I think, 'This is a piano piece,' then I will play it as a piano piece.

"And I think that's important. I've been very lucky with different record companies that they've understood when they called and ask, 'What are you doing?' and I'd say, 'Well, I'm in the middle of a piano album,' and they'd go, 'Fine!' Or if I'd say, 'I've got a sort of a prog album or whatever it is.' So they're all different. But one of the reasons they started to become a bit different was in the '80s, different countries asked for different things. For example, Japan still wanted very heavy synth albums, so I produced some synth albums. A lot of Europe—Germany, Austria, Switzerland—suddenly wanted almost a meditation-type of music, so I did the *Aspirant* series for them. And then South America wanted big prog rock extravaganzas for the orchestra and choir."

October 29 – December 12, 2009. Yes tour Europe intensively, hitting points east and west, along with the UK and Ireland.

December 1, 2009. Yes play the Bourse du Travail in Lyon, France, the show captured for eventual CD and DVD release in 2011. The show features new singer Benoit David and also, on keyboards, Oliver Wakeman.

Oliver Wakeman on how much freedom he had to alter things:

"Um, not a lot. Dad for many years had been with the band and he had been changing parts and doing things differently, because he was there originally and he had the right to change things around a little bit. But the rest of the band were very keen to play things exactly as they were on the record. And I thought, well, I don't have a problem with that, because I didn't want to turn up and start pretending to be dad, making things up and changing things, as I don't have the right to do that. So I was quite happy to go back and perform the music as it was recorded, because people hadn't heard the original solo from 'And You And I' for an awful long time, because dad always made something different up every night or did a different solo. So the thing that I could bring to the band was the authenticity back to the music. And as we developed on the tour, there were little moments where I got to add things and do things but I tried to stay true to the music as much as I could."

6

2010s

•••

Incredibly into their sixth decade now, Yes seem unstoppable, whether ganged-up or going it alone. Jon Anderson, now exiled, is touring in his own sweet way; Asia continues to work, and with nobody a stranger to multitasking, Asia keysman Geoff Downes returns to Yes.

The task at hand is the recording of the first studio album without Jon Anderson since *Drama*. *Fly From Here* emerges in 2011, and it is a fine record, featuring Benoit David, and it is the band's first album in ten years. Touring necessarily is next, amidst all manner of Yes and Yes-related output, including *Union Live*, plus a similarly archival Anderson Bruford Wakeman Howe live album, from Asia came *XXX* (their third in a row with original lineup), a Jon Anderson solo album, and Squackett's *A Life Within A Day* from Chris Squire and Steve Hackett, two elegant singers paired to perfection.

From the "You couldn't make it up" school, Benoit David is sidelined with his own respiratory illness, but there is a whole tour booked for the spring of 2012. A band meeting takes place and it is mutually agreed that a replacement would be needed to fulfil the dates, with Benoit giving full consent to look for a singer. In February 2012, it is announced that Jon Davison would replace him, and like last time, the show goes on despite a blow that would fell less hardened road warriors.

In 2013, the band scratches its collective art rock head and comes up with a bombastic new twist on the idea of playing one's hit record in its entirety, front to back, the naturally long-winded Yes figuring they'd perform three of their labyrinthine records back to back. Putting further twist to the idea of playing live, Yes starts playing cruise ships. Also in

2013, original Yes guitarist Peter Banks dies, which serves to remind us how fairly fortunate this band has been concerning mortality rates.

In 2014, the band was back with another album, most pertinently, with Jon Davison on vocals. *Heaven & Earth* is produced by transformed prima donna Roy Thomas Baker, who the band had tried to make a record with back in Paris in 1979. The expected long-haul of tour dates kicks off, with fans breaking into bickering camps debating whether they can hack yet another lead singer that isn't Jon Anderson, or more specifically, one that isn't the creator of the literary canon atop all these classics that must be played and relived in communion—it's a valid point.

Into mid-2015 at 70 years old, Jon Anderson is on the verge of another new record, this time collaborating with violin legend Jean-Luc Ponty, while his ex-band of space travellers channels its inner Grateful Dead with the release of *Progeny: Seven Shows From Seventy-Two*, a whopping 14 CD box set. Life goes on, with more tour dates announced, but also with the sad news that Chris Squire, the only Yes member on every single Yes album, has been diagnosed with an acute form of leukemia.

2010

February 2 – April 6, 2010. Yes return to the US for another set of dates, closing off in Mexico.

April 2010. Steve Howe Trio issue their second album, *Travelling*, a live recording documenting dates in the UK and Canada.

April 3, 2010. The original Asia lineup issues a second record, *Omega*, after reforming.

June 8 – July 15, 2010. Yes perform more US dates, with Peter Frampton as support.

August 16, 2010. Jon Anderson continues his regular touring schedule, formally billed for this US leg as *An Acoustic Evening With Jon Anderson (The Voice Of Yes)*, which he uses on some gigs moving forward, also interspersing dates as a duo with Rick Wakeman.

Jon Anderson muses on acoustic songs and US citizenship:
"I just enjoy the form, you know? I love singing and during the last couple of years, I've been out to Europe and South America. It's just good to get out in front of a new audience and play the new songs and some classic songs. I love them and I love singing them and it's always a good evening and it pays the mortgage [*laughs*]. We were out in the US last year. It was just me and my wife,

Jane, in the car with a couple of guitars. We drove from Indianapolis through Chicago, Detroit, up through North New York State and then eventually down to Georgia. We drove 3,303 miles by the end. It was just a lot of fun. Two people in love and enjoying life and then when you do performances, people are just so respectful, you know? We put on a good show.

"I've lived in America for 20 years, and now I'm in central California. I became an American last year, so now I can sing the national anthem at the Super Bowl. It's good to be an American. I always like to do songs that the audience wants to hear, and the songs I did with Vangelis are always good to do. And of course new songs, like three songs from the new album, but you always want to give the audience some songs that they know so it's important to balance it out. And I just sing the songs as I originally took them to the band."

October 2010 – February 2011. Yes conduct recording sessions at SARM West Coast Studios, Los Angeles, crafting the material that will become the *Fly From Here* record.

Geoff Downes on "Fly From Here":
"I think we attempted a pretty monumental piece, 'Fly From Here,' where we had the basic idea quite some years ago, but we crafted it and work on it to what became ultimately, Yes's longest ever piece, which clocks in at 23 minutes. But it sits well in the Yes catalogue. It's got a lot of the hallmarks of Yes; it's probably more likened to early period Yes, rather than some of the stuff in the '90s like *The Ladder* or *Open Your Eyes*. I think the album's more closely aligned with the earlier period of Yes."

Alan White on the same song:
"We're venturing back into what we did quite a while ago, which is have an album that is somewhat of a concept, namely the storyline in 'Fly From Here.' It's a suite, basically, and we haven't had a piece of music that's 23 minutes, or thereabouts, for quite a long time. The original song was from the early '80s. There's a live version of it from that period, but it's actually constructed more like a pop song, like Yes playing a pop song. So that was the original concept. But the idea was re-developed, and expanded upon through the lyrics, and made more in-depth by writing other pieces of music around it. Trevor Horn's at the helm really, for a lot of the album. Him and Benoit had a relationship where Trevor would have an idea and then he would get that across to Benoit, and then Benoit would try to develop it into something of his own nature. But most of the time, it was pretty much as Trevor had it in his head. Even lyrically, with slight modifications done by Chris. I think Benoit in one case modified some stuff, but a lot of the concept and the way the words rolled off the tongue, that was Trevor."

Chris Squire reveals "Fly From Here" has 1980s origins:

"Well, the whole thing didn't originate from there. I think that was just a connection from when I asked Trevor Horn to produce the album. The connection that we first had was that we did have this unfinished business, that we had never done a proper studio version of the original six-minute song, 'Fly From Here.' So that's how we started off, weaving that together. And then as we went on, we didn't just want to emulate a better version of what we had done in 1980—we wanted to turn it into a much larger, long-form, piece of Yes music, and that's when we decided to bring 'Fly From Here' into existence as a suite. So some of the material hails back to those days, that Trevor and Geoff had been working on, but other parts are brand-new stuff that we had come up with in the studio. So it was a mix."

November 17 – December 4, 2010. Yes take a break from working on the next record, and conduct their most extensive South American tour yet.

Chris Squire on reconvening with Geoff Downes:

"Geoff has a certain style, a certain texture, and a certain way he puts chords together; he's a very individual kind of keyboard player. And, of course, I have fond memories of that all working very well for the *Drama* album. And Trevor Horn really thought that we would make a better album if we got back together with Geoff, and I have to say he was probably right about that."

November 20, 2010. Anderson/Wakeman issue, on Voiceprint, *The Living Tree*, which was available previously only during the duo's UK tour. The album is a collection of new keyboard and vocal songs, augmented variously by Jon on guitar and Rick on synthesizer.

Jon Anderson discusses his *modus operandi* with Rick Wakeman on *The Living Tree*:

"He would send me music. I was on tour and I'd hear the music and sing in the hotels and send it back to him. By the time I finished the tour, I'd finished the album, and it's really a beautiful thing. It's got some beautiful energy and Rick's playing is beautiful. My lyrics were good and I honestly don't think I've ever sang better in my life. I'm even singing about the war in Afghanistan. The song '23/24/11' is about this guy who can't wait to get out of the army. He's had enough of that crap, and that's what I sing about. There are different songs in there; it's just a question of people spending time to listen, I suppose. It's not fast food."

Rick Wakeman on live dialogue with Jon Anderson:

"We did three tours: one in America, two in England. He's a great friend, Jon. But the funny thing about Jon is, he has a very addictive laugh and once Jon starts to laugh he can't stop. So I used to try and get him to laugh. We had such fun in those days, because he said to me before the very first tour, 'What should we talk about between our pieces?' And I said, 'It doesn't matter. You start talking and I will interrupt you.' He said, 'Will it work?' And I said, 'Trust me. I do this all the time on British TV.' So that's what I did. And we had just great fun."

November 22, 2010. Kanye West issues his fifth album, *My Beautiful Dark Twisted Fantasy*. The lead track, "Dark Fantasy" includes a clear and prominent sample of Jon Anderson's voice, from Mike Oldfield's "In High Places," a co-write by Oldfield and Anderson.

Jon Anderson's current musical tastes and Kanye West:

"I love Mahavishnu, Weather Report. I love some new songs now and again. I enjoyed Nirvana and bands like that. I've seen U2 and Bruce Springsteen. They're great! There's great music out there, but don't hit me over the head and say, 'You've got to have a hit record.' Of course I'd love to have a hit record. I mean, my voice is on a #1 album right now. Yeah, it makes me feel like, 'Hey, I wrote a rock opera 20 years ago and I've got to get Kanye West to sing on it. Or rap on it.' He's got a great producer. I think some of their producers have their heads screwed on because it reaches so many different people. They've woken up and realized that there are different kinds of music; it doesn't have to all be about sex, drugs, rock 'n' roll, and bling-bling. It's all about money, money, money, money, money. But then they think, 'Wow, that band is so cool, man. Let's sample them.'"

2011

January 6, 2011. Yes issue a two CD and single DVD package called *Union Live*, documenting the band's 1991 tour in support of *Union*, featuring a show at the Shoreline Amphitheatre in Mountain View, California, August 8, 1991.

March 6 – April 4, 2011. Yes conduct their Rites Of Spring Tour of the US.

May 28 – 30, 2011. Yes play two dates in Mexico.

June 6, 2011. Jon Anderson issues *Survival & Other Stories*, on which he writes lyrics and sings them in accompaniment to music provided to him.

Jon Anderson talks about working with people all over the world:

"I think it was about six years ago that I put an advertisement on my website for musicians to send me one minute of their music; if I liked it, I would get back to them, and I wound up working with a couple dozen people around the world. And of course they were very talented and so I started writing songs and coming up with ideas, like operas, symphonic music, guitar concertos and violin concertos. You start working with people who are interested in developing musical ideas and it's never-ending. It's quite amazing, really, and once I got that going I actually got really sick in 2008 and so I didn't do anything for a year. After that, though, I started thinking that maybe I should put together some of these songs. I had about 30 or so that were very good, and I picked out 11 to put on the album. It's just me working with people around the world, and you come up with some very interesting styles of music, you know?

"I think that because I got so sick and nearly died, I'm very thankful to be alive and I'm more appreciative of nature. We're all spiritual beings and we're all on a sacred journey anyway; it's whether we want to believe it or not [*laughs*]. It's a natural thing for me to want to sing about it. As you get older, you get wiser and a little bit more creative in terms of lyrical content. You tend to be a little bit more inspired, and that inspiration just always appeared."

June 22, 2011. Yes issue *Fly From Here*, featuring lead singer Benoit David, who had been touring with the band at this point for nearly three years.

Chris Squire discusses *Fly From Here* and breaking in Benoit David:

"It's actually our 20th studio album of original material, and we're just making the best of it. And I think we pulled that off quite well, actually. As you know, we had Trevor Horn producing it, and he has a certain style. It's also that he has a team that he's worked with for the last 20 years or so that he knows what kind of sounds he likes and the way he likes things mixed. And, of course, actually, strangely enough, there's a guy named Tim Weidner who's an engineer, who is also a producer, who co-produced *Magnification* for us. So in fact it's the same engineer. So the Trevor Horn production was a very important part of the mix. I'm very happy with everything.

"As for Benoit, we had to make that move, because the band had been stagnant for about four years, and we were about to go on tour with Jon, in 2008, and then he took a turn for the worse with his respiratory problem. So at that point, really, we had to just decide that if we were going to carry on with Yes as a live, working unit, we would have to bring somebody else in. And that's basically what we did. I mean, we could have held on longer for him, but it seemed like we weren't really moving forward. Especially not doing any new music, and not doing anything to keep the Yes machine moving forward. You know, the ifs, ands or buts about whether he wanted to stay on, but not tour... who knows? I can't say what his physical ability would have been. But it's worked out the way it has worked out.

"Writing-wise, I tried to encourage him on *Fly From Here* to get into writing melodies and lyrics, and he had a go with that. We came up with some successful ideas that were used, and I hope that he continues now. He's got a bit more confidence in that area. Because originally, when he got in the band, he said he'd never written a thing in his life. He said he didn't know how to. So I've been encouraging him. Primarily we really wanted him to be able to perform the vocal arrangements of Jon Anderson—let's be specific. But funny thing is, on the new album, a lot of people have said Benoit actually sounds more like Trevor Horn than he does Jon Anderson! But to give him his own credit, he did very well in this album, and I think he sounds like Benoit David."

Alan White's take on Yes's 20ᵗʰ album:

"I think the production is great on it. Trevor just seems to know how he wants things to sound, and he gets a lot of clarity, especially from my point of view, which is the drums and the rhythm section. We spent half a day on each track, on the right drum sounds for the right song. And that's what we do, usually. So the attention to detail, as far as the drums go is pretty fundamental in what the band does in the studio. Tim Weidner, the engineer, works very closely with Trevor, and he has a lot of great ideas too. He's done lots of albums with Trevor, and they pool their thoughts together. No real big tricks or anything; it's just having an ear for what it should sound like for a band like Yes in 2011.

"Actually, quite a lot of it was a concept done by Trevor Horn but, in addition to that, Chris got more involved with Trevor, on writing the title track. Of course Geoff Downes is on keyboards, so we have some really, really great chords. And then Steve had a solo guitar piece that he wanted to present, and then he also had one song and Chris had one song, and then we all wrote a thing called 'Into The Storm' together.

"As for the artwork, I didn't really see it until most of the album had been done. We were just finishing some of the overdubs in London, and Roger came by and he had an idea he had talked about and started on a while back. And then he presented it to us and we all liked it and he updated it a bit. Roger's almost like another member of the band. He reads into and listens to our music, and sees what that is, and then portrays it visually. And he's a big fan—he loves pretty much everything that the band puts out."

July 4 – August 4, 2011. Yes, in support of *Fly From Here*, conduct a co-headlining tour of the US with Styx. Geoff Downes returns as keyboardist, replacing Oliver Wakeman.

Geoff Downes on the magic and challenge of Yes music:

"It's been a big learning curve, because I've studied it in great detail, and realized that a lot of the parts are very, very well-crafted. And I can see why Yes had such a big following, because not just the keyboard parts, but you put all the different instrumentalists together, and you have counterpoint. And it all revolved around Jon Anderson's voice. Then you were left with this great music that had so many subtle elements to it. And certainly a lot of Rick's stuff is very,

very interesting. Tony Kaye's stuff is probably a bit more basic, I'd say, more chord parts rather than virtuosity and lead lines. Nonetheless, on the impact, in terms of Yes's music, Tony did great work on *Time And A Word* and on *The Yes Album*, and Rick, obviously on *Close To The Edge* and *Fragile* and *Going For The One*, which are very experimental albums."

Jon Anderson reflects on not singing on the Yes/Styx tour:
"They don't want me in the band because I'm too much—what's the word?—I don't like it when they're not playing good, and I would tell them. They're nice guys and they're doing what they want to do, going around the world like Journey. It's just gigs, you know? They make money and do their thing and that's OK. The fact that they moved on when I was sick was very disrespectful, but I've said that before and that's the way life is sometimes. They're a group of guys out there trying to make money, so God bless them for that, and they're playing music that I didn't write so what do I care? I don't mind Benoit singing the songs. The only thing that really bothered me when it happened was that they should've told people who was in the band and they didn't. They just went out as Yes, and obviously, without me or Rick, they're not really Yes. People would go to see them and think, 'Gosh, Jon looks very young.' And he doesn't really even look like me. It's just that when people pay to see their favourite band, they want to see who they want to see, of course. But people get sick and die and that's life; the music carries on."

September 13, 2011. Music Club Deluxe issues the two CD *Wonderous Stories: The Best Of Yes*, which is reissued with Roger Dean-approved artwork in 2014.

November 3 – December 9, 2011. Yes promote *Fly From Here* with European dates.

Alan White praises Benoit David:
"Benoit, he's not writing lyrics so much, but his voice sounds really good on the album. His voice is very, very similar to Jon Anderson, but not exactly like Jon. Some people say if you close your eyes, you can see Jon. And he was the only guy we considered. It seemed as if what we were doing matched what he was doing and so we decided on not pursuing anybody else. It takes a year, or more like two years, to break a new singer in. It's hard enough working with Yes, but it seems to work."

Chris Squire on his bass sound:
"That's a big question because in actual fact, I'm using different sounds on different songs on *Fly From Here*, on different tracks. On 'Into The Storm' I reintroduced the use of the Neutron pedal, which actually hails from the '70s, as an effect. And I did use it at the end of the '70s, on the *Tormato* album quite

a bit, and I haven't used it since. So I pulled that one out from the archives and had a go with that. So that's good, and then my Rickenbacker; I used the classic sound quite a bit on the album, and then I'm also using a different bass on 'The Man You Always Wanted Me To Be,' and on other tracks I used an eight-string bass. So yeah, there's combinations of sounds, quite a varied collection on the album. I'm pretty happy with my performance and arrangement of the bass parts. We covered a number of different approaches to sounds, and then of course I sing, 'The Man You Always Wanted Me To Be', which I thought turned out well, so I'm happy with that."

November 28, 2011. Anderson/Wakeman issue *The Living Tree In Concert Part One.*

Jon Anderson's motivation to continue making music:

"Well, everybody has the same light inside; they might be horrible, cruel people, but they've got to live with that and live with the karma of their darkness and sleepless nights. People that screw people always get their comeuppance. The challenge is to be a good person and to give as much as you can. That's why I tour. I love singing and I love spreading good energy. I'm gonna do it until I decide to go to another planet [*laughs*]. I can't believe I'm doing this. I started my first band in 1963, so I'm almost 50 years in now, coming up. It's an incredible life and dream. I've loved every moment, and the next 20 years are going to be better in my mind. I mean, what am I gonna say? 'Hey I've got a new album out and it's crap!' No, it's great and I love what I've done. I believe in it and I believe in my next project and the next one after that and so on. I'm just happy to be alive."

November 29, 2011. Yes issue a two CD and single 55-minute DVD package called *In The Present – Live From Lyon*, which features short-lived Yes vocalist Benoit David, from a show in 2009.

2012

February 2012. Jon Davison is announced as Yes's new lead singer, replacing Benoit David, who initially is sidelined with a respiratory infection. Benoit is replaced when it is determined he won't be able to perform the upcoming booked spring dates.

Geoff Downes on the two Jons – Anderson and Davison:

"It's hard to say where we are at the moment, but since Jon came in, it's really given the band a huge boost. Benoit did a very good job, and we did an album with Benoit. But since Jon came in, it's really reinvigorated a lot of the older material, and he certainly delivers it really, really well every night. Who knows, as regards Jon Anderson? It's something that's not really in my control. I've not really ever worked with Jon Anderson. I know the other guys speak to him from time to time. People say it was an acrimonious departure, but it's probably not as much as people might think. People get on. When you get to your 60s, nobody wants to be carrying too many grudges around with you [*laughs*]."

Steve Howe on being asked if Jon Anderson and Rick Wakeman will be back in Yes:
"Well, how in hell do I know? I wouldn't particularly say that it is on the agenda. People have said the cliché like we have burned bridges and all of that. We are realistic people, so in the sense of realism, for Yes to evolve we had to be a strong group and we had to have people who were committed to it to warrant a position in the band. In other words, if you come in and say to Yes, 'I play the drums but in Yes I am going to play the bongos,' we would say, 'But we want a drummer.' You've got to be able to provide the full story.

"Everybody in this group needs to accept that we look at the entire career of this group. We don't just look at little pockets when certain people were in the group—we don't do that anymore. We look at the group as a whole. Of course, we do focus a lot on the '70's but there were a few lineups there. In a way, that is the commitment. It is not about Jon and Rick now. It is about who can do these tours and who can perform the repertoire from 1968 to 2012. If you can do that, then you have an opportunity to be in Yes. I'm not going to say Rick and Jon can't do that. I will say that I don't think that is what they want to do. But that is what Yes demands. We want artists who can come in and perform with an open heart right across the board. I guess that is the key to it."

April 1 – 29, 2012. New vocalist Jon Davison is put through his paces in New Zealand, Australia, Japan, Indonesia and Hawaii.

Alan White's pleased Jon Davison is in the band:
"It's very easy, he's great, Jon. He fit like a glove immediately. He's a big fan of Yes music from the past, and he was just really tuned into what the band was doing, and he's got an absolutely great voice for Yes. And he's a really, great, all-around musician. He plays bass guitar and a little bit of keyboards. He's a very, very talented guy and just an all-around nice guy."

May 8, 2012. Trevor Rabin issues his first new set of solo studio material since 1989, in the form of *Jacaranda*, a diverse and mostly instrumental album of jazz, rock, world music, prog, classical and bluegrass.

Trevor Rabin on stepping away from soundtrack work to make *Jacaranda*:
"There is a group of middle-aged women who have followed my career; they keep in touch with my assistant. They keep asking him, 'When is he going to put an album out? He has not put an album out since 1989.' My God, I've put 17 albums out since then. They don't consider my movie soundtracks music.

"I never get to do anything challenging on guitar anymore, I really look at it like I am a session guitarist. I do what is specifically needed for the movie but I don't get to stretch out and really play. I decided to finally do this album and I consciously didn't worry about genre or what kind of songs they were going to be. I would do three weeks on the album and then I would do two movies and then I would come back to it. It really didn't take long to do the album; it just took a long period of time to finish because of all of the other things I had to do.

"I haven't enjoyed anything as much as this, ever. I did a lot of stuff with Yes, Manfred Mann and with my solo career, but I never have enjoyed playing as much as I've enjoyed playing on this album. I not only played the guitar, but I played piano and organ. I got great drummers to come in and Tal Wilkenfeld is a fantastic bass player and was a joy to work with.

"I love my work, and my work for the last 12 years, or so, has been making song scores, but I love going on vacation. I really do enjoy doing the movie stuff and I'm not going to stop. I am also not going to let that side of things get in the way of doing this, which is my favourite thing to do.

"I expected to get a lot of flack that there is no demographic to focus on with this album. I think it is a good thing because I like all kinds of music. Essentially, I am a guitar player and I love many styles. If you put a gun against my head and said that I could only play one style of guitar for the rest of my life, then I would probably say some kind of fusion. It would have to have a big sound and I would have to be able to dig in a little bit. I would hate to be restricted to I/IV/V type patterns. I've always been one to sit and play for hours upon hours. To find something challenging and difficult leads me to play it until I get it down and then I get bored with it and go to something else. I have always been really heavily into sound and how that influences what you play. If you have a sound that leans one way, then you're going to play that way."

May 1, 2012. 101 Distribution issue the 17-track *Yes Family Tree*, an assortment of Yes tracks from archival compilation *Beyond & Before* plus solo, collaborative and offshoot band work.

May 28, 2012. Chris Squire and ex-Genesis guitarist Steve Hackett, recording as Squackett, issue an album called *A Life Within A Day*.

Chris Squire explains how the Steve Hackett collaboration came about:
"We'd finished the album actually in 2010, but both of us got so busy with our individual lives that we weren't chasing a record deal particularly hard. But we eventually put it all that in place and signed a deal. We're singing together and sound pretty good together!

"But the story began when Steve originally played on my Swiss Choir album. Obviously, the friendship was a very important element of the situation. We had already become very good friends, so it was easy to work with Steve and, of course, with Roger King who was involved as a keyboard player and producer. So it went very easily along, with no pressure, and it was easy for us to write music together. There was no plan. It's just we liked each other's songs and I was playing on some of those already—Steve gave them to me to play some bass on—and after a while, we just realised that we were making an album, in a way, together. And we agreed to carry on in that direction as a friendship and also a musical journey.

"It's strange but when we first met, in 2007, I thought Steve was a guitar player. I did not know that this guy was actually a good singer. I realized that after he played me his demos. And the good thing that happened was that after we started singing together and doing harmonies together it sounded very good. And once again, thanks to Roger King for his production of the vocals. So yes, the harmonies are important."

July 10 – August 21, 2012. Yes tour the US, along with solitary dates in Canada and a Mexican date, supported by Procol Harum.

July 20, 2012. Asia issue their 13th album, *XXX*, which reaches #134 on the Billboard charts.

Geoff Downes on *XXX*:

"Whenever we make a new album, it's always a challenge. Not only to write the material, but also make sure we can do it justice in the live setting. The reward is knowing we have new music to play to people, not just relying on the early 'classic' material. Simply, nothing has really changed since we began the band. The main suspects are all still there—alive and well, thankfully! Historically a fair percentage of the band compositions have emanated from John [Wetton] and me. That's not to say that that diminishes Steve's contributions. Actually, Steve has three co-writes on *XXX*, which is the same as he contributed on *Asia*.

"But yeah, a full group composition might be interesting for the next album. The music is usually jointly collated. It's quite rare that any of our songs end up as being the whole of one of our individual ideas. I think that's the beauty of it and why it works so well, is that we weave together two of our ideas and come up with something different. John does most of the lyrics, but I'll throw in the odd title or line here and there. I think it's important for John that he believes in what he's singing about.

"The thing with this band is that we are all very different personalities. In the early days, this could at times cause conflict, or conversely work in a very positive fashion. Since we got back together, we have focused collectively on the latter. There's a very strong level of respect between the four of us, and the chemistry is still there. That's what's important. But aside from recording the new Asia CD, my return to Yes has been a real privilege—great fun to be back, involved with those guys again."

November 13, 2012. Gonzo issue a two CD Anderson Bruford Wakeman Howe set called *Live At The NEC Oct 24th 1989*, which features King Crimson and Peter Gabriel master bassist Tony Levin.

2013

January 13, 2013. Steve Howe leaves Asia.

March 1 – April 12, 2013. Yes embark on the Three Album Tour, on which, for most dates, they played in their entirety *The Yes Album*, *Close To The Edge*, and *Going For The One*.

Geoff Downes on reproducing these three albums live:

"It's all quite difficult. Yes music is complex by default. You look at stuff like 'Awaken' off of *Going For The One* and some of the stuff off *Close To The Edge*, it's quite demanding material. Not just for a keyboard player, but to get the whole band gelling together, to be able to perform it. So it's been a lot of work to get it up to speed, but I think we've got to the point now where we're actually playing the albums very well, and it's very rewarding to come up on stage every night after delivering these monumental pieces of work.

"As a record, *Going For The One*, the production is quite different. Obviously, Eddie Offord didn't do *Going For The One*, so in some ways that's a very different album in terms of its context and production. Whereas I think *The Yes Album*, *Close To The Edge*, *Fragile*, *Topographic* had much more cohesion in terms of that early period, with *Going For The One* representing quite a departure. Not in a bad way—I think in a good way—but that was one of the reasons why we chose that album as opposed to something like *Fragile*, because it showed Yes in another light, and it was important for this tour that we could do that. The other idea was to do *Drama* or *90125* or even some of the later stuff, but I think we settled on these three albums as a sort of definitive Yes."

March 7, 2013. A sad day in Yes annals. Original Yes guitarist Peter Banks dies of heart failure at his home in Barnet, London, aged 65.

March 25 – 30, 2013. Taking a break from regular tour dates, Yes play the Cruise To The Edge Prog Rock Festival, on the MSC Poesia cruise ship.

May 16 – May 30, 2013. Yes perform nine dates in South America.

July 6 – August 12, 2013. Yes conduct a US tour plus one Canadian date, continuing with their full album concept.

Geoff Downes on the pacing of the show:

"It's a combination of trying to keep it fun and entertaining, but it's also paying homage to these three great albums they recorded back in the '70s. The crowds have been enormously receptive, because they get to hear these more obscure, hidden gems like 'Perpetual Change' and 'Wonderous Stories' and things like that that probably they wouldn't normally play, and did not play for a number of years in the context of a live show. It's like putting on the vinyl and playing one side and then turning it over and playing the next side; you try to stay to the original order. Bands that we were listening to back in the '70s, they'd come out and they'd hear these albums in their entirety, and it brings back a lot of great memories for them, either at school or college or whatever, or in their cars or wherever they were when they were hearing this stuff when it was actually originally conceived. Bands have done two albums, but three is a monumental challenge. Some of this music is very, very complex, but I think we pull it off. And the fact that they've booked another tour for us starting in July, I think shows that there's an appetite for it, and people are liking it."

December 24, 2013. Atlantic issues a Yes box set called *The Studio Albums: 1969 – 1987*. Fans complain about the quality of the 12 individual card sleeves (particularly that the discs fall out of them), along with the tiny poster and lack of booklet. The discs however are remastered, and there are bonus tracks.

2014

January 6 – March 14, 2014. Yes work at Neptune Studios in Los Angeles on material for their projected 21st album.

Chris Squire on making Yes's 21st album:

"It was a bit of a whirlwind experience. Normally, when we go about making a new album, it's usually over a period of four or five months, maybe six. *Fly From Here* was done over a period of sort of six months. And this album, we've done all the recording so far in a two-month period, which is stepping up the pace for us.

"Of course, the difference is it's the first one with Jon Davison, our new vocalist, who has come in, and we welcome his songwriting ideas. Because unlike Benoit, who was a non-writer, Jon Davison is quite prolific. And, of course, he's had ideas probably for a few years now that he's been eager to put into action, and we've been giving him the opportunity to do that. So, Jon ended up working with each of the rest of us over a period of time, writing on a different couple of songs each. That was a good way to go about it, because we went with Jon's new injection of ideas, with each of the original members. Jon certainly brought a broad spectrum of taste when it came to the music. We've also kind of looked more at the strength of the song, the song power on this album, and I think you're going to be pleasantly surprised. There are some really good songs, actually, and all in one place, all in one album."

Alan White on producer Roy Thomas Baker:
"He's a great guy and he knows the band really well, and he knows what Yes should be doing now, kind of thing. Everybody got along really well with Roy; he's a good friend. The drugs aren't there any more, that's for sure. But he's still 'extreme' in some of his manners. He only makes his own coffee, because he only drinks it if he makes it. But from the sound end of it, he knew what he liked. And he would tell us when there was something that didn't quite fit in. And he spent a long time getting the drum sound. I think I had something like 18 or 20 microphones on my drums when I was recording this one. So it's pretty extensive."

Jon Davison on the extent of vintage technology used on the record:
"It's actually a hybrid of the two. There was a lot of emphasis on using traditional gear in the studio. Roy reinforced this by implementing the use of analog gear that he personally brought in. I think this approach translates quite well in the overall sound of *Heaven & Earth*. Upon hearing the record, Taylor Hawkins also pointed out that he thought the sound of the album was very organic. We've been so subjectively involved in the making of the album that it has been great to hear other people's outside perspectives."

Steve Howe on his approach to songwriting on what would become *Heaven & Earth*:
"Well, I had plenty of songs. I could have written, like Jon could've; either of us could've written the whole album. But we didn't want to—that wouldn't be Yes. And so we had plenty to collaborate on and plenty for my next project [*laughs*]. But, having said that, it's what people go for, you know, in the songs. The guys heard 'It Was All We Knew,' Jon liked it, and we did 'It Was All We Knew.' I didn't know whether it was going to make it through the sometimes dubious course of being talked about, being recorded, and then being overdubbed and then being mixed. There were places along there, with all the songs... there were risky moments.

"But that's the way albums are constructed. I mean, I have not changed. I just do the same thing. It just so happened that 'It Was All We Knew' was a song that stayed like it was originally, more or less. Then the other two songs that I helped with... I wrote most of 'Step Beyond' and Jon collaborated with me. And in reverse, Jon wrote most of 'Believe Again' and I collaborated with him. So, you know, we have done that and maybe we'll do that a lot more together in the future.

"So, as a guitarist, we make albums. I held back a lot 'cos I said we need a lot of material. Well, we only had enough for an album by the time we were ready, but most of it had been semi-approved and very, very little had been throwback because we thought that the material needed to be fresh. And, for the most part, that's what we did. So that material was not only comparatively fresh, it was recorded starting January and then it was released in, what, July-August. So, the fact is it could be the freshest Yes album ever as far as it being created and then released.

"Whether that's a good thing I can't say. In a way it isn't totally a good thing because we could've spent a bit more time on it. We were up against the wall. We had a tour coming and we just tried our hardest. We worked incredibly hard to bring the album in. But we could have spent another week on mixing and refining it. But, there again, we didn't; and we couldn't. So, we had to kind of move on. That happens."

March 19 – April 5, 2014. Yes conduct an extensive Canadian tour, throwing in two US dates for good measure.

March 25, 2014. Asia issue their self-produced 14th album, *Gravitas*, featuring three-quarters of their classic lineup, with Steve Howe replaced by Sam Coulson.

April 7 – 12, 2014. Yes play the Cruise To The Edge Prog Rock Festival for a second time, this time on the MSC Divina.

April 29 – June 5, 2014. Yes mount an extensive European tour.

July 5 – August 24, 2014. Yes undertake a US tour on which they play material from *Heaven & Earth* as well as playing *Fragile* and *Close To The Edge* in their entirety, plus assorted hits.

July 16, 2014. Yes issue the Roy Thomas Baker-produced *Heaven & Earth*, featuring Jon Davison on vocals.

Alan White on new singer Jon Davison's lyrical world:
"In some ways he's quite similar to Jon Anderson but he's got his own style too. He knows not to tread on that kind of stuff too much, and so he talks about reality a lot within the framework of Jon's cinematic lyrics, as it were. Overall, *Heaven & Earth* is a very song-based album, but it has a lot of Yes-isms built into it as well, some intricate playing. But the song values on this are really, really good. Jon Davison writes really great melodies, memorable melodies which you'll be singing if you hear them a few times. It's the kind of thing if you're walking around, you'll find yourself singing it. At least I did [*laughs*]. But then there's some experimental stuff. 'Subway Walls' has some very strange time signatures in it. I think there's one section where everything is in 17/8 time. So

you can call that experimental, if you want, but it swings as well, which is the main thing. Yeah, it's a way to divide up what's happening in the framework of what the song is at that moment. Where if you count it, it works out to 17/8. Some of those things, I don't even count until afterwards."

Jon Davison on bedding into the band:
"I got to know them really well and their composing styles and patterns and pace. And I was really quite comfortable with it especially because we started one on one. I started in Phoenix with Chris, we solidified a few ideas together, then I went up to Seattle and worked with Alan, and then to the UK and went out to the countryside with Steve. I was there for about a week. We got a lot done as well. Then I went to Wales and worked with Geoff one on one. It was really very comfortable and very exciting too."

Journalist Pete Pardo:
If you've been reading reactions on the internet, the band are really taking a pounding with this new one. While some of the criticism might have some merit, *Heaven & Earth* is actually one of those albums that takes time to grow on you. It's clearly not a symphonic prog masterpiece by any stretch of the imagination, and for many the songs here will be way too laid back and "safe" by Yes standards, but the songs are actually quite pleasant and memorable. Davison's vocal performance is reason enough to check out the CD; in fact, he's easily the MVP here, and I'd go so far as to say that he overshadows the rest of the band, who overall sound just a tad too relaxed.

"With dazzling cover art from Roger Dean, one quick look at *Heaven & Earth* and any Yes fan hopes and prays for an album that brings that classic sound that the band are known for. Sadly, that doesn't really happen here. It's a shame that Yes have not been able to capture the magic they created on the studio tracks from the two *Keys To Ascension* albums, but you have to wonder if the absence of Rick Wakeman on all these studio efforts since then is the reason the band has lost their 'proggy' touch. End result is that *Heaven & Earth* is an OK album, more of a nice pop record than a prog masterpiece from these legends, which, considering the high standards of their fan base, isn't going to cut it. More keyboards from Downes would have helped things out greatly, and perhaps a few more adventurous passages woven into some of these songs also couldn't have hurt.

July 25, 2014. A Kickstarter campaign begins at 2:00 p.m. Eastern to fund an album by Jon Anderson and Jean-Luc Ponty, a.k.a. Anderson Ponty Band.

Jon Anderson on the formation of his new band:
"I think most artists sort of get into looking at the next ten or 20 years ahead, and that's what I do; I've always done that. And it's a progression of music.

You think artistically and musically, you always want to develop. And that's the way I feel. I got in touch with Jean-Luc in 2014, and we kept bumping into each other. We got in touch and then, basically, I sang on one or two of his early, what do you call them, hits or commercial songs that he had out, music in the '70s, and I just sang on top of them, some ideas, and I was just singing along with him. And I sent the ideas to him, and we sort of hit it off and had a strong connection about music. I loved Mahavishnu and Frank Zappa, and he actually worked with them, plus Stanley Clarke, all these really very exciting musicians he's worked with over the years. So it just seemed a natural event that we could actually write together. And that's what we did. Over a period of a couple of months, we wrote some things, and then said, well, 'Why don't we get together and maybe do a couple of shows?' And that's how anything starts—it's a natural progression.

"As far as lyrics go, it's ever-expanding. I think you get to a stage in your writing where you're getting to that place of being a bit clearer [*laughs*], if you like, more defined about what you're trying to say on every level. Part of the Anderson Ponty project, we've worked with people who have helped with the project through Kickstarter. And part of the deal with some of the people who have invested some money in Kickstarter is that they wanted lyrics that I'd written, handwritten, as a present, you know? So the other day I was rewriting lyrics that I wrote in 1978. I think it was 'Song Of Seven,' the song. And to re-read and then write out what I'd written—because I'd never really looked at it for 30 years, 40 years—it just seemed like, 'Wow, what was I thinking in those days?' It's very spontaneous. Although I'm still very spontaneous when I do lyrics."

September 20, 2014. The newly christened Anderson Ponty Band play their first show, in advance of a full Kickstarter-funded album and a slate of tour dates for 2015. The concert, performed at the Wheeler Opera House in Denver, Colorado, is recorded for future release.

Jon Anderson enthuses about his new bandmates:
"Yeah, the rhythm section, you've got Rayford Griffin and Baron Browne. Rayford, this drummer is seriously hot [*laughs*]; he's really amazing. And Baron is just pocket bass—he just does it. It's like when we're rehearsing, I never talk to him about what to play. He just plays everything correctly. And it just flows beautifully, you know? And Wally Minko is a brilliant keyboard player. And, of course, Jean-Luc is a master. He truly is a master of the violin, and he's very, very musical. And we were just... we're really just getting to know each other. We spent a couple of weeks together, and made the video, and made the record, and it's turning out to be very, very exciting. It's taken its time, like anything. But when I spoke to Jean-Luc last week, I just talked about when we're on tour, we're going to be able to spread our wings. Now that we know the music, the

songs, we need to spread our wings and find out who we truly are on tour, as a band. And he agrees. He just says, well, that's why we got together."

November 10 – November 29, 2014. Yes play New Zealand, Australia and Japan, continuing with the set structure from the summer US tour.

How Jon Davison keeps his voice in shape on the road:
"I've been meditating for years and, on tour, my meditation routine is definitely an important role in helping me to acquire a clear perspective of the situation. I follow a strict diet and vocal warm-up routine daily."

November 15 – 19, 2014. Yes play the Cruise To The Edge Prog Rock Festival for a third time, this time aboard the Norwegian Cruise Line's Norwegian Pearl; as usual, around Florida and points south.

December 8, 2014. Yes issue a CD and DVD live album called *Like It Is: Yes At The Bristol Hippodrome*, capturing a show from May 11th, earlier in the year on the Three Album Tour. It is the band's first live album featuring Jon Davison. Although the live show featured three albums played live in entirety, for the purposes of the recording, *Close To The Edge* is omitted.

2015

April 11 – 18, 2015. Induction week at the Rock and Roll Hall of Fame. Yes is snubbed yet again, but a revolution is brewing similar to the populist demonstrations concerning Rush and the Hall. The author writes a piece for *Goldmine* magazine arguing for Yes's qualification credentials, as well as Deep Purple's, his #1 pick for overdue induction. But others talk about Yes as well, including industry guru Bob Lefsetz.

Billy Sherwood argues for Yes's induction:
"Why they're not in the Hall of Fame is beyond me. It's just crazy. After all these years, in service of the music business, and record sales and touring and just making phenomenal records that you continue to hear on the radio today... for Yes not to be acknowledged, it just seems stupid. But I mean, the idea of voting between two bands or whatever, put them all in. What are you doing? It's like a dinosaur museum going, 'Which dinosaur should we bring in?' Well, bring them all in [*laughs*].

"But for legacy, with Yes, at the top of that column would have to be the musicality involved in all of the records, and the writing and how creative it was. No one has done it—and continues to do it—quite like they do. They are a unique band that has a sound unto itself, and a creative process that yields amazing works. It was pushing the envelope with music in a way that hadn't been done before, and walking the line between rock 'n' roll band and the orchestral. I guess that's where prog rock comes in to it, and lends an identifier to all sides of symphonic music, mixed with jazz and rock 'n' roll. Yes is definitely a band where each member was a virtuoso, and the writing came together in a unique way that was just magical."

Jon Davison wades into the debate:

"I too have wished this honour for Yes. They've certainly earned it. Will it happen? Despite all the success Yes has achieved throughout the years, progressive rock has yet to be accepted as a legitimate genre to the majority. If that day comes, no doubt, Yes will be acknowledged as one of the most prominent and successful pioneers of the movement."

March 10, 2015. Rhino issues a two CD Steve Howe package called *Anthology: A Solo Career Retrospective.*

May 19, 2015. Yes issue *Progeny: Seven Shows From Seventy-Two,* a 14 CD box set consisting of seven full show's from the band's Close To The Edge Tour. There is also a highlights version formatted as two CDs or triple vinyl.

Jon Anderson on his legacy:

"Well, I'm amazed, frankly. I get a lot of young people coming to my concerts... I was playing with the San Antonio Youth Group just a few weeks ago, and these kids love to do 'Owner Of A Lonely Heart' and 'Roundabout, 'And You And I,' or 'State Of Independence.' They don't really know 'State Of Independence' but man, they're loving playing it. And the audience loved it. We did 'Starship Trooper' and some new songs, like a reggae song. Everybody had a great time, and that's my legacy—I'm still up there enjoying life."

May 19, 2015. Pre-Yes outfit The Syn see the release of *The Syn Live Rosfest.* In conjunction with the 2009 live set (which also includes a DVD), re-released are *Syndestructible, Original Syn,* and *Big Sky.*

May 19, 2015. It is announced that Chris Squire has been diagnosed with Acute Erythroid Leukemia and will be undergoing chemotherapy in his hometown of Phoenix, Arizona. Filling in for Chris is Billy Sherwood.

June 23, 2015. Asia issue a live two CD and DVD called *Axis XXX Live In San Francisco MMXII,* on Frontiers. The set celebrates a show by the original lineup at the Regency Ballroom from November 7th, 2012.

July 3, 2015. Yes issue a two CD/DVD live set called *Like It Is: Yes At The Mesa Arts Center,* featuring *Fragile* and *Close To The Edge* performed in their entireties. It gets its US release on July 10.

Alan White on his retirement plans:

"None really. I love living in Seattle. I have a nice house by the lake, and I've got a really nice boat—I spend a bit of time boating. I have my own band here in Seattle, and I do shows with that band on occasions, just to keep my foot in the local scene here. But most of my life is taken up with Yes. I mean, we're touring a lot of this year. And then I'm enrolled in a lot of charity functions around the area. I'm one of the founders of Music Aid Northwest. We do charity events and we raise money for music in schools in the state of Washington. So we've made a lot of money for the schools. Because with education, music is the first thing that gets cut. So, we kind of fund schools for buying instruments and things like that. It's a worthwhile situation."

August 7 – September 12, 2015. Yes tour North America with Toto as co-headliner.

Steve Howe on projecting spirituality through his playing:

"That is the easiest thing. There is a channel that I don't ask too many questions about, prophesize about or speculate about. I open myself up to the world and I get ready to play. The opening is really just playing as well as you can with as much concentration and purposefulness as you can. I think that is a reasonably easy channel, but I am a professional musician and I have been doing it for years. I don't think a guitarist should just walk in a venue and play. I don't think any musician should treat himself that poorly. He should center himself and get ready in a disciplined way. He should think about the show in his mind. You want to get on there and have everyone pull together and accelerate, not just go out there and play. If you think like that, it helps. Other people might have four beers and go onstage [*laughs*]. There are different ways of doing it. It depends how important it is to you."

Jon Anderson on creating a musical style:

"People thought Mozart was an idiot, you know, and he died with no money. And people didn't like Van Gogh because they thought he was an idiot, and he died with no money. I'm so happy that I'm still alive and that people still come to my shows, like these young people. I can see in their eyes that they're really inspired to hear songs that they've just learned about, and they're 16 or 18 years old and you can feel that energy. They're digging it. I've always believed that Yes's music was, and still is, a very different style of music. It's very hard for a band to create a style of music, and I'm so proud that we did. We created a style that was unique, and there are always going to be critics, but I don't make music for critics. I just make music hoping someone is going to like it, and if they don't, well then, go listen to other stuff, man, and don't give me a hard time [*laughs*]."

Time And A Word

•••

June 27, 2015. Christopher Russell Edward Squire passes away, after his mercifully brief battle with leukemia. Chris's wife Scotland issues a statement on July 1st indicating that his cremation had been set for 3:00 p.m. Phoenix time. She quips that the time is tentative, given that Chris is well known for being late. "Fish" leaves behind the distinction of being the only member of Yes to have played on every album, to have been in every incarnation of the band, and to have been the heart and soul of Yes.

Steve Hackett's tribute to Chris Squire:
"We were great friends and the last thing that Chris recorded was on my current album, *Wolflight*; he played on a track called 'Love Song To A Vampire.' My feelings are, emotionally, it was terrible to say goodbye to Chris. Oddly enough, we've just had a communication from Chris's widow this very day. We wrote to her and we've just heard back this very day, my wife and I, Jo, from Scotland (Chris's wife) and it's nice to know she's coming out of that dark tunnel now. Chris will be missed. He was a fantastic character, a wonderful bass player, tremendous bandleader, and he was great fun to be with. I loved working with him. We had great times, both in the studio and recording in my home. And also we had great fun doing the *Squackett* album together, Squire and Hackett.

"Sometimes [*laughs*], we were recording in an apartment that I had in London, and very quickly, I came to realize that, at the time, Chris often didn't surface until about four o'clock in the afternoon. So then I'd drive from Twickenham to Chelsea, where he was living, pick him up, driving him the ten miles, and we would arrive some time between five and six o'clock, by which time my engineer and famous keyboard player, Roger King, was ready to finish work and ready to go home. But we had to work on Chris's time, and so we would record into the night with him. And so, yeah, he was a little bit switching day for night, at the time. But then that all changed, because he then had a young daughter called Xilan, and suddenly he was up at 8:30 and calling me. And I thought, what's going on here? He's going through a change here.

"But I'm sure we would have recorded more stuff in the future. We just naturally seemed to gravitate towards each other. He was larger than life, a great force in music, and I miss him every day."

Chris Squire, speaking with the author in 2014, on his retirement plans:
"The great thing about being a musician as opposed to being a sports figure or something, you actually can make music and perform shows, really, to some undetermined age. As long as it's all good and you're all healthy in life, there's no reason to stop doing what you're doing. And that's our philosophy, really. Touch wood, everyone is in pretty good physical shape, and so we're good to go

for a while. I don't really have any plans. Most people say, 'Yeah, I want to travel the world.' Well, done that [*laughs*]. I don't really see things changing, other than just carrying on doing what we're doing... "

Selected Discography

•••

A few points of methodology are in order. By necessity towards compactness, I've prioritized along the following lines.

• Most important, in my opinion, are the studio albums in their original form and the songs on them (no double quote marks, as is the normal convention, for neatness). This makes for a useful cross reference tool as one reads the trunk of the book.

• I thought timings were of interest as well, given the band's often radically long songs.

• I've used a note section as a catch-all for anything else I thought important, i.e. mostly lineup changes. For personnel, I've simplified and credited the performers with their main role or duty only, establishing the full lineup for the debut and then just noting alterations as we move from album to album.

• As well, albums released in the vinyl era get a side 1/side 2 designation, and CDs, just a straight numbered track list.

• Finally, in order to allow mention of as many live albums and compilations as possible, I've omitted the naming of songs, plus listed only what I thought were key compilations.

Studio Albums

Yes (July 1969)
Produced by Paul Clay and Yes
Side 1: 1. Beyond And Before (4:50) 2. I See You (6:33)
3. Yesterday And Today (2:37) 4. Looking Around (3:49)
Side 2: 1. Harold Land (5:26) 2. Every Little Thing (5:24)
3. Sweetness (4:19) 4. Survival (6:01)
Notes: Jon Anderson – lead vocals; Peter Banks – guitar;
Tony Kaye – organ, piano; Chris Squire – bass; Bill Bruford – drums.

Selected Discography

Time And A Word (July 1970)
Produced by Tony Colton
Side 1: 1. No Opportunity Necessary, No Experience Needed
2. Then (5:42) 3. Everydays (6:06) 4. Sweet Dreams (3:48)
Side 2: 1. The Prophet (6:32) 2. Clear Days (2:04)
3. Astral Traveller (5:50) 4. Time And A Word (4:31)

The Yes Album (February 1971)
Produced by Yes and Eddie Offord
Side 1: 1. Yours Is No Disgrace (9:36) 2.The Clap (3:07)
3. Starship Trooper a. Life Seeker b. Dissolution c. Würm (9:23)
Side 2: 1. I've Seen All Good People a. Your Move
b. All Good People (6:47) 2. A Venture (3.13)
4. Perpetual Change (8:50)
Notes: Guitarist Steve Howe replaces Peter Banks.

Fragile (November 1971)
Produced by Yes and Eddie Offord
Side 1: 1. Roundabout (8:30) 2. Cans And Brahms (1:38)
3. We Have Heaven (1:40) 4. South Side Of The Sky (8:02)
Side 2 1. Five Per Cent For Nothing (0:35) 2. Long Distance
Runaround (3:30) 3. The Fish (Schindleria Praematurus) (2:39)
4. Mood For A Day (3:00). 5. Heart Of The Sunrise (11:27)
Notes: Keyboardist Rick Wakeman replaces Tony Kaye.

Close To The Edge (September 1972)
Produced by Yes and Eddie Offord
Side 1: 1. Close To The Edge I. The Solid Time Of Change
II. Total Mass Retain III. I Get Up I Get Down IV. Seasons Of Man
(18:50)
Side 2: 1. And You And I I. Cord Of Life II. Eclipse III. The Preacher
The Teacher IV. Apocalypse (10:09) 2. Siberian Khatru (8:57)

Tales From Topographic Oceans (December 1973)
Produced by Yes and Eddie Offord
Side 1: The Revealing Science Of God (Dance Of The Dawn) (20:27)
Side 2: The Remembering (High The Memory) (20:38)
Side 3: The Ancient (Giants Under The Sun) (18:34)
Side 4: Ritual (Nous Sommes Du Soleil) (21:35)
Notes: Drummer Alan White replaces Bill Bruford.

Relayer (November 1974)
Produced by Yes and Eddie Offord
Side 1: The Gates Of Delirium (21:55)
Side 2: 1. Sound Chaser (9:25) 2. To Be Over (9:08)
Notes: Keyboardist Patrick Moraz replaces Rick Wakeman.

Going For The One (July 1977)
Produced by Yes
Side 1: 1. Going For The One (5:30) 2. Turn Of The Century (7:58)
3. Parallels (5:52)
Side 2: 1. Wonderous Stories (3:45) 2. Awaken (15:38)
Notes: Returning keyboardist Rick Wakeman replaces Patrick Moraz.

Tormato (September 1978)
Produced by Yes
Side 1: 1. a. Future Times b. Rejoice (6:46) 2. Don't Kill The Whale
(3:55) 3. Madrigal (2:21) 4. Release, Release (5:40)
Side 2: 1. Arriving UFO (6:02) 2. Circus Of Heaven (4:28) 3. Onward
(4:00) 4. On The Silent Wings Of Freedom (7:45)

Drama (August 1980)
Produced by Yes
Side 1: 1. Machine Messiah (10:27) 2. White Car (1:21)
3. Does It Really Happen? (6:34)
Side 2: 1. Into The Lens (8:31) 2. Run Through The Light (4:39)
3. Tempus Fugit (5:14)
Notes: Keyboardist Geoff Downes replaces Rick Wakeman; vocalist
Trevor Horn replaces Jon Anderson.

90125 (November 1983)
Produced by Trevor Horn
Side 1: 1. Owner Of A Lonely Heart (4:27) 2. Hold On (5:15)
3. It Can Happen (5:39) 5. Changes (6:16)
Side 2: 1. Cinema (2:09) 2. Leave It (4:10) 3. Our Song (4:16)
4. City Of Love (4:48) 5. Hearts (7:34)
Notes: Returning vocalist Jon Anderson replaces Trevor Horn;
guitarist Trevor Rabin replaces Steve Howe; returning keyboardist Tony
Kaye replaces Geoff Downes.

Selected Discography

Big Generator (September 1987)

Produced by Yes, Trevor Rabin, Paul De Villiers, Trevor Horn
Side 1: 1. Rhythm Of Love (4:49) 2. Big Generator (4:31)
3. Shoot High Aim Low (6:59) 4. Almost Like Love (4:58)
Side 2: 1. Love Will Find A Way (4:48) 2. Final Eyes (6:20)
7. I'm Running (7:34) 4. Holy Lamb (Song For Harmonic Convergence)
(3:15)

Anderson Bruford Wakeman Howe; June 1989

Produced by Chris Kimsey and Jon Anderson.
Side 1: 1.Themes i. Sound ii. Second Attention iii. Soul Warrior (5:58)
2. Fist Of Fire (3:27) 3. Brother Of Mine 1. The Big Dream ii. Nothing
Can Come Between Us iii. Long Lost Brother Of Mine (10:18)
4. Birthright (6:02) 5. The Meeting (4:21)
Side 2: 1. Quartet i. I Wanna Learn ii. She Gives Me Love
iii Who Was The First iv I'm Alive (9:22) 2. Teakbois (7:39)
3. Order Of The Universe i. Order Theme ii. Rock Gives Courage
iii It's So Hard To Grow iv. The Universe (9:02)
Notes: Not a Yes album in legal name only. Jon Anderson – lead
vocals; Steve Howe – guitar; Rick Wakeman – keyboards; Bill Bruford –
drums. Primary additional personnel is Tony Levin on bass.

Union (April 1991)

Produced by: Jonathan Elias; associate producer Jon Anderson.
"Masquerade" produced by Steve Howe; "Lift Me Up" and "Saving My
Heart" produced by Trevor Rabin; "Miracle Of Life" produced by Trevor
Rabin with Mark Mancina and Eddie Offord; "The More We Live – Let
Go produced by Eddie Offord, co-produced by Billy Sherwood.
1. I Would Have Waited Forever (6:32) 2. Shock To The System (5:09)
3. Masquerade (2:17) 4. Lift Me Up (6:30) 5. Without Hope You Cannot
Start The Day (5:18) 6. Saving My Heart (4:41) 7. Miracle Of Life (7:30)
8. Silent Talking (4:00) 9. The More We Live – Let Go (4:51)
10. Angkor Wat (5:23) 11. Dangerous (Look In The Light Of What
You're Searching for) (3:36) 12. Holding On (5:24)
13. Evensong (0:52) 14. Take The Water To The Mountain (3:10)
Notes: Yes for this album only is an assemblage of Yes as it exists
on *Big Generator* and the Anderson Bruford Wakeman Howe band.
Jon Anderson – lead vocals; Steve Howe, Trevor Rabin – guitars; Rick
Wakeman, Tony Kaye – keyboards, Chris Squire – bass; Bill Bruford,
Alan White – drums.

Time And A Word

Talk (March 1994)
Produced by Trevor Rabin
1. The Calling (6:56) 2. I Am Waiting (7:25) 3. Real Love (8:49)
4. State Of Play (5:00) 5. Walls (4:57) 6. Where Will You Be (6:09)
7. Endless Dream a. Silent Spring (Instrumental) b. Talk
c. Endless Dream (15:43)
Notes: Personnel is back to the five-man team that recorded _Big Generator_.

Open Your Eyes (November 1997)
Produced by Yes
1. New State Of Mind (6:00) 2. Open Your Eyes (5:14)
3. Universal Garden (6:17) 4. No Way We Can Lose (4:56)
5. Fortune Seller (5:00) 6. Man In The Moon (4:41)
7. Wonderlove (6:06) 8. From The Balcony (2:43) 9. Love Shine (4:38)
10. Somehow, Someday (4:47) 11. The Solution (23:47)
Notes: Keyboardist Billy Sherwood replaces Rick Wakeman, although
Sherman plays some bass, sings and serves as second guitarist
as well. Sherwood essentially shares keyboard duties with Igor
Khoroshev, with Steve Porcaro providing additional keyboards on
the title track.

The Ladder (September 1999)
Produced by Bruce Fairbairn
1. Homeworld (The Ladder) (9:32) 2. It Will Be A Good Day (The River)
(4:54) 3. Lightning Strikes (4:35) 4. Can I? (1:32)
5. Face To Face (5:02) 6. If Only You Knew (5:43)
7. To Be Alive (Hep Yadda) (5:07) 8. Finally (6:02)
9. The Messenger (5:13) 10. New Language (9:19)
11. Nine Voices (Longwalker) (3:21)
Notes: The band adds sixth member keyboardist Igor Khoroshev.

Magnification (September 2001)
Produced by Yes, Tim Weidner
1. Magnification (7:16) 2. Spirit Of Survival (6:02) 3. Don't Go (4:27)
4. Give Love Each Day (7:44) 5. Can You Imagine (2:59)
6. We Agree (6:30) 7. Soft As A Dove (2:17) 8. Dream Time (10:46)
9. In The Presence Of I. Deeper II. Death Of Ego III. True Beginner
IV. Turn Around and Remember (10:24)
Notes: _Magnification_ marks the only time the band recorded as a
four-piece, given the departures of Billy Sherwood and Igor Khoroshev.
The album also features a full orchestra, conducted by Larry Groupé.

Selected Discography

Fly From Here (June 2011)
Produced by Trevor Horn

1. Fly From Here - Overture (1:53) Fly From Here Pt 1 We Can Fly (6:00) Fly From Here Pt II Sad Night At The Airfield (6:41) Fly From Here Part III Madman At The Screens (5:16) Fly From Here Part IV Bumpy Ride (2:15) Fly From Here Part V We Can Fly Reprise (1:44) 7. The Man You Always Wanted Me To Be (5:07) 8. Life On A Film Set (5:01) 9. Hour Of Need (3:07) 10. Solitaire (3:30) 11. Into The Storm (6:54)

Notes: Geoff Downes returns as keyboardist; vocalist Benoit David replaces Jon Anderson.

Heaven & Earth (July 2014)
Produced by Roy Thomas Baker

1. Believe Again (8:02) 2. The Game (6:51) 3. Step Beyond (5:34) 4. To Ascend (4:43) 5. In A World Of Our Own (5:20) 6. Light Of The Ages (7:41) 7. It Was All We Knew (4:13) 8. Subway Walls (9:03)

Notes: Vocalist Jon Davison replaces Benoit David.

Live/Studio Albums

Keys To Ascension (October 1996)
Produced by Yes; co-produced and engineered by Tom Fletcher

Disc 1: 1. Siberian Khatru (10:16) 2. The Revealing Science Of God (Dance Of The Dawn) (20:31) 3. America (10:28) 4. Onward (5:40) 5. Awaken (18:29)

Disc 2: 1. Roundabout (8:30) 2. Starship Trooper a. Life Seeker b. Dissolution c. Würm (13:06) 3. Be The One i. The One ii. Humankind iii. Skates (9:50) 4. That, That Is a. Togetherness b. Crossfire c. The Giving Things d. That Is e. All In All f. How Did Heaven Begin g. Agree to Agree (19:14)

Notes: All tracks live except "Be The One" and "That, That Is." Returning guitarist Steve Howe replaces Trevor Rabin; returning keyboardist Rick Wakeman replaces Tony Kaye.

Keys To Ascension 2 (November 1997)
Produced by Yes, Billy Sherwood

Disc 1: 1. I've Seen All Good People (7:16) 2. Going For The One (4:58) 3. Time And A Word (6:23) 4. Close To The Edge I. The Solid Time Of Change II. Total Mass Retain III. I Get Up I Get Down

Time And A Word

IV. Seasons Of Man (19:40) 5. Turn Of The Century (7:55)
6. And You And I I. Cord Of Life II. Eclipse III. The Preacher
The Teacher IV. Apocalypse (10:48)
Disc 2: 1. Mind Drive (18:37) 2. Foot Prints (9:09)
3. Bring Me To The Power (7:25) 4. Children Of The Light A) Children
Of Light B) Lifeline (6:02) 5. Sign Language (3:29)
Notes: Disc 1 is live and disc 2 is studio.

Live Albums

Yessongs (May 1973)
Yesshows (November 1980)
9012Live: The Solos (November 1985)
Something's Coming: the BBC Recordings 1969-1970 (October 1997)
House Of Yes: Live From House Of Blues (September 2000)
Songs From Tsongas: Yes 35th Anniversary Concert (August 2005)
The Word Is Live (August 2005)
Live At Montreux 2003 (September 2007)
Symphonic Live (February 2009)
Union Live (January 2011)
In The Present – Live From Lyon (November 2011)
Like It Is: Yes At The Bristol Hippodrome (December 2014)
Progeny: Seven Shows From Seventy-Two (May 2015)
Like It Is: Yes Live At The Mesa Arts Center (July 2015)

Selected Compilations

Yesterdays (February 1975)
Classic Yes (November 1981)
Yesyears (August 1991)
Yesstory (September 1992)
Highlights: The Very Best Of Yes (September 1993)
An Evening Of Yes Music Plus (Anderson Bruford Wakeman Howe;
October 1993)
In A Word: Yes (1969–) (July 2002)
The Ultimate Yes: 35th Anniversary Collection (July 2003)
Wonderous Stories: The Best Of Yes (September 2011)
Live At The NEC (Anderson Bruford Wakeman Howe; November 2012)

Notes & Sources

•••

Interviews by the author

Anderson, Jon. May 14, 2015.
Bachman, Randy. October 28, 2002.
Berry, Robert. August 20, 2001.
Bruford, Bill. April 15, 2002.
Downes, Geoff. September 27, 2002.
Downes, Geoff. April 11, 2013.
Hackett, Steve. June 17, 2002.
Hackett, Steve. November 2, 2015.
Howe, Steve. September 3, 2001.
Howe, Steve. November 16, 2002.
Palmer, Carl. February 24, 2006.
Sherwood, Billy. May 6, 2015.
Squire, Chris. August 6, 2011.
Squire, Chris. March 28, 2014.
Wakeman, Rick. May 7, 2004.
Ward, Bill. May 1, 2015.
Wetton, John. April 6, 2006.
White, Alan. August 6, 2011.
White, Alan. June 16, 2014.

Additional Citations

All Access Music. Interview: Yes Singer Jon Davison Talks About Heaven & Earth Album by Mark Strickland. June 25, 2014.

Banks, Peter, with Billy James. Beyond and Before: The Formative Years Of Yes. Golden Treasures Publishing Ltd., Bentonville, Arkansas. 2001.

Circus. Squire And Howe Sire Solo Yessongs by Leo Warner. No. 108. April 1975.

Circus. Yestour '76 by Peter Crescenti. No. 139. September 13, 1976.

Circus. Yes Is Going For The Big One by Jim Farber. No. 163. September 8, 1977.

Classic Rock. Yes: Rock's True Pioneers by Sal Treppiedi. Spring 1988.

Classic Rock Revisited. Interview With Steve Howe by Roy Rahl. September 8, 2014.

Crawdaddy. Henry VIII's Yes Man by Jon Swenson. August 1973.

Creem. *Tormato* record review by Michael Davis. Vol. 10, No. 8. January 1979.

Creem. *Drama* record review by Rick Johnson. Vol. 12, No. 7. December 1980.

Gettin' Off. Rick Wakeman: Journey To The Centre. Reprinted from New World Magazine. Consumer Edition #1. 1973.

Goldmine. Yes Through The Years by Howard Whitman. Issue 796. Volume 37, No. 2. February 2011.

Hit Parader. The New Yes: The Drama Continues by Dan Hedges. No. 198. January 1981.

Hit Parader. Yes Returning With Style by Rob Andrews. No. 234. March 1984.

Keyboard. What Ever Happened To Patrick Moraz? by Robert L. Doerschuk. May 1991.

Keyboard. Bruford & White: Beating Off With High-Tech Toys by Greg Rule. Vol. 17, No. 8., Issue # 184. August 1991.

Keyboard. Rick Wakeman & Tony Kaye Face Off by Robert L. Doerschuk. Vol. 17, No. 8., Issue # 184. August 1991.

Melody Maker. YES - Now With Added Whiteness by Chris Charlesworth. July 29, 1972.

Melody Maker. *Tales From Topographic Oceans* review by Chris Welch. December 1, 1973.

Melody Maker. Yes – Over The Edge by Chris Welch. December 1, 1973.

Notes & Sources

Melody Maker. Greek Coup... by Steve Lake. August 10, 1974.

Melody Maker. Cover story by Karl Dallas. August 17, 1974.

Melody Maker. Wondrous Stories by Chris Welch. October 22, 1977.

Music Express. This Combo Buggles The Imagination by David Farrell. Vol. 4, No. 10. 1980.

New Musical Express. *Tales From Topographic Oceans* review by Steve Clarke. January 19, 1974.

New Musical Express. Wakeman - On Wembley Ice! April 5, 1975.

Phonograph. *Relayer* record review by Ed Sciaky. Vol. 5, No. 4. January 1975.

Prog Report, The Jon Davison (Yes) Interview. April 1, 2014.

Record Collector. Yes On Yes. No. 269. January 2002.

Record Collector. Yesteryears By Tim Jones. No. 269. January 2002.

Rolling Stone. *Going For The One* record review by John Swenson. September 8, 1977.

Sea Of Tranquility. *Magnification* review by Pete Pardo. November 7, 2001.

Sea Of Tranquility. An Interview with the Legendary Jon Anderson by Jordan Blum. May 1, 2011.

Sea Of Tranquility. *Heaven & Earth* review by Pete Pardo. August 1, 2014.

Something Else Reviews. 'It Was A perfect storm:' Trevor Rabin and Jon Anderson on Yes's most overlooked album by Nick Deriso. May 10, 2014.

Tascam User Guide. On Tour With Yes by Tascam Sam. No. 12. Fall/ Winter 1994.

Technology Tell. No Disgrace: Entertainmenttell.com Interviews Yes Singer Jon Davison by Howard Whitman. January 21, 2013.

Trouser Press. Wakeman Tells Yesstories by Ira Robbins. No. 20. June/ July 1977.

Trouser Press. Bill Bruford conjures up his past by Ray Bonici. No. 31. August 1978.

Universal Wheels. Alan White Talks! by Kevin Julie. 2000.

Universal Wheels. Interview with Geoff Downes by Kevin Julie. 2012.

Special Thanks

...

Besides my own interviews and material cited in Additional Sources, two buddies—Dmitry Epstein and Jeb Wright—have graciously allowed me to quote from some of their chats.

Dmitry's smart and historical classic rock scholarship can be seen at dmme.net. So proud of him coming to Toronto, pretty much cold, from Belarus via Israel and carving a good life for him and his family very, very quickly.

Jeb... what can I say about Jeb? Through his fine work at classicrockrevisted.com, he's proven himself to be the most important supporter of classic rock we've got. Without his words of wisdom and grounded perspective on all these guys we talk to when we get on an email tear or on one of our epic phone calls, I doubt I'd be able to keep plowing ahead. Friggin' inspiration, that guy. Look for his fiction—yes, fiction—soon.

About The Author

•••

At approximately 7900 (with over 7000 appearing in his books), Martin has unofficially written more record reviews than anybody in the history of music writing across all genres. Additionally, Martin has penned 52 books on hard rock, heavy metal, classic rock and record collecting, and contributed to another half-dozen. He was Editor In Chief of the now web-only *Brave Words & Bloody Knuckles*, Canada's foremost metal publication for 14 years, and has also contributed to *Revolver*, *Guitar World*, *Goldmine*, *Record Collector*, bravewords.com, lollipop. com and hardradio.com, with many record label band bios and liner notes to his credit as well. Additionally, Martin worked for two years as researcher on the award-wining documentary *Rush: Beyond The Lighted Stage* and on *Metal Evolution*, an 11-episode documentary series for VH1 Classic, and is the writer of the original metal genre chart used in *Metal: A Headbanger's Journey* and throughout the *Metal Evolution* episodes. Martin was also consultant on Banger's series for VH1, *Rock Icons*. He has lived in Toronto for 26 years, Martin can be reached through martinp@inforamp.net or www.martinpopoff.com.

Martin Popoff – A Complete Bibliography

Wheels of Steel: The Explosive Early Years of the NWOBHM (2015)
Swords And Tequila: Riot's Classic First Decade (2015)
Who Invented Heavy Metal? (2015)
Sail Away: Whitesnake's Fantastic Voyage (2015)
Live Magnetic Air: The Unlikely Saga Of The Superlative Max Webster (2014)
Steal Away The Night: An Ozzy Osbourne Day-By-Day (2014)
The Big Book Of Hair Metal (2014)

Sweating Bullets: The Deth And Rebirth Of Megadeth (2014)

Smokin' Valves: A Headbanger's Guide to 900 NWOBHM Records (2014)

The Art Of Metal (co-edit with Malcolm Dome; 2013)

2 Minutes To Midnight: An Iron Maiden Day-By-Day (2013)

Metallica: The Complete Illustrated History (2013)

Rush: The Illustrated History (2013)

Ye Olde Metal: 1979 (2013)

Scorpions: Top Of The Bill (2013)

Epic Ted Nugent (2012)

It's Getting Dangerous: Thin Lizzy 81-12 (2012)

We Will Be Strong: Thin Lizzy 76-81 (2012)

Fighting My Way Back: Thin Lizzy 69-76 (2011)

The Deep Purple Royal Family: Chain Of Events '80 – '11 (2011)

The Deep Purple Royal Family: Chain Of Events Through '79 (2011)

Black Sabbath FAQ (2011)

The Collector's Guide To Heavy Metal: Volume 4: The '00s (2011; co-authored with David Perri)

Goldmine Standard Catalog Of American Records 1948 – 1991, 7th Edition (2010)

Goldmine Record Album Price Guide, 6th Edition (2009)

Goldmine 45 RPM Price Guide, 7th Edition (2009)

A Castle Full Of Rascals: Deep Purple '83 – '09 (2009)

Worlds Away: Voivod And The Art Of Michel Langevin (2009)

Ye Olde Metal: 1978 (2009)

Gettin' Tighter: Deep Purple '68 – '76 (2008)

All Access: The Art Of The Backstage Pass (2008)

Ye Olde Metal: 1977 (2008)

Ye Olde Metal: 1976 (2008)

Judas Priest: Heavy Metal Painkillers (2007)

Ye Olde Metal: 1973 To 1975 (2007)

The Collector's Guide To Heavy Metal: Volume 3: The Nineties (2007)

Ye Olde Metal: 1968 To 1972 (2007)

Run For Cover: The Art Of Derek Riggs (2006)

Black Sabbath: Doom Let Loose (2006)

Dio: Light Beyond The Black (2006)

The Collector's Guide To Heavy Metal: Volume 2: The Eighties (2005)

Rainbow: English Castle Magic (2005)

UFO: Shoot Out The Lights (2005)

The New Wave Of British Heavy Metal Singles (2005)

Blue Öyster Cult: Secrets Revealed! (2004; updated 2009)

About The Author

Contents Under Pressure: 30 Years Of Rush At Home & Away (2004)
The Top 500 Heavy Metal Albums Of All Time (2004)
The Collector's Guide To Heavy Metal: Volume 1: The Seventies (2003)
The Top 500 Heavy Metal Songs Of All Time (2003)
Southern Rock Review (2001)
Heavy Metal: 20th Century Rock And Roll (2000)
The Goldmine Price Guide To Heavy Metal Records (2000)
The Collector's Guide To Heavy Metal (1997)
Riff Kills Man! 25 Years Of Recorded Hard Rock & Heavy Metal (1993)

See martinpopoff.com for complete details and ordering information.

Also Published by Soundcheck Books

Sail Away
Whitesnake's Fantastic Voyage
By Martin Popoff
ISBN: 978-0-9575700-8-5

A Passion Play
The Story Of Ian Anderson
And Jethro Tull
By Brian Rabey
ISBN: 978-0-9571442-4-8

Do You Wanna Play Some Magic?
Emerson, Lake And Palmer In Concert 1970-1979
By Garry Freeman
ISBN: 978-0-9566420-8-0

All titles available in paperback
from all good booksellers. Kindle versions,
where applicable, available from all Amazon sites.